Bamboo Hirst is a Chinese-Italian writer whose books draw on her unique overlap of East and West.

'Blue is the colour of the Miao, the ancient people
to which I belong on my mother's side.
Blue is the wind rousing old memories,
shaping them and making them new.
Blue is the China thousands of *li* from here.
Blue is the colour of my nostalgia.'

She has written *China Ink, Passage to Shanghai, Rice Doesn't Grow on Trees, The World Beyond the Peach Blossom River, Postcards from Beijing, Daughters of China.*

LOKI BOOKS

www.lokibooks.com

First published in Great Britain as a Loki Books paperback original in 2008 by **LOKI BOOKS LTD**, 38 Chalcot Crescent, London NW1 8YD

Printed and bound by Antony Rowe Ltd, Bumper's Farm, Chippenham, Wiltshire SN14 6LH

A CIP catalogue record for this book is available from the British Library.

ISBN - 10 -   09529426782
ISBN - 13 -   9780952942689

Cover design by Alexandra Baraitser

BLUE CHINA

Bamboo Hirst

Translated from the Italian
by Sue Rose

Series Editor: Marion Baraitser

LOKI

Xinran Xue was born in Beijing in 1958. From 1989 to 1997, she worked as a radio presenter at Nanjing Radio Broadcasting Station, where she invited women to call in and share their life stories. These appeared in Britain in *The Good Women of China*, which has now been published all over the world

In 2004, Xinran set up *The Mothers' Bridge of Love* (www.motherbridge.org, 9 Orme Court, London W2 4 RL, UK Charity Registration Number 1105543) that reaches out to Chinese children in all corners of the world.

Sue Rose is a freelance translator and poet (*Travelling Light*, 2008). She has an MPhil in Writing (University of Glamorgan), and a Diploma in Translation (Institute of Linguistics).

Marion Baraitser is an award winning playwright (*The Story of an African Farm*, Young Vic; *The Crystal Den*, New End; Oberon Books), short story writer, lecturer in English Literature (Birkbeck, University of London), and editor.

She founded **Loki Books** in 1997 supported by the Arts Council of England, UNESCO, Women in Publishing, the European Jewish Publication Fund, and the British Council.

Introduction

A Chinese Bamboo Growing in the West

In April 2007 I met Marion Baraitser, a London playwright and founder of Loki Books, a small independent press that 'voices the unvoiced'. She asked me to write an introduction for the English version of *Blue China*, a memoir written by Bamboo Hirst. The daughter of the love between an Italian diplomat and a Chinese singer, Bamboo was born in China but has lived in Europe since 1952, coming to Italy when she was thirteen. As a result of living between two very different cultures, she chose a Chinese name for herself to use in the West—Bamboo. Bamboo is not only a very popular name for Chinese women along the River Yangtze where most of the landscape is beautifully 'dressed' by it, but its image has appeared in Chinese poems and ink paintings for over three thousand years.

I met the writer at a book launch party for the Chinese writers Fan Wu (*February Flower*) and Dian Weiliang (*Eye of Jade*) at Asia House in London. Bamboo was wearing an elegant Chinese black silk dress, which reminded me of the image of a Shanghai beauty in the 1930s. We talked in a typical 'overseas Chinese' way, mixing English, Mandarin and our own local dialect. (She spoke my home town Shanghai dialect which, I am ashamed to say, I never learned to speak since I grew up in Beijing—which is much nearer Shanghai than Italy!)

At the time of our meeting, *Blue China* was still in translation from the Italian to English, so on my return, after reading some background information about her writing, I decided to have at least three telephone conversations with Bamboo in her house in the Ligurian hills where she was staying, in order to further understand her personal voice and the book.

My first question was: 'In ten minutes flat, what do you want to tell your readers about who you are, and what is your message in *Blue China*?' In fact, no one can tell the story of over 60 years of life in such a short time, or put one life into a book even though it is over thousand pages. As one Chinese grandmother told me: 'Life is at first like an exclamation mark without the dot—it is nothing, not even an unfinished mark. But the 'dot' can be a happy family, a successful career, a book you have written, a tree you have planted, or a way of cooking.' She said she had been thinking a great deal about what her last words would be to her children, as they will be her 'life mark'—her '!'.

Bamboo answered my first question in eight minutes, but we did not hang up for more than an hour. She said: 'My only message is that with some luck and determination, one can turn the negatives of one's life into positives. Being half-Chinese and half-Italian threw me into the position of people discriminating against me in my early years, but because of my 'different look', I was able to enter the fashion world and build a career. I would also add that the difficulties I had to face have given me rich material to turn into my books. Apart from the disillusionment I experienced in my childhood, especially as a result of my father's abandonment of me, I still have faith in people. I have met many good ones and they are all in my books. I shall never forget their acts of kindness. In China the peasants hid me from the Japanese. In Italy certain teachers gave me free tuition, and my schoolmates wrote some essays I was not capable of doing so that I could participate in school trips they funded with their pocket money. All this kind-heartedness taught me a lot. As a consequence I am always willing to help anyone who needs it. I am very open-minded to everybody from whom I continue to learn, and this keeps me young at heart.'

She also told me that she sees herself as Chinese, but with 13 years in China and 55 years in the West, I asked her how she can be so sure that she is a Chinese woman. 'Yes, I have been living in a double culture since childhood. For example, as a child, on Saturdays I went to a temple with a Chinese *nainai* (Chinese old lady), then on Sundays I went to church with French missionaries. Or again, in China I had to hide my big nose in front of Japanese invaders, but in Italy children were surprised that my nose was so small. Later in my life, during the day I worked in Italian fashion public relations, yet in the evening I dressed in Chinese clothes, drank green tea, and read and talked about China. But I know I have a Chinese heart to feel China. I was angry when some Westerners tried to 'blacken' China, but I felt sad when I saw China making so many mistakes because I am so proud of being a Chinese woman in many ways.'

The emotion in her voice over the telephone brought back to me many memories and images of Chinese women whom I have met both in China and the West. All of us have been struggling to be good and to be proud of being Chinese women since we were born, but how many of us have been recognised for who we really are? The renowned Canadian director Robert Lepage has an unfailing depiction of the issues around understanding Chinese women. *Dragon's Trilogy*, his masterpiece in which East meets West, creates an imaginary China in 1930s Quebec, with a group of faceless and silenced Chinese laundry women doing Tai Chi and martial arts. It is fairly true that 'faceless' is perhaps the first impression gained by anyone who is unfamiliar with a foreign culture. But at the same time, Lepage also indicates that, with heads bent down, the first Chinese women who settled in North America were invisible.

So what do the faces of the once weakened and lowered Chinese women look like now? We see the confident smiles on Chinese businesswomen, the serious faces of diligent Chinese students in London colleges, the glamorous faces of Chinese film stars on international silver screens, but we also see the dirty and sad faces of Chinese peasants in the countryside who have been used as 'the evidence of Communist abuse' in Western media since 1949. Actually, not only Westerners find it difficult to get a clear picture of recent developments, but Chinese women themselves have been confused by the standards of women's rights, liberation, freedom and democracy since the 1980s, when China was opened to the world for the first time in more than three thousand years of recorded history, and Chinese women started to learn these words. Bamboo is like someone who can read your mind, and when I was thinking the above she said: 'Mao Zedong let Chinese women hold half the sky, which made a huge change in China compared to the situation of Chinese women before the 1940s when they were not allowed go out and take part in any social and culture activities according to traditional Confucian customs. I saw these changes when I went back to China 30 years later in 1987— Chinese women's faces were much happier.' I know that Mao did terrible things to Chinese people, including my family and Bamboo's, and though he decreed that Chinese women should take part in the world apart from housework, he did not create a modern education system to help Chinese women, who were left to carry a double work burden.

After this conversation with Bamboo, I thought a great deal about Chinese women's faces. As a Chinese person who has lived 'in the China door' for over 40 years, I have come to accept that Mao Zedong empowered hundreds of millions of Chinese women to be the most liberated among those in the East Asian countries in 1949, through the establishment of the People's Republic of China and his fevered proclamation that 'women hold up half the sky.' Criticising the traditional Confucian view of the roles of each sex, Communist ideology pushed women into farmyards, factories and even construction sites to positions that were usually occupied by men. Indeed women were regarded as equal makers of the revolutionary fruits. However, to keep to the facts, after women were introduced to paid work, the traditional roles of women in the domestic scene have not been affected much by egalitarianism. The problem of working women carrying the major burden of housework and childcare is not a problem in China alone: it is universal among liberated Western women as well. Structured by gender stereotypes and cultural clichés, society looks down upon housewives. In fact, in almost all countries, including the developed ones, 'housewife' has become an adjective for uneducated or less knowledgeable women without a modern sense of civilisation.

If education is the key for women to open a professional door, then proving their capability could be a bridge between traditional chains and the new freedom. Unfortunately, in today's China, with more than half the population only educated for less than ten years, most women in the countryside hardly have a chance to either be educated or trained to enhance their capabilities. In the last twenty years millions of teenage girls have moved into the cities and taken over low-skilled labour and service work from urban people. They are stuck between their dreams and the facts, between a strange city with a better life and a familiar rural home.

If anyone wants to be able to understand today's Chinese women, no matter from what perspective, I think we have to work from the premise that in the past, certain social phenomena that are accepted all over the world, have never really been accepted or put into practice in China: these are freedom of religious belief; freedom of the press; proper functioning of the legal system; sex education.

For the last 3,000 years, the Chinese have regarded their emperors and leaders as their gods whose every word could mean the difference between life and death. In the early twentieth century, China was plunged into chaos as the feudal system came to an end, and in all this bloodshed, the role of saviour was taken over by the warlords. They all understood that the Chinese could not do without their gods as props to their spirit. In the eyes of most Chinese people, the emperors and party committees were the legal system, and the judicial system was just a fiction from Western films. Most modern Chinese only know of the police, not of lawyers or judges. The only information ordinary Chinese people can obtain from the public media—radio, television and newspapers—are the orders of those emperors and political parties. If you are born blind, no matter how others describe the beauty of colours to you, you still have no way of imagining the difference between yellow and blue. For people who have lived all their lives in China without any chance to travel anywhere, it is impossible to imagine the right to the freedom to read, watch and listen to what you like, and to communicate with the rest of the world. The drab, drained information they can glean has numbed the natural desires of most Chinese for any information at all.

Sex, which is regarded by the rest of the world as a basic part of human nature, was a defining characteristic of hooligans or delinquent behaviour in China until the 1990s, and sexual education in schools only started in 2002. Touching or hugging someone of the opposite sex could lead to criticism or even imprisonment. Even at home, pillow talk between couples could be used as proof for one of them to inform against the other after a quarrel, which could result in imprisonment or dismissal from their jobs. In addition to all this, from 1912 to the 1980s, the Chinese education system never had a chance to improve or to build itself up to international standards because of the domination of the warlords, the anti-Japanese War, the Second World War, the Civil War, the Korean War and endless political movements including the Cultural Revolution. So very few Chinese really understand the difference between democracy and the governing system, freedom and law, human rights and personal behaviour—even between human beings and animals. What is more, writing containing sexual content was criticised as sexual hooliganism, and erotic literature was thought to 'water down' educated people's minds, generation after generation. There is growing sexual curiosity on the part of China's middle classes. Before that the sexes were segregated, overt sexuality in dress or behaviour was frowned on, and kissing in public could bring condemnation. This is why, when China's door opened in the 1980s, Western sexual relationships, the naked human body and sex CDs and DVDs flooded into China with cheap Western culture and fast food, as a very early consequence of 'study and improvement'. Sexual education and the social welfare system were set up almost twenty years later.

What is the price of this unbalanced development and sexual freedom? Thousands of babies are born without families and a warm welcome into the human world. Before the year 2,000 most of them became orphans, and nearly one hundred thousand baby girls have been adopted by over 58,000 Western families across 27 countries since 1993. As a report from the UN in 2002 stated, the number of Chinese women committing suicide was the highest in the world, family rows increased between generations, and public judgement became lost in the confusion over what constitutes good standards of Chinese society. Of course the developed West has taken more than two hundred years to walk towards today's democracy and freedom, and away from religious control. How much can we expect of liberal knowledge and thought in today's China, which opened to the world only twenty years ago, after three thousand years of recorded history and five thousand years of civilisation, when most families still believe McDonald's is the best Western food for their children?

Happy faces need good food, rest and the right spirit, and this is exactly the same for Chinese women's faces. From later interviews with Bamboo, I could see a happy Chinese woman's face and a great 'I' from her life. She married an Englishman and they have a lovely daughter. They move between Britain and Italy—one is a cultural centre of the world, the other has the best food in the world (except for Chinese food, in my view). Bamboo has had forty years in a successful career in Italian fashion public relations, and in addition to all this, she has published her seven books in Italy. They are about China from her Chinese heart. Bamboo said to me: 'In these books I have tried to focus on the situation in my country of origin. However, as Chinese scholar Lin Yu Tang wrote: "China cannot be understood, only sensed ." The China I write about is not a literary concept, nor a pretext for writing, but an important part of me. I am sure that readers will discover it from the pages of this book, *Blue China*.'

I asked Bamboo why she called her book *Blue China*. 'Those Chinese women who were dressed all in the blue colour brought me up. Blue is the colour of the Miao, *not* Mao. Miao is one of the minority people in China: they were my mother, nannies, wet-nurse, and cooks. They gave me my inspired Chinese heart. Blue is the wind that awakens the memory, shapes it and renews it. Blue is the China, which is an infinite distance away. Blue is my nostalgia.' Bamboo said this as if singing a poem.

Bamboo and I both believe that people should have

different stories and talk in different voices about today's China, and we take any opportunity to be its students. Yes, the value of China is not just economic numbers in newspapers: the real value of the Chinese is our more than five thousand years of rich and beautiful culture.

I knew we could have gone on talking about Chinese life for days, the conversation ranging from calligraphy and Yin Yang balance to food and herbs. The last thing we talked about was 'the handkerchief rat' – a 'running' rat made from a handkerchief with which women played with their babies before computer games were invented, and *jiu niang* (fermented rice)—the best *pu ping* (tonic) for women's health along the River Yangtze. Bamboo said these are all in this book. I believe *Blue China* is a path to a Chinese heart with many Chinese mothers, *ayi* (aunties), and *nainai* (grandmothers) in it.

Xinran Xue, 2008

Blue is the colour of the Miao, the ancient people
to which I belong on my mother's side.
Blue is the wind rousing old memories,
shaping them and making them new.
Blue is the China thousands of *li* from here.
Blue is the colour of my nostalgia.

Blue China was written about the most important period in
my life. I have reconstructed the past with the aid of a wide
range of reference material obtained by word-of-mouth and
my own research. The characters, backgrounds and episodes
described are all true. The book is divided into three parts.

The first part tells my father and mother's story: the meeting
of East and West.

The second part deals with the culture shock of arriving in
Italy, where I had to put down new roots.

The last part refers to my return to China, in search of the
sights and sounds that were familiar to me, even though I
know that desperately wanting to find these places again was
pure fantasy.

I no longer need to run my fingers over the red lines marking
China's borders on the map, because all the memories and
desires, everything that China once represented and still
represents for me, has now become internalised.

'China cannot be understood, only sensed. Syllogisms and
schematic, statistical deductions cannot help us if we don't
accept its difference', wrote Lin Yu Tang. The China I am
describing isn't a literary place or a narrative pretext, but an
integral part of me.

Blue is the colour of the Miao people, the ancient ethnic
group from which I'm descended on my mother's side.

I'm also half-Italian. And it is in Italian, the language that
has become mine over the years, that I have decided to tell
my story.

B.H.

PART ONE

Just the smell of it made me feel sick. So I sat there gazing at the large bowl brimming with milky coffee they were determined to make me drink, even though it had gone cold hours ago.

The nuns thought I was just being naughty. I couldn't explain that in China only babies drank milk, and then only mother's milk, and that cheese and dairy products didn't exist.

I didn't offer any explanations because I didn't want the other girls at the Istituto to make fun of me. They already called me "Lady Mandarin" after finding out that I'd been "sold" to a Chinese governor, whose nickname was the "Mandarin".

This governor was actually a very important man with the same privileges and powers as the mandarins of the past. According to custom, he was a polygamist and his sumptuously dressed wives and concubines lived with him in his mansion.

The big house was surrounded by camphor trees and oaks and there were tuberoses and forsythia in all his rooms.

He was a benefactor of the Mission that was my home during those years and had met me while I was playing in the shady garden.

When he wasn't in military uniform, he wore a long, blue silk robe that showed the tips of his shoes. These were a masterpiece of craftsmanship with embroidery along the sides and velvet edging that matched his clothes.

I was impressed by his aura of authority. On one occasion, I rode in his rickshaw. There was a bell near the footrest that he sometimes impatiently pressed with his foot, as if to say to the driver: "Keep going straight through the crowd". And all the people bowed, lining up on either side to let him pass.

He seemed to be a very kind, wealthy gentleman and I loved him like a daughter. I thought he wanted to adopt me when he learnt of my father's presumed death and I had no idea there was nothing paternal about his feelings for me.

It was only later that I found out he didn't mean to adopt me, that he'd earmarked me as a future concubine: at the age of fifteen, I would have become his fifth "little rose".

When I realised his intentions, I was genuinely disappointed.

He had only ever shown me kindness and generosity: I was too young to know that there are two sides to every coin.

1

The House of Distant Fragrance, as my family's residence was called, sat on a hilltop in Hangzhou overlooking the West Lake. Since 1855, it had been home to three generations of the Blue Miao ethnic group to which my Chinese ancestors belonged, a delicate silken thread linking them to me, a half-Italian woman and the only female descendant of that line still to bear the family name. Their story has no fixed start: the further back I go, the more I'm left groping in the dark after elusive facts.

According to many scholars, the founders of the Miao ethnic group date back to 4,000 B.C. They lived in the southern valley areas of the Yangtze, the Long River, mainly in the region of Wuhan. For a very long time, they led a tribal existence with no specific social structure. It was only between the 3rd and 10th centuries that these tribes, bound by family ties, settled and spread, establishing permanent villages.

During the Tang Dynasty, the Miao people divided into different social classes and experienced considerable economic and social development as a result of their contact with the culture and economy of central China. In the days of the Sung Dynasty, many Miaos were appointed Prefectural Governors of the Imperial Court, thereby building a political base for their economic expansion which reached its apogee between the 14th and 17th centuries, a period marked by the rule of the Ming Dynasty. When the Manchu overthrew the Ming, many Miaos fled to the distant mountains in the southwest to escape the ensuing massacres. There they lived in the forests with the monkeys or hid in the caves along the

Yangtze. Some became soldiers or farmhands and others changed their name and settled in places that were not so hostile. As a result, they dispersed as far as Siam and Indochina, present-day Thailand, and Vietnam.

The Miao people were divided into different groups—Blue, Red, Black, Green or Flowery, depending on their costumes. In fact, to this day in China, their clothes are considered to be among the most vibrant and most sumptuous of the many ethnic groups that once existed.

The name of the Blue Miao group to which my ancestors belonged, came from their preference for the indigo blue dye they used for their clothes, obtained from a plant known as *lan cao* or "blue grass", particularly widespread in the upper Yangtze valley.

They had settled in a fertile valley, green as a garden, in a village on a plateau in Wuhan called Celestial Harmony, where nothing had changed for many centuries.

The families of landowners, like my ancestors' family, had at least five members, while the peasants often did not even manage to raise a family, due to extreme poverty. The major landowners were also merchants and moneylenders; many were administrative officials and tax collectors who owned granaries, oil presses and shops. This made them extremely powerful and it was only in the 20th century that their authority declined, then completely petered out.

One of the landowning families in the village of Celestial Harmony was that of my Revered Ancestor, who was born in 1840, during the first opium war.

When he turned fifteen, having lost his father at the age of ten, several "old men under the moon", as matchmakers were called, showed up to give his Honourable Widowed Mother a list of families with available daughters. Each name had the relevant horoscope marked next to it. The family astrologer was then summoned to examine and compare these horoscopes with that of my Revered Ancestor. In the astrologer's opinion, the girl's sign had to be the Snake, because the year in which my Revered Ancestor had been born was governed by the Dragon. After all the necessary checks, the girl was chosen and betrothed to him. Her name was Wise Phoenix: she was a descendant of the Han line and her surname was Chou.

A robust, energetic man, my Revered Ancestor was a prominent figure in the village: his family owned a great deal of livestock and their lands were mainly given over to the cultivation of poppy fields and rice fields, while huge piles of manure were sold for fertiliser. He only wore silk tunics, and he allowed his nails to grow extraordinarily long. He also devoted himself to social activities such as the Temple Society, an organisation set up to keep open the village school, to which the villagers were also expected to make offerings. He organised the annual village festival and it was he who had to hire the wandering players to perform the show without which the festival would have been incomplete. Last but not least, he supervised the administration of the Buddhist Association to which most of the villagers belonged and to which they paid large sums of money in order to speak with the dead. The ability to arrange such verbal "encounters" with the departed gave my Revered Ancestor a particular power over everyone practising this rite.

This marriage to Wise Phoenix produced my great-grandfather, and the family again consulted an astrologer to interpret the heavens on the occasion of his birth. The Chinese believe that human beings are composed of five natural elements—metal, fire, water, earth and wood—and the astrologer's task was to discover which element the baby might lack. Once identified, the ideogram for this element had to be added to the boy's name. However my Revered Ancestor's son lacked none of the five elements, so he was called Accumulated Virtue, and he was presented before the Ancestral Tablets at a lavish ceremony during which his name was officially acknowledged. The astrologers declared that the eight circumstances of his birth were all propitious and that he would experience only two difficult phases during his life: the first at the age of ten and the second at thirty, but the configuration of the planets showed that he would overcome these difficulties.

Subsequent events proved the astrologers right, at least with regard to one of these difficult phases. The Miao people lived through some extremely anxious times, coming under French rule after the Sino-French war, which broke out in 1884 and ended in 1885. My ancestors lost much of their property during this time: their small-scale opium production business and the marketing of the tea harvest were swallowed up by large foreign groups, depriving them of a hefty chunk of their income.

The major foreign powers gradually divided China into different geographical areas with different commercial interests. Shandong was given to the Germans; Mongolia to the Russians; the Yangtze basin to the English; Fujian,on the southeast coast, to the Japanese; Yunnan, in the southwest, to the French. During these years, the Chinese retained only two major sources of income: river and maritime customs duties and the salt tax, although their administration came under constant supervision by the foreign powers.

As a result, in 1885, my great-grandfather Accumulated Virtue, left the land of his ancestors for Sichuan, where he was appointed Water Inspector. For several years, he lived in the small city of Ziliujing, built over a large salt works near the Lu River, a tributary of the Yangtze.

Accumulated Virtue had married Spring Orchid, the daughter of a high-ranking Imperial official and a man ahead of his time. He came from a family of scholars that had spawned many intellectuals of the Mandarin class, reformers who had broken with tradition and who were seeking to change China.

The official had even given his daughter the same education as his sons to demonstrate his open-mindedness. A famous poet and calligrapher from Jiangxi province had been appointed Spring Orchid's tutor, and he had taught her the expressive beauty of the Chinese language through the study of calligraphy and the different disciplines of painting. Her father had also hired a foreign priest to teach her European languages, saying: 'Things are changing and what was once enough for our ancestors is no longer enough for us.'

Her feet were not bound, in the manner still demanded for young girls from good families. She read widely and her tranquil way of life seemed to be upheld by her reading. Nevertheless, despite her family's modern stance, she had married according to tradition, at the age of sixteen. She probably would have preferred to decide her own fate, perhaps continuing her studies, but her marriage to Accumulated Virtue, despite being arranged by the two families, turned out to be a happy one: the couple fell in love and discovered a great many shared interests.

Living in her husband's house on the hill above the West Lake overlooking the city of Hangzhou, Spring Orchid led the typical almost reclusive life of a Chinese woman of her rank, a life filled with the chores and duties occasioned by the large number of family members living under the same roof—a life described in the unusual, personal account she left behind.

2

In 1895, when my great-grandfather left on one of his long missions to inspect the watercourses, Spring Orchid wrote him a series of letters in which she described her feelings, her sadness at her husband's prolonged absence, small everyday occurrences, family births and weddings. These letters, which were never sent, became a diary—an honest, heartfelt document in which Spring Orchid, writing as if chatting to her husband, was actually talking to herself, recording the daily events that punctuated her life regularly as clockwork. She did this with unusual candour for a Chinese woman. Although she wrote with the uninhibited spontaneity of someone not writing to be read, her letters were also characterised by the typical self-discipline and serene detachment of the Chinese.

My First Uncle was of the opinion that this unusual diary of letters was the product of circumstance, since women of rank were not allowed to write private letters and notes, which was traditionally the job of the household clerk or head of the family. As a result, her letters were genuine, private, unposted letters to her husband.

Written on rice paper using a brush dipped in China ink, they are undated and each is distinguished from the other by a charming sketch. My great-grandmother kept them in a lacquered box under her bed.

'The house on the hill,' wrote Spring Orchid, articulating her sadness at her husband's absence, 'has lost its soul. It is a house without windows. At the thought of not seeing you coming home from the city, I tell myself that there'll be no more dawns for me and no sunsets will be able to warm my heart. Meiling, the housekeeper wanted to put away your desk chair because it takes up too much room, but I haven't allowed him to do so. It must remain where it is, so that I can still picture you sitting there smoking your water pipe.'

'My days are all the same. The mornings fly by with the tasks that are the lot of all women and, in the afternoon, I sit on the terrace with your sister after taking your Revered Mother for her nap. Then the peace and quiet is truly wonderful. Your sister and I take our embroidery out onto the terrace where we spend hours watching the people in the valley opposite. The weather is lovely. The hill is covered with the deep red flowers of autumn and the air is filled with a golden haze... The wild geese flying south carry my thoughts to you!'

Then there are the diary letters relating everyday occurrences in the family: the jealousies, petty arguments between relatives: strained relations between mother-in-law and daughter-in-law.

'Your younger brother is to be married soon. His betrothed's beauty is a frequent topic of conversation and we know she's very well-read. Your Revered Mother is not very happy about this last quality. "Too much education," she declares, "is not good for a woman: she would have done better to stick to embroidery instead of reading books." Your sister and I are secretly pleased because there will soon be three of us to put up with her and listen to her lectures. I say this not because she talks too much or because her words lack wisdom, but because she talks and we have to listen… The atmosphere changed from the moment your sister-in-law arrived. Still, I like Bao Yi, which is her name. She's so childish, although she's only three years younger than me. She's always laughing and in disgrace with your Revered Mother, and since she also makes your sister laugh, your Revered Mother has decided that from now on we must both learn texts by Confucius as a punishment. At the moment, between peals of laughter, we're studying the *Six Shadows That Attend The Six Virtues*. I fear we will never learn the verses at all. Your Revered Mother told me off unfairly. As you know, I can't reply to her in kind, even if her words were aimed at me "like arrows from the taut strings of a bow"... Your sister-in-law, Bao Yi, is in trouble again. I'd written to you earlier that she had brought a few servants from home, including her *amah*. In common with everyone who doesn't have much to do, her *amah* enjoyed sitting around and gossiping. So I ordered her to come to my garden and I told her: "The sheaves of rice have been beaten against wood for the last time. It's time for you to leave!" She left the house, but immediately used this as an excuse to reveal everything she knew about everybody. Everyone has found out about your illustrious ancestors' vices. I didn't know your family had such a long list of ancestors. She began with the ones from the Ming Dynasty and certainly hasn't mentioned their virtues. You're lucky to be so far away because this means you were out of range. Your Revered Mother strode from one courtyard to another in a fury and I feared she would call the police. Then she stopped, because she realised that the woman was entitled to shout her anger from the rooftops. You know your Mother has never practised the virtue of self-control, especially when it comes to controlling her tongue. That evening she was so agitated that we sent for the medicine man to apply the cupping glass to draw out the hot air from her body.'

One of the letters revealed a certain amount of wifely jealousy. Accumulated Virtue had sent a photograph depicting himself at a banquet given for the opening ceremony of a waterworks. My great-grandfather may never have known Spring Orchid's reaction: 'I received your letter and photograph. You say it is the plate from a party given by the Governor. I don't understand its precise importance, but I seem to make out a large number of people, particularly a large number of women. I didn't show the photograph to your Revered Mother because she might order you to come home immediately. I won't take the liberty of criticising your colleagues, nor do I think that the Governor could take you to a place not worthy of his rank, but in my humble opinion, the women appear to be too scantily dressed.'

There are also letters that recreate the impact of major or

minor events outside the family: these are lively letters that reveal not only her ability to share in other people's lives but also the serenity of someone who is happy with their lot. Last but not least, there are letters expressing her joy and pride at falling pregnant and giving birth to her first son, my mother's father: 'In the courtyard, I can hear the women chattering. I have sent for the seamstresses and embroiderers who spend their days preparing everything our son will need. So we are very busy, your sister, your sister-in-law and myself. Even your Revered Mother has picked up a needle. The pile of clothes grows daily: I touch them and stroke them and can already see them enveloping his little body. There are coats, little pairs of trousers, little shoes and little hats, and thick, warm eiderdowns. I have sent for the blind man and the ballad-singer who help us pass the time with their tales... Here is your beloved son. He is strong and handsome. When I hold him tightly, the wind blows through the pine forest carrying the music of the gods. I see the reflection of your face in his eyes, as in a mirror. Could anything be more wonderful than motherhood? Now I know the complete cycle of love. I didn't know everything there was to know about it until I could hold the boy in my arms. Now that you are also the father of our son, you have a new place in my heart. The bond uniting our hearts is stronger than rope made of plaited bamboo, a bond of love that will never break. I'm the mother of your firstborn... Your brother is a man of little discernment. He doesn't see the wonders of your son. He says that these are normal beauties. All I can say is that I feel sorry for him. The gods have definitely placed two veils in front of his eyes. I don't bear any grudge, there's no room for anything but love in my heart. I spend my days with the baby. I sing lullabies that make everyone laugh. When he sleeps, I watch him and see his face becoming more and more like yours. I want him to become a strong noble man like you and bear your name with honour, so that one day people may say: "Your wife's firstborn is a great man." At night, I lie down beside him and I'm jealous of his sleep, because it takes him away from me. While waiting for your return, your sister and I have nicknamed him "Ten Thousand Springs" because he was born in the spring. But I wouldn't want the gods to hear and become jealous, so we call him "Little Blockhead" when talking aloud. The gods will think that I'm not that bothered about him, so they won't decide to take him away from me.'

When Accumulated Virtue returned from his long mission on the Yangtze, my grandfather, "Little Blockhead", had already celebrated his second birthday and the family, with all the pomp and circumstance demanded by the occasion, officially named him Radiant Wisdom.

Young Radiant Wisdom grew up in difficult times for his country. The late 19th century saw the rise in China of the anti-Imperialist Boxer movement, which made its appearance in Shandong in 1899. The Boxers, formed mainly by peasants, artisans and labourers, were so called because they were diligent practitioners of boxing. Initially the movement appeared to be a protest against the Christian Church and the missionaries sent by the foreign powers. From Shandong, the struggle spread to the neighbouring provinces and the demonstrations became more violent, culminating in the sieges of Beijing and Tianjin. In 1900 there was a decisive attack on the foreign legations, churches and missions. Italy also became involved and King Umberto I was forced to send a military force to protect his diplomatic staff and the Italians living in China. The other foreign powers concerned followed suit. With superior weapons and greater experience, the eight besieged nations prevailed over the Boxer rebels following a bloody, ruthless siege. In 1901, immediately after the rebellion was quashed, Empress Cixi, who had imprisoned her nephew Emperor Guangxu, returned from Xian, where she had taken refuge, to Beijing to sign the peace treaty. From that time onwards, a large part of China became a colonised country, divided between the major powers of the time: the foreigners enjoyed every kind of privilege, while China as a nation, became more a geographical term than a sovereign state.

As a result, my grandfather did not have a straightforward

life like his father, Accumulated Virtue. On the contrary, he found himself struggling to knit together a patchwork of various businesses to ensure his and his family's security. The political and economic situation in which the bourgeoisie found themselves in both town and country, meant that the Miao family lost part of its property. Silk production entered a substantial decline that led to huge financial losses. My grandfather, however, managed to control this situation and slowly rebuild the family fortune by focusing on the cultivation of tea. In fact he was convinced that the food market was never hit by disastrous crises.

He did not have the aggressive spirit necessary to turn a gentleman into a successful entrepreneur. He was an extremely mild-mannered man and, in the three years he spent at the military academy, he was renowned for his refined, courteous manners, unassuming nature and the sense of irony that emerged in the witticisms he liked to make. Although he graduated from the academy honourably, it was not with particularly brilliant results. He loved flowers, particularly his own. His life was in the family home in Hangzhou, where he was better able to give rein to his fine sentiments and quiet dignity. He preferred to leave the fighting, conflicts and battle for ideals to his brother True Wood, who, many years before, had chosen his own path, having decided to espouse the Marxist cause for which he would later give his life.

World War One provided burgeoning Chinese capitalism with the opportunity for modernisation on a national scale and industry experienced considerable growth. A working class emerged and gradually began to gather strength as millions of peasants, keen to turn their backs on imminent hunger and death, became factory workers, flocking to the big city from the countryside that had historically been plagued by droughts, famines, floods, swarms of locusts and the presence of bandits. Many who worked for the Miao family left their service for the factories because the new work was more profitable.

'They want to be factory workers, so we must change the way we think', said my grandfather thoughtfully with characteristic composure. Anyone who heard him wondered how he always managed to stay so calm. But as the years went by, he took great comfort in manual work. He said that his gardener had taught him that every tree and bush had its own mood. In China the landowning classes were beginning to relinquish control and my grandfather's attitude reflected this situation.

The house of the Miao family on the Hill of Distant Fragrance was in the part of the city where the Chinese were not allowed entry to the parks and good restaurants. The foreigners in the Concession had their own post offices, law courts, even their own police force. They enjoyed a wide range of privileges connected with industry, trade, railroad transport, navigation on the Long River and mineral riches, and my family survived owing to Radiant Wisdom's good personal relationships with the English.

My grandfather married Splendid Gem when he was young and their marriage produced a little girl whom Accumulated Virtue wanted to name Green Bay, to commemorate the coves bordering the Yangtze where he had sheltered so many times during his travels on the Long River.

The passing of the seasons brought bright patches of peonies, camellias, peach and plum blossom to the garden of the House of Distant Fragrance.

I spent hours there watching the little birds, and scattering corn to attract the sparrows that hopped in circles around the grain. It was from the garden of that house that my first kite blew away, soaring in the sky till sunset when it came to rest in a tree; and it was there that I first saw a butterfly, jet black from its big wings to its swallow tail, fluttering above an orchid.

Like a mirror, the house still absorbs images and reflects them back from a time long ago, as if it were an extension of my identity. But if I am to tell my story from the beginning, I must take a huge mental leap back in time to the period when the Chinese people were learning new names: Mao Zedong, Chou En-lai and Chiang Kai-shek, already regarded in 1925 as the head of the nationalist republic.

Those years also witnessed the growing presence of the European powers, whose economic prospects and pseudo-colonial prestige were on the up. Italy had also decided to enhance its diplomatic and commercial presence in the country, increasing staff in the Tianjin Concession and the Beijing diplomatic legation to ensure it was on equal footing with the other powers. Mussolini sent Galeazzo Ciano, who was engaged to his daughter Edda, to Shanghai then Beijing, marking the start of a meteoric diplomatic career that allowed him to take Edda to China, where they remained until 1934. When they returned to Shanghai on board the luxurious liner, the *Conte Verde*, the couple were also accompanied by Il Duce's sons, Bruno and Vittorio, on a short visit.

One of the officials who arrived a year later was a Venetian whose life, after landing in China, might have been lifted from the pages of a novel.

3

It was the winter of 1935 and, after stopovers in Bombay and Singapore, the transatlantic liner was approaching Shanghai. With its cargo of passengers from every nation, the *Conte Verde* under Captain Camelli was almost at the end of the long journey begun about twenty-three days previously in Italy.

The ship's arrival coincided with the Chinese New Year celebrations, and the festivities in Shanghai were so exuberant that even the 50,000 or so foreign citizens were involved. For the ship's passengers, this festive occasion unexpectedly prolonged the endless round of parties that had begun in Europe before Christmas and had continued on board until now, when they would end after landing, with a bang.

As soon as the vast bulk of the ship had veered left to enter the Whangpoo river near Woosung, thirteen miles from the river port of Shanghai, the passengers could hear the crackle of hundreds of firecrackers exploding along the banks; as the *Conte Verde* neared its final port of call, the detonations began coming thick and fast, sounding ever more deafening.

Shrouded in a dawn fog that seemed to hover between turning to mist or lifting, the ship, swept along by an icy wind from far-off Mongolia, was surrounded by a flotilla of junks, sampans and waterbuses. From the decks, they could see men and small boys on the small crafts lighting the fuses of firecrackers and fearlessly letting them explode between their feet, since they were unable to throw them to a safer distance to avoid the explosion, and they were unwilling to watch them guttering silently in the water.

The four-day holiday had coincided with a bitterly cold snap, so the representatives from the foreign colony were holed up at home, and almost all the Chinese population were hidden away in shacks or boats. The only people to be seen on the quay running parallel to the Bund, the major thoroughfare, the buildings of which lined the port, were the docking and disembarkation staff who were keeping themselves busy to avoid being frozen to the spot. Meanwhile the ship, propelled by two tugs and towed by two others, slowly approached its cylindrical mooring buoy, its now motionless propeller blades barely visible.

Various launches equipped for transporting passengers, pulled away from the riverbank carrying police and customs officials, health authorities, representatives from Lloyd Triestino, and shipowners. Tall tower blocks lined the Bund like rows of motionless sentries protecting the fortunes they represented—strongboxes clad in European marble which had been purchased with Chinese money from the financial activities carried out in these very buildings.

On the other side of the river soared the steel turrets of the menacing, sleepy grey dragons, positioned there to defend the Japanese Imperial navy's armoured cruiser *Itzumo*, surrounded by its swift escort.

On board the *Conte Verde* actions, voices and words regained their full weight and meaning now that the heavy wood and metal structures, no longer in use, had fallen silent. From the heated deck, sheltered from the wind, an Italian woman responded to a remark made by her companion: 'So they're all banks! But which one is our hotel?'

'That one over there, the Cathay Hotel... the highest building in the middle with the pyramid-shaped top. It's the most famous one.'

'I can just make out the ninth floor where we're going to be dancing this evening.'

A cloud of swirling mist carried on the wind suddenly enveloped the ship, hampering mooring operations as the officer on the empty bridge found himself unable to see the mooring buoy. The men fastening the robust cables, numb with cold and stiff as underwater divers, continued their work like cheerful robots.

'Symbolic mist,' remarked a missionary. 'When we go ashore we can reckon on having crossed an ethereal span of centuries. The mysteries of the Chinese and their problems are enclosed one inside the other, like the carved ivory spheres some of them like to fashion.' The other passenger, a tall, slim Italian with a chiselled profile, alert expression and a confident air, turned to the missionary, smiled and said: 'Father, you're here to help them find an answer. You'll be here for years. You're not telling me you're already losing hope?'

'You've only just landed. The Chinese people are the most downtrodden, ailing nation in the world. Their poverty begins where that of other nations ends. You'll have the chance to witness it with your own eyes. I think this is your first time here, isn't it? We don't see poverty like this anywhere in Europe.'

The Venetian passenger gazed at the quay for a while, then looked up at the marble and cement colossuses towering above it.

'You're right, Father. This is my first time in the East and I'm not going ashore in Shanghai. I'm taking another ship tonight, to the Italian Concession in Tianjin.'

'Don't be fooled by what you can see from here,' remarked the missionary. 'Even if you did go ashore for a few hours, your impressions would be very misleading. During these four days, people behave as if they are possessed. It's their new year and they celebrate it as if they want to thank their Buddha for helping them survive the year that has just gone. They cast off the sorrows they've left behind and they don't think about the year to come. They don't want to spoil their enjoyment of the festivities.'

The Venetian passenger repeated that he wasn't intending to go ashore. Perhaps in the spring he might visit Shanghai, when the icy wind had dropped and the city had returned to normal. He could never have guessed the role that the city would play in his life in the next ten years.

While waiting for instructions to transfer to the steamer taking him to Tianjin, he spent a few hours in the peace and quiet of the *Conte Verde*'s neoclassical-style reading room, ensconced in a comfortable leather armchair with a book.

Later he went out onto the lifeboat deck to stretch his legs. He was tempted out into the open air despite the cold, by the grey dragons—the Japanese warships. He had a Kodak bellows camera with him and he took some photographs of the *Itzumo*, the flagship of the Japanese Imperial fleet, which might be of interest to the naval officer at the Italian Mission with whom he would be making contact as soon as he landed in Tianjin. Then he waited for the ship.

It had been arranged at the Palazzo Chigi that he would continue his journey by sea from Shanghai. It was now too risky to go by train because the Japanese were continuing their advance across the country in the north, and in several places along the railway line they had put up roadblocks that often resulted in clashes with Chinese armed formations. In 1931 the Japanese invasion of Manchuria's territory (later known as Manchukuo), had actually galvanized resistance by the two main opposing military and political factions, the Kuomintang and the Communists, who would join forces when necessary, to prevent the Japanese invaders from making a final advance. As a result, it was better for anyone needing to travel north to south, or vice versa, from Shanghai to Beijing and Tianjin, to use coastal services. The service offered by ships belonging to English shipowners, which were neutral and so were safe, was the best bet. For more than half a century, a heavy maritime traffic of merchandise and passengers had been conducted from Hong Kong along the whole stretch of coastline running from Singapore on the equator to the fourth parallel, with the exception of China's Yellow Sea and Korea.

The steamer boarded by the young Venetian was in fact English. The relatively small craft was moored alongside a quay; nearby, the long arm of a crane worked with the ship's cargo booms to transfer to the hold the assorted merchandise still piled on shore.

When he arrived in Tianjin, the New Year celebrations were

just a distant memory and the city's appearance and pace of life had returned to normal. Although the entire foreign colony was waiting for the imminent arrival of the Japanese troops, no one seemed to regard this as a matter of great importance.

The cold had not lessened; if anything, Tianjin, being much further north than Shanghai, was even colder, and for the first few days the Venetian was glad to be able to stay in his lodgings or in the office, immersed in long conversations and meetings.

It was only after a week that he decided to get to know the lively town and began to venture out more frequently, but his outings became increasingly solitary because it was as if a wall existed between the foreign citizens and anyone not linked in any way to the presence of the foreign colony, even in casual encounters. His conversations were nearly always limited to exchanges of views with Italian colleagues and officials from the various diplomatic or consular offices of the other Western countries.

His impatience grew over the next few weeks and months. The political and military situation was extremely fluid, preventing him from drawing any useful conclusions that would enable him to suggest a specific course of action to his superiors. He was left with the covert mission entrusted to him by the Ministry of Foreign Affairs before he left Rome, which he realised would be easier to carry out more effectively in Shanghai.

One evening, while at a cocktail party given by a powerful Franco-Russian Jewish businessman, a Jew who was "decamping" to Shanghai and making that city the base for his operations, the Venetian ran into Jean-Jacques de Turenne, the French Inspector General at the Ministry of Foreign Affairs, whom he had met during the voyage and with whom he had repeatedly discussed the current political situation in China. De Turenne made no move to greet him. The Frenchman seemed to be very much in the public eye and was surrounded by high-ranking people at all times. Only when the opportunity for a seemingly casual encounter presented itself did he come over and, out of earshot, began talking as if continuing an earlier conversation

'We were right, *mon ami*,' he said, 'Gunther Stilke was in the company of another agent, an engineer who left Telefunken and now works full-time for the Nazi secret services; he's responsible for radio installations at the Ministry of Foreign Affairs in Berlin, and he and Stilke were here to work on the transmitters and improve the technical quality of radio messages sent to Tokyo. At this moment in time, our two friends have already gone back to Shanghai to carry out the same job on the transmitters there.'

'But why is Stilke spending so much time on a job that the other German is better equipped to do?' asked the Venetian, pleased at the unexpected encounter and admiring the ease with which the Frenchman talked about secret matters as if he were weighing up France's chances of winning the Davis Cup that year with Jean Borotra and Lacoste.

'Because Stilke was reappointed to the post by Colonel Meissinger, head of the Gestapo here in the Far East, and he's now responsible for the smooth running of all departments. There you are, *mon ami*, this is your chance to show your superiors just who has his ears open! *Bonne chance*,' he said, walking away to mingle with the guests, as if he had just spotted someone more interesting to chat to.

The Venetian was not overly surprised to gain confirmation that Jean-Jacquesde Turenne was also involved in international espionage. He was more surprised to learn that this man seemed certain that he was also one of them.

Even more convinced that Shanghai was the nerve centre where his mission should be carried out, he asked to be sent on a visit to other Chinese cities with an Italian diplomatic presence, and then on to Shanghai. At the end of June that year, he was ordered to go straight to Shanghai on a mission, and after that to Nanking to meet the officials of the Italian naval units maintaining a presence in those waters.

When he arrived in Shanghai, the heat was overwhelming and the city was permanently wreathed in a heat haze. In the garden of the Italian Consulate, the new blooms on the magnolia trees were already edged with brown, and dropping their petals like wax flowers. The streets were filled with scantily-dressed people who only returned at the dead of night to their homes where they were still too hot. Information from Rome crossed with news from Tokyo and Berlin and, in the oppressive heat it was not easy to assess accurately their importance.

Before leaving Tianjin, his new destination required him to travel to various parts of the city to establish confidential contacts and carry out enquiries. The pavements were crowded, the streets swarming with rickshaws that wove between the cars to the continual sound of horns as the drivers made their way through the frantic hustle and bustle. It did not take him long, though, to find his way around and spend the minimum amount of time needed to attend the various meetings that filled his working day.

One Saturday in August, he visited the Zikawei Observatory to meet Father Gherzi, an Italian Jesuit renowned throughout the Far East for continuing the work begun in 1871 by the observatory's founder, Father Frac.

A series of meteorological data collection points had been built along the coastal strip of China; this data was communicated to the observatory and was examined for signs that could be used to identify new typhoons. This made it possible to predict their course and provide timely warnings to the area in question and the boats at sail there. However, Chinese junks did not receive radio signals and were in danger of shipwreck, even though the fishermen seemed to have a special instinct warning them of the danger; when a typhoon was approaching, it was customary to put a paper junk in the sea hoping that the wrath of the Dragon of the Waters would fall on the tiny model and spare the real boat.

The work carried out by the Italian Jesuit that saved thousands of lives every year, could also be useful for the naval units stationed along the coast and in the internal waterways. This was why, on that sultry Saturday in August, the Venetian had to go to the observatory. As soon as Father Gherzi saw him, he walked over to him with a smile, immediately recognising a fellow countryman.

35

'I'm simply the last link in a chain of signalmen,' he replied when asked if he was "the typhoon signalman".

'Nevertheless, Father,' replied the Venetian 'you must admit you're the mainspring of an extremely large and complicated instrument.'

'My work is linked to the more important and more inscrutable work of Divine Providence,' commented Father Gherzi, stroking his grizzled beard.

'Your name works its magic throughout the Far East,' insisted the Venetian. 'Minister Ciano has also spoken to me about your work; he would have come back here to pay his respects before returning to Rome, if urgent new commitments in the capital had not prevented him.'

'I remember the Minister's visit well and how interested he was in our work. I'm delighted that this magic, as you call it, should be linked to the name of an Italian like me, a poor priest, a modest scholar, doing his best to uphold the glorious tradition of Italian science in China, brought over by Father Ricci many centuries ago. But I owe my fame less to any scientific merit, and more to the publicity afforded by—'

'—the typhoons?' interrupted the Venetian.

'Exactly! The typhoons. Or rather, the typhoon warnings. And in many respects, the responsibility for those warnings—which entail taking into account the typhoon's unpredictable deviations—is huge. You only have to consider that it can cost hundreds of thousands of dollars to bring the port life of a city like Shanghai to a halt.'

'So nothing is more dangerous than raising a false alarm?'

'Well, one thing is more dangerous—not raising a genuine alarm.'

'Isn't it possible to be absolutely sure?'

'The only sure thing, my friend, is faith. Science also has its grey areas. There's always an unattainable benchmark of scientific excellence.'

'But apart from typhoon warnings, what other activities are carried out here in Zikawei? His Excellency Ciano mentioned general forecasting and meteorological research,' said the Venetian with feigned indifference. His visit to the observatory was actually part of a bigger plan to gather all possible information about the various Chinese provinces. With the international political situation in ferment in China—where too many countries had formed a complex framework of alliances—it was essential to ensure that the systems for gathering and distributing information were as efficient as possible. When he had visited the Zikawei Observatory, it had seemed to Galeazzo Ciano that it possessed the greatest technical and operational potential for retrieving information that was more than just meteorological data. However, the best way to harness this potential represented a delicate problem that necessitated making cautious enquiries to avoid the risk of sparking off a diplomatic incident between the Italian State and the Church. There was also a danger that other countries might have realised the potential represented by the observatory and might already be hard at work carrying out manoeuvres no different from those being undertaken at this very moment.

Adjusting his spectacles, Father Gherzi unrolled the geographical map of China on a desk,

'Hundreds of aides wire preliminary material to us on an hourly basis so that we can compile a daily analysis of the weather. Here at Zikawei, various priests take shifts even through the night: you could say that we keep watch on China, Japan, Mongolia, Siam and the Philippines with about a hundred meteorological stations—particularly the Philippines, because typhoons almost always begin forming east of that archipelago. Near land, the typhoons may move in one of three possible directions: down towards Hong Kong, up towards Japan and Korea, or straight towards the interior here in Shanghai. In theory, their course is predictable; in practice, typhoons unfortunately head towards us like a blinded raging Cyclops that, unable to see, careens out of control and often unexpectedly changes direction.'

While Father Gherzi was explaining this, the Venetian examined the map, following a hand-drawn belt of curves that started close together, then spread out in various directions at the other end.

'Typhoons are quite rightly seen as living, breathing monsters and it's ironic that they come from a sea that we humans have named the Pacific,' he remarked, his mind on other things.

In the observatory, the prevailing silence high up in the mountains was broken only by the faint whistling of the wind. Father Gherzi spent all his time here, religion and science united in the work and mind of a great Italian. But, the Venetian wondered, was his patriotism as strong as his religious faith? The organisation headed by Father Gherzi really had enormous potential: the network of data collectors located in the farthest reaches of China, in many cases in Communist-occupied territories, could make this a remarkable centre of espionage. In fact, the daily task of broadcasting messages to Zikawei provided an excellent cover for gathering and distributing information about movements that were anything but weather-related.

But how was he going to find out how receptive Father Gherzi might be? The Venetian weighed every remark, every phrase the clergyman uttered, ready to seize the right word to make a timely interruption and prepare a possible get-out as soon as he sensed any adverse reaction on the part of Father Gherzi.

After a long series of questions to which the priest, with a patience characteristic of his vocation, replied with a serenity tinged with pride, the Venetian was about to utter the decisive words, when Father Gherzi said: 'Would you believe that even the Japanese know about us. This winter, on a bitterly cold day in January, a Japanese admiral came to see us with the captain of the cruiser on which he was sailing, and two other officials. The name of the ship was the *Itzumo*, if I remember correctly. They seemed very interested in our work, but at a certain point, they asked if I would be willing to collaborate with them, placing some of my data-collection stations at their disposal. They would no doubt have been used for broadcasting coded messages here, which would have been picked up by one of their envoys. It's just typical of the Japanese and Germans to think that I'd have gone along with them! I include the Germans too, because they paid me a visit last year. They came from Shandong to ask the same question. How could they imagine that the Society of Jesus would accede to a request like that?'

This was a severe blow for the Venetian: his mission had come to nothing and he could only hope that Father Gherzi had not been wise to his real reasons for asking to visit the observatory. All he could do was to politely take his leave from the Jesuit and return to the office to report that his mission had failed. His one small consolation was knowing that, although two other nations had beaten him to it, both had suffered a quick and humiliating defeat.

The evening of his visit to Zikawei, the Italian Consulate was organising its usual party at the Cercle Sportif.

Back at his lodgings, after a short rest and a long bath, the Venetian donned a white raw silk suit and black shirt. They were made by the Chinese tailor who worked for the navy officials and staff of the Italian Legation and whom everyone called *Foderetto* because he had initially made his name changing the lining or *fodera* of sailors' caps. Smartly attired from head to foot, the young man left for the party at the Cercle Sportif.

These clubs are all the same, he thought as he gazed around. To tell the truth, the premises of the Cercle Sportif offered a level of luxury that was hard to find even in Europe, with its vast oval ballroom and steel-sprung dance floor, its huge swimming-pool covered in winter and used as a badminton court, its 36 tennis courts, extensive lawn, beautiful terraces, and its restaurant serving excellent food. But here, as elsewhere, members wore Panama hats and white suits; after work, or playing polo or tennis, they relaxed in wicker chairs drinking ice-cold cocktails brought by the Chinese bellboys, their conversation revolving *ad nauseam* around the same subjects: horseracing, women, business, and the temperature.

This evening, however, there was a surprise in store for the bored young official, a small surprise with far-reaching consequences. Shortly after he walked into the club, he was approached by a small, plump woman of around fifty, her blonde hair gathered in an elaborate chignon.

'We haven't met, have we?' she asked immediately. 'I'm a great fan of Italy. I lived in Milan for two years, in Via Rovello. Do you know it? And I've always spoken, or rather, sung in Italian. Yes, I'm a singer. Or rather I was. I haven't sung for three years. I was an opera singer and so I decided to go to your country to study when I was very young... Olga Aleksandrova, from Leningrad. You are from which part of Italy?'

'Marco Polo's city,' replied the Venetian, smiling, 'but I only followed in his footsteps six months ago, and I chose a faster and much more comfortable means of travel! What about you, Signora, how long have you been in Shanghai?'

The woman needed no prompting to reply, and the Venetian, perhaps regretting this rash question, soon learned everything there was to know about her life.

She had been in Shanghai since the end of 1925. Her husband was a jeweller. Life in Russia had been getting harder because work was no longer as plentiful, and her career as a singer had been very precarious. So after her parents died, the pair had decided to move to Moscow in a bid to improve her husband's work situation. This had not panned out for either of them. No one at the academy would help her because she was not from Moscow and, with Lenin's death, everything became even tougher as Stalin began to take absolute control of the country, and the pogroms made life unbearable for Jews like themselves. Tens of thousands of Russians began to leave the country, and they, too, wanted to make a new life in America. Instead of attempting to go through Europe, her husband had decided to take the Trans-Siberian railway to Vladivostok, believing this would be an easier route. When they had arrived on the Pacific coast they had encountered enormous difficulties; it had been a miracle that they had been able to board a ship bound for Yokohama from where they had continued their journey to Shanghai.

At this point in the story Olga Aleksandrova broke off to sip her champagne.

'We had no idea,' she immediately continued, 'that when we got here we'd be arrested and detained in a camp for

Russian refugees. The local authorities had adopted this measure with all our fellow countrymen: they feared the danger of a rebellion on the part of Communist factions that had formed here and there in China. So they placed us in a kind of quarantine and kept us under surveillance to see if we acted suspiciously.'

They were released about a year and half later, after proving they could earn their living and that they had no intention of giving the Chinese authorities any trouble.

It was not easy to get by, but both of them managed to restart their careers in Shanghai, after a fashion. All the best hotels of the city employed orchestras to entertain their guests in the main dining room during meals, as well as at teatime on public holidays, so it was not difficult for her to convince hotel managers to let her sing selected arias from Italian lyric operas for their customers. Her husband, on the other hand, had tapped into a "gold vein", as she put it, when he started to repair, alter and clean the jewellery of the wives of officials, then went on to sell his own jewellery.

'But now I've practically given up singing,' the woman finally concluded. 'My voice isn't what it once was—I realise that—and in my view, there's nothing sadder than a singer's voice that has lost its brilliance. I have found a way to turn my experience to good effect, though, and I now have an enthusiastic group of students who love Western singing: men and women of varying ages who are passionate about the art.'

She talked at length about one of her pupils in particular: a young Chinese woman with an extraordinary voice and a very promising future.

4

After spending a few days in Nanking on business, the Venetian was now on his way back to Shanghai. The Italian Consulate's Fiat drove at a snail's pace between the colourful crowd walking down the middle of the street. The Venetian watched with curiosity, the confusion created by the noisy hustle and bustle.

The sergeant of a patrol of soldiers with flat helmets, brown uniforms and long bayonets fixed to rifles dating back to the Manchu dynasty had stopped the car and asked to see the two occupants' papers. The first inspection was a searching look inside the car to ascertain whether the passenger was Japanese or European. The driver, a trustworthy man from the Consulate, had an impressive pass that the soldiers recognised at first glance. The Venetian, to speed things up and minimise the ever-present risks these checks represented, flashed his own business card. Whether genuine or forged, it was the most influential form of pass in China and a sure-fire way of getting through street checks, especially if it was embossed. Immediately after, the car was waved through with a string of orders.

The car suddenly speeded up, arriving at the railway station just before the disembarkation of the *Falcon*. This ferry provided a shuttle service across the Yangtze to Nanking, which was the departure point for the direct line to Shanghai and carried around 1,000 passengers from Beijing. If the car had been a few minutes late, it would have been hard to find any room on the train.

Now the Venetian sat quietly gazing at the landscape through the small train window. The countryside gave the impression of majestic, peaceful serenity. Green mulberry trees and willows stood among blossoming almonds, cherries and medlars that basked in the gentle warmth of spring. Everywhere he looked, he saw vast expanses of sky and water, immense rice fields crisscrossed by canals, cultivated fields, thickets surrounding ancestral tombs, promontories against which the vast mass of the river silently pressed, forming looming gorges. On the horizon, he could make out the low, grey silhouette of the hills of Hangzhou, its pagodas and temples introducing an artificial note in this vast natural setting.

Junks sailed up the river hugging the banks with the wind behind them, while large tree trunks like rafts were swept along by the current. In no other part of the country had the Venetian ever had such a strong impression that time was a figment of the imagination and that past, present and future had merged into one.

As the Chinese countryside silently unfolded before his eyes, creating a feeling of solitude, he cast his mind back to Nanking—the city he had just left to return to Shanghai—and the meetings and conversations he had had with friends there.

Little more than half a century earlier, the Taiping rebellion had decimated the whole city so Nanking seemed like an empty shell. Now it was a mishmash of neo-Chinese and American-style buildings. Attractively situated against a backdrop of hills on the promontory formed by a loop of the Yangtze, its marshy plain was covered with lotus flowers to the south, between the Long River and the walls. In the 1920s, the Central Government had decided to completely rebuild it, but unfortunately, the plans lacked an adequate infrastructure and the city was showing signs of decline. The Ministries were surrounded by vegetable gardens; there were pools near the Legations where it was not unusual to see a smartly attired city dweller watching a poor fisherman with his bamboo rod; leafy branches and roots were nibbling away at the corners of the tennis court where the Venetian had played.

He remembered how he had dined with a group of former colleagues from the Academy on board an Italian gunboat, the *Carlotto*. Anchored thirty feet from the riverbank, the ship had recently returned from its usual mission protecting on the Yangtze steamships sailing under the Italian flag from attacks by pirates. Beneath a canopy sheltering them from the humid heat, the friends had chatted about the complex international situation, relations between the big powers, and the spread of Communism in China, which was opposed by the Japanese and Italians and supported by the Russians. Every now and then, the shouts of unexpected disputes echoed from the surface of the river: steersmen of junks and rafts in danger of colliding, applied themselves to oars and tillers as the shallow water restricted the amount of available space, increasing the danger of collisions in the darkness. Above them, migratory birds sporadically uttered mysterious chirps and whistles. Two junks collided and he and his colleagues heard a voice calling for help while other voices continued arguing. The calls for help drifted further and further away, until they stopped altogether, swallowed up by the Yangtze. The mist rolled towards the water and the penetrating humidity prompted the three friends to go their separate ways after making tentative plans for another meeting and toasting each other Chinese-style, shouting *'Gan bei'*

On the first Sunday afternoon after his return to Shanghai, the Venetian walked into the lobby of the Park Hotel. He looked in the various reception rooms of the hotel in the hope of seeing his friends from the *Carlotto*, whom he had arranged to meet there. He checked the lounges on three floors, then told the lift boy to take him up to the nineteenth floor, where he headed for his favourite room, the panoramic orchestra lounge. As always, the band was playing music from the operettas. He carefully examined all the tables—with a bit of luck this was where he would find his friends.

Luck must have been on his side that Sunday afternoon, but not in the way he had expected. Three people were sitting at a table at the back of the lounge, virtually hidden by the plants placed near the band. His gaze alighted on the familiar face of a woman whom he did not recognise at first, but after a couple of seconds remembered as the Russian singer he had met at the Cercle Sportif party. The man beside her was probably her husband, but he wondered who was the attractive Chinese woman with them.

He walked over and gladly accepted their invitation to join them at their table, ordering a pot of Lapsang Souchong tea, his favourite blend. He might have been in two minds about it if he had not been so very curious to find out more about the young Chinese woman, who was introduced to him as Green Bay. Like the other two, she also spoke English, so it was easier to involve her in the conversation.

He soon found out that she was one of Olga Aleksandrova's students, the talented young Chinese woman she had told him about at the Cercle Sportif. Green Bay was hoping to study in Italy and the singer's contacts at the Italian Consulate had come in useful when asking for information about the possibility of obtaining a study grant for her to attend a singing school in Italy. All that remained was the problem of the Italian entry visa, but Green Bay's parents had excellent *guanxi* (connections) that would cut through red-tape and enable her to obtain exit papers from China without delay.

While the Russian singer told him what she had done to enable Green Bay to study singing in Italy, the Venetian could not stop looking at the young Chinese woman. He had been in China for almost a year, but had never before had the opportunity to talk to such a pretty Chinese woman, who kept abandoning her timid demeanour to make enthusiastic comments about a plan that had until now been all hopes and dreams. It was difficult to imagine that a young woman who looked so delicate might have the kind of powerful soprano voice that, so Olga Aleksandrova said, was a rare gift in China, and destined her for a bright career.

'Are you happy?' Green Bay suddenly asked the Venetian in English. The question, as unexpected as it was unusual, caught him off guard, but the Russian singer immediately chipped in to save him from embarrassment.

'In China, you see, it is a sign of politeness to ask someone if they're happy. Perhaps Green Bay is asking because she has noticed that you still haven't drunk your tea, so maybe you don't feel well.'

'Yes! Very much so, thank you,' replied the Italian to Green Bay in English, with a broad smile and, even before he could pick up the teapot, Green Bay had beaten him to it and poured his tea, as is customary in China.

'Pouring tea or arranging morsels of food on a man's plate,' explained the singer, 'are also regarded as a sign of good manners for Chinese women.'

The Venetian listened carefully to her words; he would remember everything said at that table. He did not know whether to take his leave so he could arrange another meeting with the lovely Chinese woman, or stay with them all so that he could go on speaking to her. He was afraid that the Russian singer and her husband might get up from the table and disappear with her. He had to take the initiative. He made as if to rise and, resting his hands on the table, turned to look at Green Bay.

'If you remember the name of the official you spoke to about the papers you need for your visa,' he said, 'I'll try and find out tomorrow why they still haven't been in touch. If you'd be so kind as to phone me late in the morning, I should have some news for you about your application.'

'But Doctor Venturini has already told us that the application would have to be reviewed by the Consul General,' replied Green Bay with obvious apprehension.

The Venetian shrugged. 'That's of little importance,' he retorted. 'Tomorrow I'll meet with the Consul General and take care of it. That's settled then. I'll look forward to your phone call, Miss Green Bay. Signora, Signor Aleksandrov, please excuse me. Good evening.' Turning again to Green Bay he took her hand and squeezed it very gently, almost afraid he might hurt her. He fancied he could still feel the Chinese woman's light touch on his right palm, so he took out the money to pay the waiter with his left hand. In the lift, he examined his palm closely, as if to read his own future. He sensed he was master of his own destiny, and that the first page had already been written.

5

In the autumn of 1936, the newspapers were full of news about floods, famines and civil wars. The international political context was becoming increasingly complex. Due to the African question, Italy was being hit by sanctions imposed by many European and non-European countries in the League of Nations; and because some of these countries were also maintaining an active presence in the Far East, Italy's position in China was becoming increasingly difficult. The checkerboard of alliances was changing.

The Venetian's private life had changed so agreeably in the last few hours, it appeared to be cushioning him from the impending crisis, though he realised that the deterioration of the political and military situation could have an impact on his private life.

Consul Venturini remembered Green Bay and he soon managed to track down the copy of the file that had already been forwarded to the office in charge of cultural relations; it was the job of that office to screen all applications, make an initial selection, and send them to Rome for the visas to be issued. There had been no answer yet, so the Venetian sent an immediate reminder.

On the dot of eleven that morning, a phone call was put through to him.

'If you please, did you find out whether my application has been received?' It was the young Chinese woman, her voice more vibrant and confident than he remembered from the evening before. He also liked the fact that Green Bay went straight to the point, without indulging in the lengthy preambles and polite remarks to which the Chinese were accustomed.

The young woman's confident tone made it impossible for him to think up a less-than-honest reply, and there would be no point in simply telling her that the application was waiting attention in Rome since he wanted an excuse to see her again.

'Signorina,' he said slowly, 'it would give me great pleasure to tell you in person what I've found out this morning.' Without giving Green Bay time to interrupt him, he continued. 'I know a quaint restaurant where we can eat *dim sum* and excellent sweet pastries—the Xinja at 719 Nanking Road. Why don't we meet in the dining room on the first floor around quarter past one and I'll tell you all about it then? Is that OK?'

There was a short silence on the other end of the line. Green Bay was taken aback: in Hangzhou, it would have been unthinkable for a young man she had only just met to suggest lunching alone with him. Things were obviously done differently in Shanghai.

'That's very kind of you,' she replied, after a short silence that felt like torture to the Venetian. 'I'll be there on time. Goodbye!'

What she said was simple and succinct, but to his ears her words combined courtesy with a compliment, and a promise of receiving more.

After further research that morning, he discovered, with a mixture of disappointment and pleasure, that it was very rare for a Chinese citizen to succeed in obtaining a study visa for Italy, let alone a study grant. What was more, all the successful applicants had been men. He would be very upset if, because of the follow-ups he himself had initiated, Green Bay ended up obtaining her visa straight away.

When it was time for their meeting, he straightened his tie, smoothed down his hair, turned up the collar of his jacket to protect himself from the wind sweeping down the Bund, and without attracting attention, left the office, walking quickly towards Nanking Road.

He arrived at the Xinja restaurant on time and went directly upstairs to the first-floor Guangzhou dining-room, renowned for its delicious Cantonese *dim sum* specialities.

He could not see Green Bay among the people waiting by the door. He had barely passed through the heavy red velvet curtains, when he noticed her near a column.

It was the first time he had seen her standing. She was wearing European dress and he took in her slim build, graceful stance, and long black hair framing a pale face that was even more beautiful than he remembered from the previous evening. He was bowled over by her beauty. He walked over to her, his heart racing.

'How are you? he asked. "Have you been waiting long?'

Banal words compared to what he would have liked to say, he thought, holding her hand in greeting, the sensation immediately reminding him of the previous evening at the Park Hotel. Gently keeping her hand, he looked around for a table.

She replied unselfconsciously, looking at him directly: 'Before I find out what you have to tell me, let me thank you for showing an interest in my case and taking time away from your work.'

There it is again, thought the young man, the same firm, decisive, musical voice he had heard on the telephone several hours before.

Weaving his way between the tables, he led her to one that was unoccupied, and they sat down without bothering to attract the waiter's attention. The other tables around them were occupied by Chinese and European diners, all of them bent over, their faces immersed in their bowls, intent on conveying small pieces of meat and grains of rice swiftly to their mouths with whirling chopsticks.

'I'd also like to thank you for buying me tea yesterday afternoon,' she added, slipping her overcoat over the back of the velvet chair.

'It was a pleasure to have your company. I was hoping to meet up with two Italian friends whom I'd seen again in Nanking. You can imagine how happy I was to find Signora Aleksandrova instead and to make your acquaintance. Is this the first time you have been out with a European man?'

She smiled. 'This is the first time I've been out with a man. Have you met any other Chinese women since you've been in Shanghai?'

'Work keeps me very busy and I still haven't done anything to meet people outside Legation circles. But I was forgetting that I arranged to see you specifically to talk about your application,' he lied. 'Unfortunately, the news isn't good,' he went on. He was sure a woman like her deserved sincerity and not the polite illusion of false hopes. He was right.

'I appreciate your honesty, I'm not labouring under any illusions. Dreams are like flowers in the mirror and the moon in the lake,' she said.

'In any case,' he said, 'everything that can be done at the moment has been done. All you can do now is wait. I'll put my heart and soul into following the matter up personally, I promise.'

Green Bay's eyes, full of surprise at his last words, met the Venetian's tender gaze.

Only the arrival at their table of a waiter pushing a trolley laden with an assortment of *dim sum* made them change the subject. The continuous succession of tasty morsels chosen each time with consummate skill by the Chinese woman, kept them engaged in a lengthy interplay of glances and unexpressed emotions. Finally she softly repeated the same question in English that had taken him aback the evening before.

'Are you happy?' she asked, leaning towards him.

'More than you,' came the reply.

Green Bay's breathing quickened as she confessed, pointing at her chest: 'I felt the same pain here when I sat for, and passed, my exams for the singing diploma.'

'And after? What did you feel afterwards?'

'The fluttering of a thousand herons' wings,' replied Green Bay, lowering her eyes, surprised at her own words.

The meal over, they said goodbye reluctantly and, when he was back in the office, the young Italian tried to put his thoughts and feelings into perspective. Again he sensed that

51

this meeting with Green Bay was momentous.

The next morning, at the florist in the marble lobby of the Cathay Hotel, he ordered for her a bunch of tuberoses, along with a box containing a small spray of the same flower. He nervously wrote an awkward note: 'Make this happy: wear it this evening!'

Their rendezvous was in the ground-floor lounge of the Cathay Hotel, on the corner of Nanking Road and the Bund, regarded by many as the most luxurious hotel in the East. Its restaurants, wines and ballroom orchestra could compare with the best in Europe.

Green Bay had been raised to be extremely punctual and was already there, waiting. The Venetian, like many Italians, exercised his unspoken prerogative to be late for appointments, even if they were to do with affairs of the heart. He found it impossible to break the bad habit, despite the discipline instilled in him at the Academy.

Green Bay was sitting in an armchair in the lobby. She saw him striding in, before he saw her. She noticed that other people stepped aside to let him pass.

Green Bay had abandoned Western clothing that day, and when she rose to meet him, her elegant figure drew everyone's attention. She wore a blue silk *qipao* (the close-fitting Chinese tunic), the tuberose bud pinned to her right shoulder, her long black hair framing her face. A faint smile on her lips, she walked over to meet him, moving with incomparable grace. Her long slender legs could be glimpsed through the side slits of the *qipao*.

The Venetian, thrown by this unexpected vision, hesitated a second before taking her hand. They held hands gazing at each other, both conscious of and unconcerned about being the centre of attention.

'You look ravishing.'

Green Bay lowered her eyes, blushing, while she sought some word of greeting. She only managed to smile at him.

The young man continued almost without drawing breath: 'Do you want to eat first, then go upstairs? The ballroom will be more crowded then.'

'It'll be easier for us to feel alone in a crowd,' replied the young Chinese woman. So they headed towards the dining room where the *maître* showed them to a corner table.

They ordered a small selection of classic Chinese dishes, accompanied by tea. They sat there at the table for a long time, talking and telling each other about themselves. The Venetian learnt that Green Bay came from Hangzhou, where she had always lived before moving to Shanghai to finish her singing lessons and specialise under the guidance of Olga Aleksandrova. Her stay in the city had lasted longer than expected because of the delay in obtaining her visa for Italy, but she occasionally went back to Hangzhou to visit her parents and enjoy a respite from the hustle and bustle of Shanghai.

The young Italian told her a great deal about his life, too: the childhood years spent in Venice—his mother had died and he had two siblings, Pierluigi and Maria; his training at the Naval Academy in Leghorn; his transfer to Rome.

The unexpected love that had already blossomed between them, true love at first sight, was far too intense for the young couple to be able to consider the obstacles to a mixed relationship in China. Otherwise they would have noticed that their table, so pleasantly isolated, had remained so even though the dining room had gradually filled. The *maître* had assiduously avoided showing Western guests to tables near the one where an Italian man was sitting with a young Chinese woman. This most prestigious hotel in the city was regarded as the exclusive domain of Westerners: Chinese guests were not welcome—young, attractive Chinese women even less so: at least officially, *"can do"* girls (prostitutes) were banned by fashionable establishments. Green Bay was too inexperienced and the Italian had spent too little time in China for either of them to be aware of the true situation, or the obstacles facing their love.

They danced all evening on the circular dance floor of pink-veined marble, completely wrapped up in each other, oblivious to the looks they were attracting. At one moment, two Italian navy officers broke in while they were dancing a foxtrot and asked the Venetian if they could be introduced to his beautiful companion.

'Later, later,' he said with cheerful self-confidence, 'Let us finish this dance first.'

'Everyone in town knows you,' joked Green Bay.

'They want to meet the most beautiful girl in Shanghai. I'm the lucky man who met you first. And I intend to keep you all to myself.'

The band finished the popular excerpt from the film *Rose-Marie* with Jeanette McDonald and Nelson Eddy and, while the musicians enjoyed a short break, the pair crossed the room side by side. The Venetian was conscious that everyone was looking at them.

Outside the hotel, they found a Chrysler taxi.

'Windsor Court, opposite the race-track, on Bubbling Well-Road,' the Venetian told the driver and lapsed into a silence that seemed to last forever, although it can only have been a few moments. He had now fallen into "the tender trap" and he could not, and would not, try to escape; he banished the uncertainties that had crossed his mind earlier and remembered how, as he held Green Bay in his arms on the dance floor, she had spontaneously returned his embrace. When he had buried his face in her hair fragrant with tuberoses, he had frequently brushed his lips against her forehead and she had not pushed him away. Yet she lowered her eyes at his compliments and blushed. Innocent and wise, honest and passionate, mysterious and serene, old-fashioned in the elegance of her traditional attire, yet thoroughly modern in the unaffected way she conversed or in the ease with which she had accepted his invitations, she fascinated him, binding him tighter with every passing second. He took her hand and, fingers intertwined, they stayed like that as the taxi drove through the brightly-lit streets of wide-awake Shanghai, not talking, each wondering if they would part when the taxi reached its destination.

When they drew up in front of Windsor Court, the young Italian agonised whether he should leave with the taxi or accompany Green Bay to her apartment. But he sensed this was not the time to rush things and that he should proceed with caution. Green Bay seemed enclosed in a delicate shell that would break if held with force.

He left. Carried away by the intensity of his emotions, he walked through the night, returning only at dawn.

6

The next day, the Venetian would never have met Zhang if he had not tried to avoid a rickshaw. Tired after a night spent walking the streets of the city, his heart and mind full of her, he did not move away quickly enough, and one of the rickshaw shafts grazed him. He collided with a Chinese man in the crowd and they fell to the ground, locked in a clumsy embrace. When they got up, dusting themselves off, they did not exchange imprecations or insults as neither was sure whose fault it was. The collision was met by a peevish 'Sorry!' in English from the Venetian and a 'Solly!' from the Chinese man.

'But Master not English!' exclaimed the latter in surprise.

The Italian was just as surprised to hear these words: he had only said one word and had pronounced it better than the individual in front of him.

'You're not English, you're Italian' said the Chinese man confidently, switching to Italian.

'What makes you think so' retorted the Venetian crossly, in his native tongue. He was irritated that the Chinese man would not meet his eye, unaware that it was actually a sign of respect in the Chinese code of behaviour.

'I worked for the Salesians of Don Bosco in Suzhou and all the Italians wore a thin chain with a small medallion of the Madonna. Only the Italians—not the English or the Germans,' he added.

'Yes, I am Italian. But what interests you more—the fact that I'm Italian, or the chain around my neck?'

'I don't want your chain. If I'd wanted it, it would already be mine and I'd be long gone,' replied the Chinese man with a winning smile.

The Venetian thought for a moment, then pointed to a less crowded area of pavement stretching from the Bund to the river. When they started walking, the Italian who brought up the rear, noticed that the Chinese man moved like a mime artist, walking fast and silently, shifting a little to the left, then to the right, every move creating the impression that he had disappeared, only to reappear a moment later.

Since his arrival from Tianjin, the Venetian had felt the need to find a trustworthy messenger to help him with the secret part of the task given to him in Italy before he left for China. Something told him now that this individual who had accidentally landed up on top of him could be the person he had been looking for.

'What line of work are you in?' he asked, as soon as they had reached a quiet place by the Whangpoo River.

'I'm a waiter at the Heron Fountain near the station, past Suzhou Creek.'

'And what type of inn is it?'

'A place that opens in the evening and closes in the morning. It's frequented by many foreigners and sailors, and others who do all kinds of work.'

'Such as…?'

'I don't ask,' replied the Chinese man, still with his eyes downcast. The Venetian pressed the question.

The Chinese man sensed that it was prompted by more than simple curiosity. He suspected that the Italian might be a member of the secret police, but decided to trust him anyway.

'A variety of work,' he said. 'There are fences of goods stolen from foreigners,' he began with deliberate roguishness. 'There are smugglers who come down from the port, currency traffickers, opium traffickers, bent policemen, police informers, the boyfriends of the *can do* girls, and there are always people looking for work. There are Chinese and foreign sailors from the ships, informers from secret societies who are spying on those from even more secret societies. Do you want me to go on? I don't know what to tell you because I don't know what you're interested in.'

'Are there are any Westerners—who are not drunken sailors?' asked the Venetian.

'Yes. They come sometimes, and only ever talk to the men from the secret societies.'

Hoping his intuition had not let him down, watching the Chinese man closely, the Venetian asked: 'Are you married? Do you have children?'

These questions surprised the fellow.

'No! No woman wants to marry me because I'm always out and about in Shanghai when I'm not working at the inn. I live with my grandfather on a sampan in Suzhou Creek. Perhaps when I have a shop, or a house.'

'Would you like to work for me without the risk of losing your job at the inn?'

'What would I have to do?'

'Follow some people, then report to me where they went and the people they met. I'll give you ten dollars now, but first you must come with me so I can show you who I want you to follow. OK?'

'But where are you going? You need to tell me where to find you afterwards so I can tell you everything.'

'Don't worry. I'm not running away. I wouldn't give you ten dollars then just disappear. What's your name?'

'Zhang, Master Italy. What's yours?' he timidly asked.

'Just call me Master Italy. Now,' he added, looking at his watch, 'Let's go!'

Zhang followed the Italian with his strange side-stepping dance that reminded the Italian of Spot, the English setter he used to take hunting in the countryside of Breda del Piave: the dog had run in front and behind, to the right and to the left, but never straight ahead—he would disappear, reappear then disappear again.

The two men took a taxi and stopped where the road widened near some impressive buildings from which a swarm of employees was pouring, like ants. The Venetian told the taxi to pull over near a line of luxury cars parked by the kerb, in which the drivers waited for their employers to emerge from the main doors opposite.

'Zhang, get into the back,' he ordered. 'Tell the driver to keep an eye on the second car in the first row, the one with white wheel trims. Get him to follow it as soon as it does a u-turn from the other side of the street and draws up in front of the main entrance. Stay here in the taxi and keep watch to see who gets in the car. The person I'm interested in is the fair, almost bald man wearing spectacles. Don't let him out of your sight. The car will stop in front of a red building with two magnolia trees, which is his house. Keep out of sight and take a look around. If the car remains parked there and waits for him in front of the house, it means he's bound to go out again. Wait for him and watch who he comes out with. If it is a Western woman, let them go. If he comes out alone though, watch what direction the car takes. I'll leave you now.' He added after a moment's thought: 'See if he sends the car away immediately—that means he'll be working from home. You'll notice that the house has very large radio antennae on the roof. Keep a close watch on the house and anything taking place in the garden and at the back. Make sure you remember the face and build of the fair man. You Chinese think all Westerners look alike. I'm off. Let's meet tomorrow at midday on the Bund, where we caught this taxi. Good luck!'

'*Can do*, Master Italy!' replied Zhang with his captivating smile, rolling up capacious sleeves concealing long arms that, slender as they were, could break an adversary's bone with one martial arts move.

Satisfied, the Venetian moved off, disappearing into the crowd of people getting off a bus. He was now in a safer position to keep closer tabs on Gunther Stilke, the head of German espionage in China. He had come across him before— on the ship and in Shanghai, but he had never been keen to tail him. Stilke only needed to see him face to face once, and his cover would be blown, and such behaviour would not be officially excused in view of current good relations between Italy and Germany—he might actually jeopardise Italian diplomacy. But the Venetian's brief went way beyond his official diplomatic activities. Galeazzo Ciano, Mussolini's emissary in China, had particularly asked him to provide proof of the Germans' suspicious behaviour there, and assess how likely it was that their shady dealings might place Italy at a disadvantage to the other foreign powers that had active political, economic or military interests in the country.

The next day the Venetian headed for the prearranged place on the Bund, anxious to find out how Zhang had fared. He wondered if this was the last he would see of the cunning person he had recruited on instinct alone. He knew he should keep out of sight in case Zhang double-crossed him and had him followed.

As soon as he arrived at the taxi rank, he heard a voice behind him saying: 'Me speakee you, Master Italy.'

'Not here, Zhang,' replied the Venetian without turning round. 'Let's go and have a beer.'

They walked over to a drinks stand near the Customs House, crowded with Westerners and Chinese men and women waiting for sampans or launches that shuttled between the city's shoreline and the larger ships moored to gigantic buoys. With the Bund behind them, obscured by a stack of cases of empty bottles, facing the port, the Italian prepared himself to listen.

His companion told how the fair, balding man had left the office block with another Westerner, a fat man wearing a white suit and a Panama hat. When they arrived at the junction of Peking and Yates Road, the fair man had climbed out of the car and had entered a building. Zhang had swiftly sent away the taxi and rushed over to the door through which the German had disappeared. He had seen him walk into the lift as the boy closed the gate—he was the only person to do so—and the lift pointer indicated that he had stopped on the third floor. As soon as the lift had returned, Zhang had asked to be taken to the third floor saying he had an urgent message for the gentleman who had just gone up. As he could not read, he asked which office the German gentleman had entered. Once out of the lift, he laboriously copied the letters on the nameplate as best he could. Then he ran downstairs and stationed himself near the entrance. He noted that the German was driven back to his home and that the car had left.

Zhang passed the slip of paper on which he had copied the letters to the Venetian, who read it, recopied it, ripped it up and threw it into the water.

'Well done,' he said, smiling at Zhang. 'I'll give you five dollars a week to work for me. You might also have to work at night. What happens if you occasionally don't turn up for work at the inn?'

'If you speak to my boss and tell him you need me to work as a waiter for an evening and give him ten dollars, he'll say OK. Money's the only thing he's interested in. *Can do*, Master Italy!' He added that the lift boy also had said that the German gentleman had been going there regularly for some weeks.

The Venetian thought perhaps this was because the German no longer felt confident about a previous meeting place with his contacts, and had set up another with a different cover. If so, the Italian could consider himself one of the luckiest men in the whole of Shanghai for literally bumping into a Chinese man who understood what had to be understood, and showed such initiative. The Venetian was left in no doubt that Stilke was like an octopus with tentacles reaching in every direction.

The next day Zhang was not only able to provide him with a detailed description of the man he had seen go into the office visited by Stilke, but also information on the two Chinese men who ran the firm based there, a company with an English name that traded in machinery. This information he had obtained from the Chinese secretary of a small English sales firm in an office on the same corridor by pretending he was looking for a third person. Apparently the two Chinese men were visited by two Europeans three or four times a week. One was the German who always arrived late in the afternoon; the other—a thin, tall man—dropped by on foot, just after lunch, when things were busier: the secretary had often seen him near the junction of Peking and Yates Road.

The Venetian needed one final confirmation. He asked Zhang to keep a look out for the tall, thin man.

'If he turns up, see if he's holding something, and if he still has it with him when he leaves the office, follow him. Don't worry about the German. I'll wait for him. We'll meet here tomorrow at the usual time.'

When the offices began to empty, the Venetian set off towards Peking Road, stopped at the corner of Yates Road, and waited in the entrance of a building opposite. From that vantage point he could also watch the flow of traffic from Siemens and spot Stilke's large car.

After waiting half an hour, the Venetian saw the car drive up slowly and stop opposite him. The now familiar figure of Stilke got out and disappeared in a flash inside the building. He was carrying a leather briefcase.

After less than an hour, the Italian saw Stilke hurry out of the main entrance and get into the car, which drove off towards the International Concession area where Stilke lived.

He did not move immediately, curious to see if he could recognise the other two Chinese men described by Zhang. Suddenly, with a jolt of fear, he sensed someone behind him.

'No more. All finish, Master Italy,' came Zhang's voice.

With a sigh of relief, the Venetian turned round.

'Tell me everything about the tall, thin man,' he demanded. 'Did you follow him? Where to? What was he carrying?'

He now understood that the office was being used as a "post-box" between Stilke and the German diplomatic mission. They examined all information received from Stilke, then sent it on to Berlin, in turn delivering messages and instructions to Stilke.

They took a taxi to a bar beyond Suzhou Creek, not far from Zhang's place of work, saying nothing as the driver probably spoke pidgin English and might overhear them. Here Zhang reported that the tall, thin Westerner had arrived in the early afternoon carrying a leather briefcase. He went into the office of the two Chinese men, staying only a matter of minutes. When he came out, he was still carrying the briefcase. He walked along Peking Road for ten minutes, then crossed over, continuing down a narrow, crowded street that led to Nanking Road. Unexpectedly, he turned into an ordinary town house, with a gate that allowed cars access into the dusty courtyard at the back. It could not be seen from the street, but was visible from the alley alongside it. There were two powerful cars parked side by side, a Horch and a Mercedes Benz. Zhang had not noticed anything odd about the place, except the silence, which was unusual for the courtyard of a house in Shanghai. On closer inspection, he had seen that the windows were all closed and there were no signs of life—no washing lines hung with laundry, no baskets, dustbins, hens, bicycles or rowdy groups of children. Only silence, and those two large black, powerful cars standing guard like tanks in elegant civilian attire.

Zhang then retraced his steps, entered a dusty herbalist's shop to ask the proprietor if he thought it was possible to knock at the door of the house opposite and enquire if they needed a trustworthy man to wash the cars. The toothless old herbalist had looked him up and down with an amused expression and had burst out laughing: 'Hi, hi, hi! Do you need a swift kick in the seat of your pants? Go ahead, give it a try! Do it now, so I can enjoy the show.'

'You're making fun of me!' Zhang had replied with feigned resentment. 'You talk as if others have met with the same fate before. Who lives holed up in that house?'

'The drivers of the German Legation. They wash the cars every morning. Yes, in person! So you see, they won't even open the door!'

'Two cars and two drivers in such a big house! It's a disgrace, when I have to sleep in a boat with my grandfather,' remarked Zhang, hoping the other man would take the bait.

'Ah, but they're not the only ones who sleep there. During the day, other people turn up and stay, sometimes all night. I know because I see the light. They also go out by the small back gate. I think they have parties at night and bring back *can do* girls. Hi, hi, hi!' With that, he disappeared into the back of the shop.

The Venetian was pleased with the progress made by his investigations. Months of work were finally being rewarded by the possibility of exposing an address organised by the new Nazi secret services. And he was confident that he could count on Zhang's help. He raised his glass of beer: 'Chin-chin, Zhang.'

'*Gan bei*! Master Italy.'

7

Green Bay deduced from many little signs that important matters often kept the Italian from her. She never asked any questions and he never told her about his secret mission. One evening, as usual, she greeted him unquestioningly, her eyes shining: no matter what had happened or might happen, the evening was theirs. And from the way he took her hand and squeezed it, the young Chinese woman could tell that he wanted to share and celebrate his satisfaction about something in particular.

'Where are we going this evening?' she asked him, coming to a sudden halt as soon as they had they left the house.

'Wherever you like,' he replied, only too glad not to have to make a decision at least once during the day.

'Then I choose not to choose and not to make you choose either. I don't want to do something we know we're doing from the start. Do you agree?'

'Show me how.'

'Watch closely and listen carefully!'

Looking serious, Green Bay stood facing him with her feet together

From the window, Olga and her husband Igor, saw the light-hearted discussion between the young couple. Igor turned to his wife and, in a slightly perplexed tone asked: 'Do you think it'll last, Olga?'

'Of course it will! Their love is perfect and perfect things last. They're a model couple. It's so simple! They'll get married because they want to stay together, not to demonstrate a theory or make a point. If they want to show that a mixed marriage can be a resounding success, it will already be a *fait accompli*. Of course there are risks. They exist in all marriages. But I can't see why this mixed marriage shouldn't be a happy one if they carry on loving each other the way they do today. Look at them!'

'You sound very confident,' retorted Igor. 'I'm less certain. I've thought a great deal about it recently and I'm sure that a mixed marriage creates serious personal problems. They should get married according to European law, the only one that counts for his career—and that won't be easy. And then, his work—he has yet to explain to me exactly what he does—because saying he's in the diplomatic service is like saying you shouldn't ask questions. His work, as I said, will take him to the ends of the earth. Their love blossomed in China with its culture, history and traditions, so he's fascinated by all that, just as Green Bay has been fascinated by him, because she's always dreamed of going to Italy and he represents a small patch of Italy that she has come to know, a sample, if you like, of what she will discover one day when she goes to live in another country. But when they leave China, if they ever leave, don't you think their feelings might also change?'

'I'm telling you, nothing could ever spoil their love. Just look at them...'

Igor might have liked to argue that the increasingly imminent war might alter their relationship, but he preferred not to undermine his wife's serenity any further, and he leaned over to look at the young couple.

'Oh! Look at Green Bay!' he exclaimed. 'What is she doing?'

'It looks like they're playing blind man's buff!'

Green Bay had put her hands over her eyes, turned round three times on the spot, then stopped, her hands still covering her eyes.

'Let's go straight ahead in the direction I'm facing to the second set of crossroads,' she said to the young man, 'then we'll take the first right, then the second left, then straight on for exactly five minutes. That's where we'll stop. There you are, I said it all at random, without thinking. Will you be able to remember the directions?'

'Of course. But what game is this?' asked the Venetian, amused.

'It's the game of fate. Since I don't feel as if I've made the decision and nor have you, let's go and see what fate has in store for us this evening!' She paused: 'Don't you like the idea?'

'On the contrary, I'm curious to find out where we'll end up.'

Holding hands, they set off in the direction Green Bay had blindly chosen, unaware of Olga and Igor's affectionate gaze as they stood in the semi-darkness of their window. Playing their game, the excited young couple spoke to each other spontaneously, light-heartedly experiencing strange new sensations and emotions

Time (only a state of mind for the Chinese) stood still for them.

They arrived at the place where Green Bay's whimsical directions had led them: a rotunda at the centre of four streets. The first had a half-ruined house with what was left of a corn merchant's shop on the ground floor, its empty windows barred with wooden boards nailed to splintered frames. To the right, lay a small dark street with a squalid inn, the entrance blocked by a group of ragged individuals intent on making fun of the withered *amah* who was 'protecting' two pale, thin, tuberculotic young prostitutes with sunken, expressionless eyes. A third street, at the corner of a rickshaw mender's courtyard with faded graffiti on the wall, led to the gasometers and factories near the mountains of coal on the riverbanks and seemed to peter out in a treacherous alley pitted with puddles of black water. The fourth street disappeared between two rows of anonymous houses.

The Venetian looked at Green Bay.

'Now what?' he asked.

'How do you feel about trusting to fate? If you want, we can still turn back.'

'No. When we were coming here, I've never felt so close to you. But where are we?'

'Take a good look around.'

'In China?' the Venetian ventured ironically.

'Bravo! I too feel I'm at the centre of China. See how the game works!' Green Bay exclaimed, exultant.

The Venetian looked at her, bemused. He did not know if she was really entering into the spirit of something that still seemed mysterious to him.

'But I was joking,' he said.

'Exactly!'

Surprised, the Venetian gazed intently at the Chinese woman, while she stared back challengingly at him. She was eighteen, her eyes were gleaming with childlike happiness, and yet there was something deeply serious about the way she was looking at him.

'I said the first thing that came into my mind,' he repeated, looking around as if trying to find an answer. 'But perhaps this area has some particular meaning for you?'

She smiled. 'To me this *is* China. I see the corn merchant's shop as a symbol of the Chinese countryside decimated by war and natural disasters; in that little street down there, the moral decay of the big city and of those who cling to vice to survive or find a little pleasure; in that other street leading to the factories and the coal, I see industrial China, black, filthy and dusty, fraught with hardship and hard work that destroys men, turning them into inanimate raw material. And the rickshaw mender?' she turned to look at that side of the little square. 'Those contraptions symbolise the slavery that is still rife in this country. They are the symbol of people who are under the yoke of a dominant class oblivious to the suffering of others, forced to bow their heads to foreign masters who wage war on each other to take possession of my country.'

They had been walking towards the rickshaw mender but at the centre of the little square, Green Bay stopped.

'There you are,' she said. 'We're at the centre of my country. We're at the fifth cardinal point and these streets represent the four other points. This rotunda marks the point of equilibrium between north and south, east and west, between vice and virtue, happiness and sadness. Which way do we go? If you want to put an end to my game, all you have to do is choose.'

Fascinated and a little puzzled by the seriousness that seemed to coexist with the whimsical gaiety of an eighteen-year-old, the Venetian elected to shatter the magical solemnity of the moment.

'My dear,' he replied, 'fate has had me on my feet all day and I don't want to walk anymore. Let's go over to the rickshaw mender and let him take us wherever he wants. That way, we won't be "choosing" the end of the game, OK?'

They crossed the square to the mender's chaotic courtyard, where the man was tightening the spokes on the two wheels of a rickshaw while the relieved owner of the vehicle stood nearby. When the rickshaw mender had finished his work, the Venetian and Green Bay, without conferring, stepped forward together and asked the cost of the work. The shocked owner allowed the foreigner to pay the bill.

Then the Italian took Green Bay's hand, helped her up and made her comfortable on the patched oilcloth seat. He also climbed up and the owner, already harnessed like a rickety nag between the two shafts, started off down the street.

The driver did not ask or say anything and began, on his own initiative, to take the route towards the International Concession. The rickshaw ran more smoothly than it had for years. Fate that very afternoon had made him go to his old friend Liu to repair the vehicle.

Full of enthusiasm, he ran fast, his sandals slapping against the pavement. On board, the young couple were jostled from one side of the seat to the other. Green Bay felt the pressure of the Venetian's leg and was embarrassed at the enforced intimacy of the slippery seat. Then, without asking permission, perhaps to make himself more comfortable, the Venetian stretched his arm behind her shoulders and held her tightly. Assailed by the warmth of his body, realising she was almost cuddled up against him, Green Bay drew away as much as possible.

In those years, habits, as well as women's morality, were changing. Young women who felt 'modern' now sealed vows of love with their bodies. This was not the case for Green Bay, who still felt bound by the moral traditions of the past. Still, she allowed the rough touch of his hands on her skin and the embrace that made her feel fragile but protected. The Venetian seemed resigned to wait, though their mutual attraction was growing. For the first time, he loved a woman with his mind as well as his body; he was still not sure he knew exactly what love was, but thought he loved this deceptively delicate young woman.

'Are you happy?' asked Green Bay in English, as the rickshaw rounded, dangerously fast, the corner of the race-track in front of her house. The Venetian's expression left no room for doubt about his reply.

They dismounted from the rickshaw and remained standing in each other's arms in front of Green Bay's house, oblivious to the passers-by.

He was the first to break the silence. 'I find it hard to talk sense when you're so close to me.'

He was surprised at his husky voice and dry throat, which made it difficult to continue. He felt that he would never be able to say what he wanted to tell her.

'Come. We can't stay here. I'll go inside with you.'

They walked up to Green Bay's door and stopped, so close together that their hearts seemed to beat in time with each other. Green Bay raised her face and looked at him. He put his hand on the nape of her neck, drew her towards him, and their lips met in a long, passionate, tender kiss.

'From the moment I met you,' murmured the Venetian into her long perfumed hair, 'I've dreamed of this moment.'

'I didn't know I could feel like this,' admitted Green Bay and she would have added more, had she not heard footsteps drawing closer. Hurriedly she opened the door and went inside. Before closing it, she turned and looked at the Venetian once more. With a smile she blew him a kiss, asking him mischievously in English, 'Are you happy?' Then he added, 'I am!'

In the taxi home, the Venetian could not stop thinking about Green Bay. How could he say to a young Chinese woman with what might seem like brutal Western bluntness, 'I'm in love with you'? He was almost on the point of asking her to marry him, but then he thought about his father in Venice, about his family. They would be against him marrying a Chinese woman. For a second he envied his contemporaries skilled at extracting maximum pleasure out of these affairs without getting involved, but the thought of treating Green Bay like a *can do* girl immediately filled him with contempt. Should he give her up then? The fear of never seeing her again chilled his heart.

All this could not distract the Venetian from the mission for which he had been sent to China. Having identified the network that led to Stilke, he still had to make his final move.

He had to settle for meeting Zhang.

'Listen to me very carefully,' he told him. 'How many times do the police come to your place of work?'

'I've already told you, Master Italy: all the time. The Heron Fountain is always full of bad cops and good cops.'

These were the terms used in the place to describe agents who were regulars. "Bad" cops were those who carried out raids and who seemed incorruptible but who, in their turn, blackmailed the shopkeepers. "Good" cops, on the other hand, were the ones who took bribes and were always willing to turn a blind eye.

'So there are almost always police there, but you can recognise someone who can be trusted. Is that right?'

'*Duì, duì* – that's right', replied the Chinese man firmly.

'When I met you, you listed your clientele. Is there anyone you really trust who is a skilled street thief, a bag-snatcher?'

Zhang's answer came as a complete surprise.

'Master Italy, if you want to steal something from one of the two Germans, use some kids I know. They're very good and if the police are called and they find out who did it, they won't launch an investigation. There are thousands of kids in Shanghai—they can vanish in the crowd like a firecracker exploding, and no one ever knows who has thrown it.'

The idea immediately appealed to the Venetian: robbed by

a gang of children, the German would never imagine that it had been organised by anyone else. Within a week, Zhang had managed to recruit his team of bag-snatchers and point out the designated victim.

On the appointed day, the German left his house at the usual time. He turned left and walked a little way in the direction of Peking Road. When he came level with the lane running parallel to the house, two boys came to meet him and bumped into him on either side. The most skilful of the two, with a barber's razor in his hand, grabbed him from behind and quick as lightning, sliced through the leather belt and the waistband of his baggy trousers, which instantly fell around his knees. The other boy grabbed the briefcase and raced away along an alley. The German was so shocked by the speed of the theft that he remained rooted to the spot, his mouth wide-open, incapable of raising the alarm. He hurriedly pulled up his trousers but not before attracting some amused looks from passers-by as he hastily turned back to the house that he had just left.

As soon as the boy with the briefcase reached the end of the alley, he rounded the corner and passed the stolen property to a third boy who fearlessly zigzagged across the street and vanished. A moment later, impatient to regain the safety of his lodgings, the Venetian was sitting under the canopy of a rickshaw, holding the briefcase tightly under his arm.

He locked himself in the house and opened the case to find it filled with bundles of American dollars neatly arranged to leave room for two files that immediately attracted his attention. He read the documents. One of the files contained skilfully forged bills of lading concerning the transport of machinery and optical equipment from Hamburg to Kobe in Japan, on a Japanese cargo vessel leaving from Shanghai. The other documents were for unloading various goods from Essen and Berlin in Shanghai, almost certainly arms. Then he counted the money. There were three thousand dollars, probably for paying the agents. Were they to be distributed by the two Chinese men from the office or by Stilke in person?

In the light of two lamps, the Venetian used his Minox for

the first time. This tiny camera, about four inches long and less than an inch wide in its protective leather case, fitted comfortably into the breast-pocket of his waistcoat. It had a thin chain to hold it more securely and had been designed to maintain the correct focal distance for copying documents placed on a flat surface. Ironically, this little masterpiece, so useful in the field of espionage, had actually been invented by the Germans, and every diplomatic office in the world had lost no time in getting hold of a model.

The young Italian photographed the documents. He had decided to give the briefcase with the documents back to the Germans, taking the dollars that might be used to finance other operations, so they would never suspect that this was not a real theft. The entire operation was very delicate because it involved money and documents belonging to a country in alliance with Italy. The Venetian decided to give only the Italian consular authorities the negatives of the documents relating to the goods being unloaded in Shanghai. It was well-known in diplomatic circles that the Germans supplied arms, munitions and the assistance of military advisers on the domestic front to help the nationalist forces of Chiang Kai-shek in their struggle against the Japanese. Documents that could show such assistance were always useful for the Italian information services in China. On the other hand, there were only occasional suspicions that Germany was simultaneously supplying arms to Japan. Now these documents concerning German cargo destined for that country provided proof of supplies of arms and sophisticated optical instruments likely to be used for releasing bombs from Japanese aircraft over Chinese targets.

The Venetian was positive that he had in his possession some very important items that Ciano had to see in person. So the negatives of the documents concerning the cargo for Japan would be sent to Rome where the Minister was waiting for evidence of the German's double-crossing activities.

Once the documents were photographed and the money hidden with the Minox, he wrapped the briefcase in a dustcoat and left for the Heron Fountain. It was Zhang who took his order for a beer and, when he brought it, he could see from the Venetian's eyes that he was there about something important connected with the theft of the briefcase.

'I know you received it, Master Italy. Is something wrong?' he asked in a low voice, as if he were asking if the beer was too warm.

'Nothing, actually,' replied the Venetian in the same tone. 'But you need to come with me, because I must throw the briefcase over the fence of the house where you saw those two German cars. Who's your boss here?'

'The man in the black cap.'

'Does he speak English?'

'Like me.'

'Then go and call him over and tell him that a journalist wants to speak to him.'

'Your waiter,' he explained to the man, 'was kind enough to ask me if the beer was too warm, which led me to realise that he speaks good English. What about you?' he asked, gazing at the proprietor with a wide smile.

'Yes, I speak it too, but—'

He didn't have time to go on, because the Venetian was already adding, 'Then you'll understand my request. I must absolutely meet my landlord to discuss the lease. I'm afraid he's taking advantage of me and I can never track him down, but this evening he's at home. My interpreter is away for a week because his father has died. If I give you ten dollars, will you lend me your waiter for an hour? You'll gain by it and so will he. What's your name?' he asked, turning to Zhang.

'Zhang, Master,' replied the latter quickly, while the Venetian, without waiting for the proprietor's reply, peeled off a ten-dollar note and asked him directly:

'What do I owe you for the beer?'

'When you come back, I hope you'll stay for another, then we'll take it all together, OK?' replied the proprietor, pocketing the ten dollars.

The Venetian nodded and followed by Zhang, walked out clutching his precious package under his arm. He began looking for a taxi and Zhang, in amazement, saw his master refuse all the taxi-cabs that he, with great effort, managed to flag down.

'Didn't you say you wanted a taxi, Master Italy?' he finally asked, looking bemused.

'Yes, but I'm looking for an old taxi. The noisier the better. Understand?'

Once again, Zhang did not entirely understand the reason for this strange requirement, but he immediately started to look for one until, with a deafening whistle that could only be produced by the irregular shape of his teeth, he managed to attract the attention of the driver of an old, aristocratic Humber. The car seemed to have no exhaust pipe at all and the noise was in strident contrast to the vehicle's dignified performance.

'You see, Zhang,' the Venetian explained later when both men were heading back to the Heron Fountain, after the Chinese man had thrown the briefcase over the low wall of the house, 'I wanted a noisy taxi for two reasons: to attract the attention of anyone guarding the house in front, and to mask the noise that might be made by the briefcase falling into the courtyard. In any case, it's done now. I can't wait to get back to your inn and get out of this deafening car!'

8

Although events in the Venetian's personal and professional life were going well, these were dramatic times for Shanghai, and he watched as the city was bombed by the Japanese.

In 1937, after the attack on the Marco Polo Bridge about 20 miles from Beijing, the Japanese occupation forces had been relentlessly infiltrating deep into different parts of the country, though not on a single front—their land armies supported by their navy and air force. Bombardments had begun again over Shanghai, heralded by a sinister rumble. In the space of a few seconds, floodlights were switched on and white beams of light scoured the sky nervously in search of aeroplanes, though it seemed impossible that a missile discharged by the anti-aircraft artillery could hit such a small target. As the bombers drew nearer, the terrible whistle of the bombs could be heard, followed by the flash and roar of explosions that left their tragic toll of casualties and damage. The Nantao and Hongkew areas were devastated. On one occasion, a single bomb falling right between the Bund and Nanking Road killed 1000 people. Thousands more died during the bombings. One wing of the Cathay Hotel was hit, and scores of Europeans who had taken refuge there, were buried under the rubble. The Palace Hotel lost its top floors. Mutilated corpses lay everywhere.

The bombings occurred as regularly as the tides that travelled rapidly up the Yangtze and gave the city back the coffins committed to the water from the funeral piers on the Bund. At night, the Chinese who could not afford the expense of a funeral, launched coffins, covered with paper flowers, containing the corpses of their loved ones, one at a time into the river to be carried out on the tide, returning to Shanghai's funeral pier on the next tide, thereby creating floating fields of flowers.

The Venetian watched this continual stream of coffins with horror. And yet it seemed that the bombings had become an everyday event. After each attack, people went about their lives with renewed energy; it seemed as if the war was strengthening Shanghai, injecting new life into the city. Like crazed insects, swarms of peasants crowded the streets with their carts, in search of relatives, and together with lines of rickshaws, they stopped cars from getting through. The entire population was out in the streets as if celebrating a festival. The tragedy of war was swept away by the great river of existence. Life went on, and with life, love.

The Venetian and Green Bay left the decimated city for a short trip through the rolling plain of the delta, and this helped them forget the cruelties of the war. Their destination was the indescribably beautiful city of Suzhou.

Situated in a vast plain, Suzhou lies at the foot of a range of hills lushly blanketed with vegetation extending as far as the tree-lined canals that criss-cross the city. The roots of willows, maples and oaks form a gigantic chain sunk in the water that irrigates the verdant hills dotted with ancient dwellings and temples.

The Venetian smiled when Green Bay remarked: 'We call Suzhou the Venice of China. That's our Grand Canal. The ancient artificial river is 700 miles long and connects my native city Hangzhou, with Beijing. Once it was a busy route plied with junks.'

The Venetian did not want to tell her bluntly that nothing here reminded him of Venice except the canals, and these ones differed from the canals in Venice because they were lined for long stretches by trees and gardens and crossed by bridges carrying traffic from all the streets of Suzhou.

'If anything,' he said, 'from the little I've seen so far, it looks like a garden city intersected by canals that enhance its beauty. In Venice, there are no wide streets, but mainly alleys, squares and arched bridges with steps. You hardly ever see any greenery; what little there is, is hidden away in the courtyards of the houses. And there are no cars. People get around on foot or by gondola. Have you seen a photograph of a gondola?'

'Yes, and they row standing up like we do: we also use *chuan* – small boats – to get from one place to another on the canals. The junks on the other hand are used to transport goods and also serve as dwellings for many families. They can form entire floating villages, like the ones you saw in Suzhou Creek and on some stretches of the Whangpoo in Shanghai, near the bottom of Tiger Hill by the Buddhist temples. My widowed aunt has lived in one of those for years—the Cold Mountain Temple in the Order of the White Swallow. I remember there was always a festival when she brought me here on a visit to Suzhou. It's a big city with almost one million inhabitants, counting the foreigners in the Concession. If the population continues to grow, I don't know how they'll find room for everyone! See those blond women over there? They're the wives of English businessmen, officials, and water inspectors like my grandfather, Accumulated Virtue. Now the Japanese are replacing them with Chinese officials, as before.'

The Venetian replied that things were very different in Venice, where the population was below 200,000 inhabitants.

They strolled along the paths of the gardens. Every corner afforded a different panoramic view, each as attractive and relaxing as the last. Not at all tired, they reached the Humble Administrator's Garden, perhaps the most famous park in China. Seeing this he imagined being at the top of the campanile with Green Bay, pointing out the islands of Murano, Torcello and Burano, looking down on the cupolas of the Basilica. 'Not to see it would be like going to Venice and missing the Piazza San Marco,' explained the Venetian to Green Bay, 'or not climbing to the top of Venice's campanile to admire the panorama of the entire Venetian lagoon.'

Impressed by the beauty of the 40,000 square metres of parkland, adorned by little bridges, verandas and pavilions where the murmur of water could always be heard, they decided to climb the nearest tower for a better view of the lakes covering three-fifths of the remarkable terrain. They gazed at the gorgeous panorama for a long time, admiring it like the central gem in a necklace of precious stones. Even Chinese writers, drawing ideograms with pens dipped in the brightest inks and moved by poetic rhythms chanted for tens of centuries, could not do it justice.

Then Green Bay and the Venetian made their way along the paved path leading to the market district. At the corner of a street, the young man stopped suddenly, amazed and intrigued.

'What's inside those enormous earthenware jars supported by those structures?' he asked, 'They're big enough for us both to hide in.'

Nearly all the jars had strange lids, as if to protect the contents from the dust of the street. Drawing closer, the young man saw that three steps had been carved into the low structure and that some passers-by were climbing them to dip a long bamboo ladle into one of the jars. At that moment, a woman *coolie* plunged in the ladle and, drawing it out with a swing of her arm, started to drink noisily. Two street urchins were doing the same at the jar nearby, one sitting on the other's shoulders so that he could reach to dip in the ladle.

'What do they contain?' asked the Venetian.

'Tea. Anyone who's thirsty can drink their fill.'

'But who provides it?'

'Prominent families. My grandparents once put one at the foot of Tiger Hill to quench the thirst of pilgrims who had to undertake the long tiring climb up to the pagoda. The city guilds make sure they are kept filled. Once upon a time, you would see them on every street corner—an employee made sure that the tea was always piping hot. In winter, a brazier was always kept lit under the structure. There are only a few left now, because when they break, they're not replaced. The tea is no longer what it was. It's lukewarm—it's only heated by the sun and the terracotta keeps it warm. It's a shame because we Chinese like to drink our tea hot.'

'What an extraordinary custom! I want to try a ladleful myself. I'm thirsty.'

'No, please don't,' begged Green Bay.

'Why not?'

'Since this morning, beggars, filthy little urchins like the two you've just seen, and who knows how many others, perhaps even lepers, have dipped those ladles in there. I'd never risk it, even if I were dying of thirst.'

'That's a shame. I would've liked to drink from a bamboo ladle,' said the Venetian, giving up the idea in the face of Green Bay's insistence.

'You can drink all the tea you want, even from bamboo ladles, but not from these jars. You couldn't explore Chinese customs for long that way because you might only have a few weeks left to live!'

'Then I'll use something else,' he said and he looked around, immediately noticing a porcelain shop. Linking arms with Green Bay, he stubbornly headed towards it.

On entering, they headed for the department with porcelain cups and bowls on display.

'You can drink that tea on condition that you drink only from the bowl I'll choose for you. Then you'll also have a souvenir of our trip to the canals of Suzhou.'

Green Bay went to find the proprietor of the shop and began to speak quickly to him. Every now and then the man nodded, then suddenly disappeared into the back of the shop. He came back with a package that he handed carefully to the Italian.

Pleased, he carried it to the foot of one of the jars. He saw a beggar quenching his thirst on the platform, then pouring the remains of the ladle back into the huge container. The Venetian stood there, looking undecided. The idea of dipping his precious bowl into the jar suddenly filled him with disgust. Green Bay immediately walked over to him. She smiled at him with good grace and barely a hint of irony, satisfied that she had dissuaded him from drinking by giving him an object too precious to be used in such a way. A little trick is worth a thousand words, she thought.

Only the Chinese know that the gentle, charming behaviour

of most oriental women usually masks a will of iron. Undemonstrative in love, they are particularly vehement when they lose their temper. The young Italian learned this soon after in Jade Temple Street, an area in the working-class centre of the city called The Place of the Scold. The street was narrow and crowded with passers-by. Few had stopped to watch and listen to the two women sitting with their backs to each other on top of a six-foot high structure. Neither of them showed any interest in the other, while the tirades they yelled at the top of their voices reached the ends of the street, the top floors of the ancient blocks of flats that enclosed it, and the backs of the two rows of shops lining it.

'What the devil are those two women doing?' the Venetian asked in astonishment.

'It's an ancient Chinese custom, publicly acknowledging a furious woman's right to shout her anger from the rooftops without causing a scandal. But this is the first time I've seen it done in one of the places set aside for this.'

'But why doesn't anyone stop them?'

'No one would dream of it.'

'Are they insane?'

'No, just very angry.'

'But what are they doing?' he insisted.

'They're doing themselves a lot of good and nobody else any harm,' replied Green Bay wisely.

'Some laundry is better washed at home, as we say in Italy,' said the Venetian.

'Have you seen the hovels where these poor people live? If they started screaming at home, all the family and neighbours would have to put up with their outbursts. It's a very effective escape valve, believe me.'

'Do men also do this?'

'It's a women's privilege. Men use politics!' said Green Bay ironically, pulling the amazed young Italian away.

She led him through a maze of narrow streets and canals from where they took a rickshaw to the hillside. The rickshaw man was quite happy to wait, having noticed an inn a short distance away.

They walked uphill, taking random paths through thick undergrowth and ferns. They decided to stop on a little plateau dominated by a shady walnut tree. The view of the city was breathtaking. Suzhou looked like an irregular grid of canals. Every waterway was a silver strip in the afternoon sun. The air was still and balmy. The tree roots offered them a comfortable resting place. The Venetian drew her next to him, her head against his chest. He tenderly caressed the back of her neck and gently lifted the hair from her shoulders. Together, they gazed outwards. Yet they were anxious, wondering if their love could surmount the obstacles facing them.

'Are you happy?' she asked him in English, pressing against him and turning to raise her face to his and look into his eyes.

He kissed her.

'I'll never look at Venice again with the same eyes,' he replied.

'Thank you,' murmured Green Bay. It seemed to her that the words he had uttered meant that Suzhou was a part of him—a personal compliment.

He took her hand gently and slowly unfolding the fingers, kissed her palm. 'I don't want to say goodnight to you anymore, unless you're in my arms.'

'Me neither!'

'All we can do is get married, darling, but I'm afraid we won't be able to choose how we get married. What's important is not to doubt our love.'

'I've never had any doubts. But you didn't know anything about me when we met and I was afraid that it might be an infatuation. You do love me, don't you?'

'I fell in love with you from the moment I met you on the nineteenth floor of the Park Hotel.'

Green Bay gave a faint smile and squeezed his hands, bringing them to her chest.

'When my heart beats hard like it is now—can you feel it? When you... hold me, then I know this is love.'

She turned away but he saw her eyes were shining.

The silence was broken by a passing bare-chested, lean boy

playing a violin as he headed quickly downhill. Suspended from the arm holding the instrument was a little cage swinging in time to the rhythm of his steps and the music. If he saw the lovers, he did not show it. With his chin resting on the instrument to hold it steady, his eyes were lovingly fixed on the violin. He continued down towards the city, playing as he walked. Descending among high ferns, he looked as naked as the figure of a young satyr from a painting of Arcadia by a European master.

'What an idyllic picture!' exclaimed the astonished Venetian, watching the boy. 'Is he a young beggar?'

'He looks well fed and well educated. The violin is valuable and it's his.'

'How do you know?'

'From the way he holds it and the way he plays it.'

He looked at her, surprised once more at her insight into details that seemed to highlight the difference between their two cultures, their two worlds.

'But what about the little cage hanging from his arm?'

'Crickets—it contains little crickets. He was playing to them.'

'He was playing that beautiful music on a valuable violin just for some crickets?'

'Just for them. He was teaching the crickets to sing.'

'I find that hard to believe.'

'I'm sure you do, but we Chinese are very fond of listening to cricket song and they can sing much more beautifully if you're patient enough to teach them. That boy must be a great music lover and he wants the crickets to sing well too.'

Amazed, the Venetian shook his head.

'Have you ever listened to the music the dragonflies play with their wings?' she asked.

He looked at her in disbelief.

'You must listen to it when the moon is a silvery reflection on the waters of the lakes and the honeysuckle and verbena flowers are filling the air with perfume. Dragonflies love this fragrance and express their rapture by vibrating their wings musically. All you need is a slight breeze and even the bamboo leaves make music, a rustling full of melody that joins forces with all the other sounds of nature.'

The Venetian felt as if he was caught in a spell. The Chinese woman's words made him feel less foreign. He looked around and the colours of the landscape at twilight reminded him of the subdued hues of ancient Sung pictures in which philosophers converse at the base of willow trees and ducks fly against smooth silk. He had always thought that he could discover the real China in these works rather than in the natural world. And the ancient pictures helped him to understand and appreciate the lines of a mountain, the trembling of a bamboo in the wind, the wondrous beauty of a lake opening like an eye in the boundless landscape.

When they arrived back at the street at the bottom of the hill, they saw the rickshaw in the distance, in front of the inn. He was supposed to take them to see a friend of Olga Aleksandrova, Ludmila, a Russian woman who lived in Suzhou and whom they had promised to visit, but the journey was fraught. The trouble began as soon as they entered the built-up areas where the streets narrowed into alleys crowded with wagons and carts of all kinds. The rickshaw driver managed to force his way through the crowd with difficulty, the throng parting listlessly as they passed through, heralded by hoarse shouts, 'Xiao xin, xiao xin!—Watch out, watch out!'

The journey continued until, trying to make room for a vehicle coming from the opposite direction, the rickshaw ended up with its two shafts inside a shop in the middle of two walls of quartered pigs. Continuing round a bend, it landed in a pyramid of candied dates but this happened so quickly that the rickshaw was already a long way off by the time the proprietor's shouts reached them.

They finally arrived at an arched bridge where the labyrinth of extremely narrow streets ended, and to their relief, they were greeted by the unexpected sight of green willows and multicoloured patches of flowering plants.

9

Backing onto a picturesque canal, Ludmila's house had several simple rooms furnished with rattan furniture and mint-green cushions. It had been given to her by the Colmans, a prominent family in the English Concession who had employed her as governess to their children until they had been sent to college in England.

Ludmila was a tall fair-skinned woman who lived alone, respected by her Chinese neighbours. Sitting in a comfortable armchair on the veranda behind the house, engrossed in her book or her embroidery, she often managed to forget the past. Or she watched all kinds of vessels—from small *chuan* to large barges laden with sand dredged from the Yangtze destined for the city's building sites—sail slowly and silently along the canal.

Her only contact with the world outside Suzhou's walls was through Olga Aleksandrova, whom she visited in Shanghai twice a year. It was on one of these visits that Olga had introduced her to her favourite student, Green Bay, who had already confessed her love for the young Venetian on a previous trip to Suzhou. Ludmila had taken their story to heart, although there had been no place for a man's love in her own life.

She greeted her two young visitors affectionately, hurrying to kiss Green Bay on the cheeks, but the young Chinese woman ducked her head in embarrassment. She was very fond of her singing teacher's friend, but it was not the custom to kiss "hello" in China.

Ludmila had decided to adopt a Russian style of dress for

her guests. Despite being made locally with Chinese textiles and silk, her clothes were European with a traditional pre-revolutionary Russian touch added by well-chosen accessories. The Venetian courteously admired her unusual outfit and the simple elegance of the interior decoration that, he said, transformed her bright veranda into the terrace of a Chekhovian dacha. Pleased, Ludmila poured tea from her silver teapot into little bone china cups. She served them Western-style, passing slices of lemon with silver tongs. The dinner table was also set with silver cutlery and an elegant Wedgwood service. Ludmila explained that the service had been given to her by Mrs Colman and that she was glad, for once, to have an opportunity to use it.

'Tonight, I want to treat you to a taste of Russia,' she said, bringing a steaming soup tureen onto the veranda and placing it in the middle of the table.

'This,' she announced 'is our national soup. You must have heard of our borscht, but have you ever tried it?' she asked the Venetian.

'No, never. And I'm delighted that my first borscht has been home-made by a Russian.'

They ate the beetroot soup with relish, along with the *piroshki* that followed. At the end of the meal, perhaps carried away by the memories awakened by those rediscovered flavours, Ludmila told her young guests about the tragic circumstances of her life.

'I was still at school,' she began 'when the revolution started. We were from Karbin in central Russia, but we lived in St Petersburg where my father was a high-ranking official in the Imperial Administration. He was sent back to Karbin because of his former position in the service of the tsar. Then, one evening, our peasants came to warn us to escape. They offered to take us by sleigh to the Chinese border dressed to look like them, but it was too late. The Mongol soldiers were already in the area and were searching for our house. The peasants fled and a few minutes later the soldiers arrived. My parents were bayoneted to death, while other soldiers tore off my sister's clothes and raped her. Half-crazed, she threw herself out of a window. I managed to hide in the secret closet in our playroom. During the night I escaped through the fields, but in the morning the soldiers found me and took me to a barn where they did to me what their compatriots had done to my sister. For several months, I lived like an injured animal, hiding so that no one could see me. I felt surrounded and in the darkness I imagined terrible enemies lying in wait for me. One evening I was driven by hunger to hide nearer the house, and an old man found me. He immediately saw I wasn't like the others. Taking pity on me, he hid me in his sleigh under a pile of rags and drove to the Chinese border along roads only he knew. Once there, he showed me where to cross to avoid being caught. I walked all night and all the next day, but in the evening I was seen by some Chinese soldiers and taken prisoner. I found out they were guards from a northern tribe with red hair, under the command of a war-lord, General Chang Tso-Lin. I was convinced I only had a few hours to live and that they would put me to death with a sabre. Instead they were much kinder than the Russians, and they treated my poor malnourished, bruised and battered body with respect. I was handed over to some women who tended me and fed me. When I began to feel better, I was taken with the other women to see General Chang Tso-Lin and his officials. We were shared out between the men and the General chose me. He dreamed of becoming Mussolini (Mu Tso Lin, in Chinese). I remember he often talked about the exploits of the Italian dictator before sitting down to eat. The General soon tired of my looks, and my indifference. He offered to pass me on to his aide-de-camp, Yu Pan, but I hinted that I'd prefer to be everybody's and nobody's, so he helped me to join a tea house in Mukden, where my job was to prepare the opium pipe. While there, I discovered that a large colony of white Russian refugees had settled in Shanghai, where I could find help in the form of food and lodgings, if I applied to a special office run by white Russians in the Foreign Concessions. So I decided to escape to Shanghai. I had to be as careful as possible. It wasn't advisable to ask one of the opium house's customers, because people were betrayed daily.

I found a way to communicate with a Russian merchant on the outside, who had no intention of returning to his fatherland. He advised me to catch a ship to Shanghai from the port in Dairen. I felt I could trust him: our patriotic feelings created a bond between us.

I learned that a French ship was loading goods for transport to Europe and that it planned a stopover in Shanghai to pick up its final shipments. Stowaways were not unheard-of and they were not always men—some cargo ships even welcomed women stowaways; the captain held the whip hand. I put up with this final humiliation as it was my last chance for escape.

Dressed as a Chinese stowaway, I boarded the ship in Dairen, and when I finally disembarked in Shanghai, as the motor boat carried me to the other bank of the Whangpoo, I held my head high, my blonde hair blowing in the breeze. The minute I was back on dry land, I walked into a department store to buy some Western clothes and heard a couple chatting in Russian at the counter. I introduced myself and asked for information about the refugee centre. This was Olga and Igor.'

Ludmila fell silent. She was dry-eyed and had talked with little emotion, as if she was recounting a nightmare, but she looked exhausted. There was a deep crease at each corner of her mouth, caused by the pain that was now part of her.

The Venetian's voice suddenly broke the silence. 'What's keeping you in this place, Ludmila? Why don't you go back to Europe? I know the consuls of many countries. There are still too many memories for you here. Can I help you to get a resident's visa. Tell me where you'd prefer to go.'

Ludmila stood up wearily, smoothing away non-existent creases on her "Russian" dress made of Chinese silk.

'You must forgive my outpourings. I'm an old woman now who'll never have the courage to stand face to face with those who have loved me. I have new friends here who don't know anything about me. I hope you'll continue to honour my house with your presence. It's the only thing I own that has never been desecrated. That is what keeps me in Suzhou.'

Despite the tragic note struck by Ludmila's story, Green

Bay treasured the memory of this trip, because it was in Suzhou that she and the Venetian had talked more openly about love. In the long months of his absence, she thought back fondly to their embrace on the hill overlooking the city's canals, under the shade of the tall walnut tree.

In the spring of 1939, the Venetian returned to Rome. He had been summoned back by the Palazzo Chigi to take part in discussions about the emerging situation in China; his comments on the work being done there would supplement the reports sent via the normal diplomatic channels. The young man also hoped he would be able to obtain royal assent for his marriage to Green Bay. He knew he was running a grave risk by requesting it: once his intentions were known, it was not unlikely that he would be transferred to a different office and forced to part from Green Bay. The dramatic worsening of the political situation in Europe was also a danger that could prevent him from returning to China, but he was determined to risk everything and do whatever it took to see Green Bay again.

The young man found the conditions in Rome extremely volatile. The war with Spain had ended just a few days before; the treaty signed in Munich between Hitler, Mussolini, Daladier and Chamberlain had already been broken by Hitler the previous September. Europe was in ferment, but in addition, there were extensive reports every day in the Italian newspapers about the Japanese advance in China. Anti-Chinese propaganda raged: 'The Chinese commit atrocities, while the Japanese rescue small children and do good works. The heroic, gallant Japanese troops are defending Shanghai against Imperialist interests.'

Events on such a large scale made it difficult for the Venetian to pave the way for his request for royal assent, and he wasted a great deal of precious time in the antechamber waiting for talks at the Palazzo Chigi. He also had a long private meeting with Ciano, who valued his disclosures very highly since they were particularly useful in analysing Germany's complex network of alliances. Flattered by this success, the Venetian resolutely resumed his pursuit of the goal that was dear to his heart. He found out about the necessary procedures and whether it was possible to speed up the process, but he was forced to realise that royal assent was out of his reach. It would have been impossible to avoid revealing the entire situation within a narrow-minded, hostile environment, and that would have inevitable repercussions for his career. Resigned to failure, his only thought now was to return to Shanghai before it was too late.

He paid a short visit to Venice, but did not mention anything to his family, knowing that his father would never approve of his decision to marry a Chinese girl. He passed his time in Venice gloomily and he received the summons for a confidential briefing from Ciano with trepidation. At the end of the meeting, the Minister looked the young man straight in the eye.

'You have a glittering career ahead of you and many opportunities are opening up, but permit me to give you one piece of advice: "It's better to marry a neighbour than a stranger." I myself have always found this to be a wise saying. It's strange the Chinese don't have anything similar—as far as I recall!' This was clear confirmation that Ciano knew everything and wanted to make sure the young Italian realised this.

The Venetian returned to Shanghai on the *Conte Verde*, a long but now familiar journey. Here, he found the situation altered. The local authorities had instructed Tong, general of the River Police, to suppress piracy on the Yangtze. Since the general did not have adequate resources to wipe out the pirates, and they, in turn, were not strong enough to dispose of the river guards, they both compromised. It suited the pirates to do their work out of harm's way, safe in the knowledge there would be no raids, while boats that the Government had a vested interest in protecting for political, military or diplomatic reasons were now guaranteed a safe passage—the pirates were told the precise route to be taken by the "untouchable" boat via a signal that changed every month.

Chaos prevailed in Shanghai. The war against the Japanese was already in its third year and various greedy, unscrupulous foreigners and Chinese citizens, intent only on amassing makeshift fortunes to cope with the difficult emerging situation, were taking advantage of the many money-making opportunities afforded by the war. On the political front, Chiang Kai-shek now had his back to the wall and in July had retreated to Chiungking, where he had set up his new headquarters.

The number of kidnappings and murders for money had escalated, particularly in the Foreign Concessions. Italian circles had been thrown into turmoil by the kidnapping of a lawyer, Nevio Franceschi, at the mouth of the Yangtze. The ship bringing Franceschi back to Shanghai from inland was approached by a pirate junk just before Woosung, but the pirates, who were acting for other parties, were there merely to provide the means for striking the blow. As soon as the ship's passage was barred, it was boarded by a group of bandits who immediately snatched their victim from among the passengers. Uncharacteristically, the brigands apologised to the ship's captain and returned to the junk with the captured lawyer. Before the police were able to reach the scene, the junk had already disappeared among the many coves in the marshlands around the river mouth. In the following week, a letter written in poor English arrived at the Consulate demanding an extremely high ransom. The prevailing mood at the Consulate was one of anxiety and amazement because the ransom figure was so high. Rodolfo Latartara, an experienced officer with the Italian police stationed in the Tianjin Concession, was brought in to assist the Chinese head of investigationsin Shanghai. He was then partnered with Hiang, nicknamed "Confucius" by Ciano for his wisdom. This Chinese clerk at the Italian Consulate in Shanghai was there to help Latatara in his dealings with the Chinese police staff. The letter sent to the Consulate demanded that a coded notice should be put into a local daily newspaper as soon as the ransom was ready. The authorities had no intention of paying and tried to stall for time in order to continue their investigations. There were no developments for two months and then, suddenly, the theory of a mistaken identity began to gain ground. Franceschi's partner, a certain Venetian lawyer, should have been on the ship boarded by the brigands, but unexpected commitments had prevented him from taking the trip and his partner had gone in his place. This fact received a great deal of coverage in the local press and an official appeal was issued by the investigators who demanded the release of the kidnapped man, warning that no ransom would ever be paid. A week later, Franceschi was found blindfolded, gagged and tied to a jetty on the Whangpoo. The "gentleman brigands" apologised for the mistaken identity, saying this was the first year they had tried kidnapping and they would no doubt be much more efficient the following year!

The city became a hotbed of Nazi activity and espionage. Most of the Italians in China were ashamed of their country's friendship with the Reich, despite the ongoing publicity campaign about the comradeship that was said to exist between the two dictators. And Ciano himself had come to realise that the alliance with Germany was a mistake because he wrote in his diary: 'Hitler is treacherous and untrustworthy; you cannot be involved in politics with him.'

10

It was against this political backdrop that the two young lovers met again. Nothing had changed between them.

The Venetian spoke about Italy, his visits to Bombay, Singapore and Hong Kong, but it was mere small talk. Finally he confessed: 'Without you, I feel like I'm withering inside. We must talk seriously. The reason I came back was to ask you to marry me, but things are complicated and I'm not sure how we'll manage.'

Green Bay could not contain her excitement. She wondered whether she would be able to live in Italy. The obstacles were like the treacherous rocks of the Yangtze which smashed junks to smithereens in the stories of her grandfather, Accumulated Virtue, had told her. But she reminded herself that many junks arrived safely at their destination despite the rocks. So Green Bay suggested a Chinese marriage to avoid the red tape required by the Italian authorities.

'We'd have to go to Hangzhou,' she explained. 'In our culture, a marriage is only socially approved if consent is given by the family. We'll celebrate the wedding in my father's house, the house of my ancestors, otherwise our relatives will object. I want all of Hangzhou to know that you're my honoured husband.'

'Afterwards, we'll marry according to Italian law as well,' he said. 'I'll buy you a wedding ring or no one in Italy will believe we're married!'

'How lovely! That way I get to marry you twice. And we can have a third one, a Buddhist marriage too, to please my widowed aunt who lives in Suzhou on Tiger Hill.'

'And after that, why don't we have a Catholic ceremony as well?' added the Venetian with a smile.

The young man gazed at her, taking in her scent of tuberoses, the strange light in her dark eyes. He drew her to him and kissed her so passionately and openly that she drew away in embarrassment.

'I'm sorry. Was that uncouth of me?'

'We Chinese hide our feelings. I've never felt like this before. I can't find the right words.'

In her understated Chinese way, he realised she was expressing a love for him as passionate as his own.

'We don't always need words,' he replied, rising and taking her hand. Their shoulders touched accidentally and he felt her shiver. He made as if to take her in his arms again, but she instinctively stiffened.

That evening, Green Bay wrote a letter to her family, thinking it best to warn them that the man she wanted to marry was a foreigner.

'We're not opposed,' they soon replied, 'We'll honour the foreign gentleman as our guest. We're living in times of historic change and we must, for our own safety, be on good terms with other nations. We're pleased to hear that he loves our country and our traditions, and that he's courteous.'

Green Bay and the Venetian decided to lose no time in paying them a formal visit in Hangzhou.

As soon as they climbed down from their rickshaw and began walking towards the house of the Miao family, Green Bay warned the Venetian: 'Don't be surprised when you see my mother limp, particularly when she's tired. She removed the bandages from her bound feet soon after my birth.'

The house was at the end of the Avenue of Everlasting Happiness, surrounded by a stone wall. On the eaves of the curvilinear roof, little good-luck figures in the shape of animals were outlined against the sky. The main door was solid wood with highly polished brass knockers.

As soon as he heard the rickshaw coming, the gatekeeper came out of the front gate, peered at them for a second before recognising Green Bay:

'Welcome home, young mistress,' he said, then told the boy at his side: 'Quickly run and tell the master and mistress that their daughter is here.'

'Old Li, I'm happy to see you again in such good health.'

'Young mistress, we're all happy. You've brought us the light of your presence.'

'We live above the West Lake,' explained Green Bay to her intended. 'See? The hills are green with tea plantations growing the famous Long Jin tea. Legend has it that from the sky a precious pearl fell into the lake, turning it the same colour. The Grand Canal, down there in the east, links this ancient capital with Beijing. The boats sail its entire length carrying silk brocades, salt, and tributes from the southern provinces to Beijing.'

Impressed, the Venetian listened.

'I don't wonder,' he remarked 'that Marco Polo admired it. We'll also be spending our honeymoon here,' he added, squeezing her hand.

They crossed the first courtyard, shaded by thick boughs of wisteria and flanked by servants' quarters, then continued across a second one, the Garden of the Peonies, finally passing through a round door to a garden where the whole family was lined up on the stone platform of the Guest Reception Room.

Radiant Wisdom, who had not seen his daughter for a long time, only gave a slight bow and walked over to meet Green Bay. Being a typical Chinese father, he did not show affection in public. Her mother, Splendid Gem, instinctively took a step forward, but then immediately stopped and remained standing where she was. Once again the Venetian was made aware of the inflexibility of the Chinese. Green Bay, bowing deeply, did not move either, and said in a low voice, 'Most esteemed parents.'

Suddenly Radiant Wisdom's highly polished shoes and Splendid Gem's tiny deformed feet moved equally fast. Her father stepped forward and held out his arms to Green Bay.

'Daughter, welcome home,' he said.

Every member of her family then greeted her according to

their rank.

Green Bay gestured to the Venetian: 'Father, I'd like to introduce "my beloved."'

There was a brief murmur of surprise, followed by silence. "My beloved" was a term never spoken in public, only in private. But her mother, Splendid Gem, took a step forward and, placing a hand on the young Italian's shoulder said, 'Welcome, a thousand times welcome.' Her father, speaking perfect English with the rhythmic intonation of the Chinese language, added, 'We're honoured to welcome you into our house.'

From that moment on, the Venetian was part of the family. Green Bay had helped him on the rules of etiquette and he, in his turn, bowed and replied:

'My unworthy person is sincerely honoured to be welcomed into your house.'

The welcome tea was served in the Reception Pavilion, a spacious room the decoration of which combined ancient Chinese and modern European furnishings. The silk lanterns held electric light bulbs and there were two European sofas and a gramophone in a corner. The Venetian was enchanted by the beautiful carved furniture and the peonies in white porcelain vases with wooden bases. Radiant Wisdom led him to the place of honour, while his wife, turning to Green Bay, smiled: 'Daughter, you've brought us a lucky omen.'

Green Bay laughed at the expression and took it as her cue to call her beloved Lucky Omen. Her father, smiling, turned to Magnolia and Fragrance, the two young *muitsai* maidservants bought the year before when a famine had struck the province of Sichuan.

'Quickly, quickly,' he said, clapping his hands 'bring some tea for our honoured guest.'

'Lucky Omen,' said Green Bay, correcting him with a laugh, pleased to have found a Chinese name for her beloved. In China, it is not unusual to have several names—a baby name, a school name, a polite name, a professional name, a name when performing an important task or when a great privilege has been bestowed on you.

After a long silence, Splendid Gem whispered: 'My daughter is young and inexperienced. You must be tolerant with her. We have failed in our teaching.'

Lucky Omen was surprised, for in all the time he had spent in China, he had still not grown used to the self-deprecation deemed necessary in sophisticated Chinese society. His surprise could still be read in his face when Magnolia and Fragrance came over to pour his tea, and Radiant Wisdom, apologising, added:

'Our tea isn't very good. Perhaps you would like some other sort?'

'No, thank you. It's excellent,' replied Lucky Omen, taking a long swallow. For this occasion, Radiant Wisdom had bought some Indian tea and even some milk from a shop in the English Concession, to please his guest.

'Is the photographer ready?' asked Radiant Wisdom, clapping his hands again. His enthusiasm made him look younger and more cheerful, while his slim figure and shiny, black hair with no trace of white in it, gave him a distinguished air.

A man wearing a Western-style black jacket and striped trousers came in with two children who set up the camera on a sturdy wooden tripod draped with a large black cloth. The family took up their poses in strict order and smiled when the photographer said in English: 'Smile, please', squeezing the rubber shutter release with a theatrical gesture. The photograph was proof positive that Lucky Omen had officially been accepted into the family. This was a historic occasion: the Blue Miao family was welcoming a foreigner into its midst.

In a few minutes, the large room had emptied. Green Bay's mother stood up and, turning to their guest, said: 'You must be very tired. Allow us to show you to your rooms. Rest well in the knowledge that you've filled our house with joy.'

Fascinated by the prevailing air of serenity, the Italian allowed Magnolia and Fragrance to lead him to the hot, fragrant bath that had been prepared for him. When he climbed out of the water, they wrapped him in a silk dressing gown, and he retired to his room to dress.

Leaving his room, he saw Green Bay coming towards him.

'Are you happy?' she asked him in English.

'Darling, your family is wonderful, and you have a beautiful home.'

Green Bay showed him the small lake covered with lotus flowers. The inviting reflection of the moon was beginning to show on the water where goldfish were still darting.

'Look, the stars are coming out; it's as if someone has turned on the sky's fountains.'

Taking advantage of this welcome, the young couple decided to marry while they were guests of Green Bay's family. The propitious day was confirmed by her father after consulting the almanac and on that day, the young bride donned a gown and ruby red jacket embroidered by her mother. It had been decided that she would not wear the traditional headdress.

'These are new times,' Radiant Wisdom had explained, 'so there must be new customs.' After all, Green Bay was breaking with tradition by marrying a foreigner.

So she arrived at the Pavilion of the Ancestors with her hair gathered in a chignon and held in place with precious jade pins and flowers. Wearing a blue double-breasted jacket, Lucky Omen stood proudly by her side. They approached and bowed to the ancestors, represented by small wooden tablets arranged in order of rank. Then they bowed to her father and mother, and drank wine from the same goblet. This gesture formalised the Italian's entry in the family as their son-in-law. The final act of respect was performed by Green Bay who poured tea during the ceremony and carried the cups to her parents:

'Father and mother, I beseech you to drink,' she said.

When the servants rang the gong, the guests sat down at their tables in the courtyard near the Room of the Ancestors; the excellent food they were enjoying was regarded as the fruit of the ancestors' good works and Radiant Wisdom addressed them by name, inviting them to eat before the other guests began wielding their ivory chopsticks. Green Bay and Lucky Omen only ate a few mouthfuls at the banquet. Both of them had to perform the established ritual: walking three paces behind her husband, Green Bay followed him round the tables, every now and then raising a small teacup in honour of the guests sitting there. Only when the guests had finished the last of the sixty-four courses could the newlyweds finally retire to the elegant room that had been prepared for them. In front of the window, the plants blocked out the gentle glimmer of moonlight. The perfume of the flowers in porcelain vases on high bases mingled with the aroma of the wood covering the walls. They were no pictures on the walls, only precious white and gold Chinese ideograms for double happiness on grey and blue lacquered backgrounds.

Green Bay and her husband entered the bridal chamber, leaving behind the sumptuous wedding celebrations. This was their time now. There was no escaping time-honoured tradition, though. On the camphor wood trunk at the foot of the bed sat a wicker basket filled with sweetmeats. It was customary for the newlyweds to eat these celebratory delicacies to ensure that their marriage started well.

When she woke, Green Bay thought she was still dreaming. She smiled, realising the dream was real, and, sensing that Lucky Omen was still asleep, she gently curled up against him and relaxed, her mind at rest and her heart filled with joy. She would never be lonely again. It is strange, she thought, how a ceremony can make you love someone more. She dozed off again and was woken by the sound of smothered giggles through the windows separating them from the courtyard. Magnolia and Fragrance were waiting for a sign that the newlyweds were awake: they were carrying a platter of different sweetmeats.

The marriage certificate was presented after being read to the bride and groom by an official. The newlyweds turned to bow to each other, the witnesses and finally everyone present. They applauded, remarking: 'Such a good-looking couple. A real pair of "mandarin ducks".'

Her new husband was taken aback.

'Mandarin ducks mate for life—a symbol of lasting love,' she explained

She looked at him with a smile, her face glowing after the

wedding night: every gesture, every look, showed how happy she was. Love had banished all her doubts, all her reserve. She felt that they were in perfect harmony with each other and she savoured the miracle of being together for the rest of their lives.

The newlyweds stayed in Hangzhou for a few more days and, during their stay, Radiant Wisdom threw many parties, because he wanted everyone to accept his foreign son-in-law.

'My foreign son-in-law is a very important person,' he would say.

Every day the Venetian discovered new dimensions to this family, which was so traditional, and yet so modern in many respects. He had found out, for example, that Green Bay's father loved Western classical music and that he had a collection of the most recent American jazz records. He also proved to be an excellent tennis player and he appeared even younger on court, skilfully placing his serves well out of his opponent's reach. The young Italian often caught him bent over the flowerbeds, intent on the pruning of plants and chatting with the old gardener who had grown up with the old man's father, Accumulated Virtue.

Radiant Wisdom had a theatrical performance staged in one of the rooms as a fitting end to the ceremonial wedding celebrations. The entire family attended the performance and seemed completely absorbed in the action. Between a sip of tea and a morsel of food, they seemed to live and breathe the verses declaimed by the actors in high voices, punctuated rhythmically by the striking of a gong.

The Italian was amazed at their total involvement in the play. Everyone knew the lines, recited them, and savoured them, along with the sunflower seeds. They listened rapturously to the high notes, surrendered to the unchanging music transfixed with emotion, then relaxed with a sigh.

As if reading his thoughts, Green Bay asked: 'Do you like my country?'

'There isn't a country on earth as wonderful as China. It's a world apart, a phenomenon,' he answered.

As they were about to leave, Radiant Wisdom gave Lucky

Omen a valuable letter opener with an ivory handle intricately carved by a renowned local craftsman. Green Bay's mother gave her a jade fish—the Buddhist symbol of longevity—on a long gold chain: 'I'm giving you this, dear daughter, just as it was given to me. Your father says that it has been in our family for many moons.'

Then the rickshaw carrying the newlyweds pulled away, followed by the luggage bearers.

'I feel as if I've just come back down to earth!' the Venetian exclaimed. 'I've been living on another planet for so many days. Already, you're like something from a dream—the ceremonial trappings, the traditions, the clothes and the eternally smiling faces at the banquets, everyone's heads bobbing up and down!'

'Every one of them out to convince you that you weren't making a mistake in marrying me,' replied Green Bay lightly, glowing with happiness and stroking the jade fish her mother had given her. Like her mother, Green Bay possessed that particular gift of recognising the quality of jade by touch alone, a "jade hand". Realising that the object she was holding was a perfect specimen, she showed it proudly to her husband. He, in his turn, began turning the letter opener round in his fingers and admiring the elegant motif carved into the ivory; he was surprised to feel the delicacy of the handle—he had experienced the same sensation of lightness on clasping Radiant Wisdom's hand when he had said goodbye. It was not the first time he had noticed that the Chinese did not give a firm handshake. At first, he had thought it a sign of bad faith, but Green Bay had put him right: 'Traditionally, we've never greeted each other by shaking hands. The Chinese always try to avoid physical contact with people outside the family. The bow is and always has been our mode of greeting; and bowing has always been the accepted sign of respect and regard. Chinese aristocrats' hands are always very small. They aren't used to convey personal feelings to foreigners. Many of us regard Westerners' hands as rough and insensitive.'

The Venetian placed the letter opener in its pigskin holder. He turned to look at Green Bay, then looked down at her clasped hands on the cushion of the rickshaw that was speeding downhill. He took one of her hands and squeezed it in his.

'Are they rough?' he teased.

'Now I think I know how a tiny swallow feels in the warmth of its nest,' came Green Bay's reply.

11

On returning to Shanghai, the young Italian was immediately summoned to Consul Parisi's house. He feared it was to answer for his relationship with Green Bay. The Consul signalled to Liu Foy, his head boy, to withdraw and turning to the Venetian, beckoned him to follow him through the house.

'I wanted to speak to you alone, which is why I asked you to come to my house instead of meeting in the office or somewhere public where there's always someone watching, then writing reports. Please make yourself comfortable.'

He pointed to an armchair which, the Venetian immediately realised, was the chair his superior flung himself into as soon as he came home: it looked well-used, the cushions were crumpled and it was placed where it would receive the cooling breeze from the ceiling fan. However, this evening the Consul could not relax as usual: he had to deal with a highly personal matter that was also of considerable official importance.

'You have a beautiful home,' remarked his guest, looking around, 'and you'd never guess you were in the middle of the city—you can't hear the traffic at all.'

'That'll be because of the trees in the garden and the plants that my wife tends with infinite Chinese patience. They completely muffle the noise from the road. May I offer you a drink?'

He was particularly solicitous, finding it an effort to hide his nervous tension.

'Thank you. A Punt e Mes.'

'Help yourself. The soda water siphon's on the desk.'

The Venetian felt uncomfortably like a prisoner at the bar,

waiting to hear the charges against him. The Consul had remained standing and was pacing back and forth, lost in thought until he suddenly stopped and looking intently at the young man asked pointedly, 'Forgive me, I made a mistake. Perhaps I should have asked if you'd like some tea... '

The Consul's sarcastic tone left no room for doubt. The young man stood up, his composure as icy as the drink in his hand.

'I think I understand—'

'Please sit down,' interrupted the Consul, placing himself directly in front of his guest. He took a silver cigarette case from the inside pocket of his white linen jacket and offered him a Macedonia.

'I don't smoke. If I—'

Again the Consul interrupted him: 'Listen to me.'

He lit a cigarette, inhaling deeply and slowly.

'There's nothing I hate more than getting involved in people's private affairs.'

The Venetian held his tongue and waited, hoping that the Consul knew nothing of his wedding in Hangzhou.

'I hear that... that for some months you've been living with a Chinese girl in the Windsor Court apartments on Bubbling Well Road. Allow me to inform you that you're making a grave mistake.'

The Venetian was surprised at the Consul's courteous tone: the Italian authorities must still be in the dark about his marriage to Green Bay.

The Consul continued: 'I wasn't the one who had you tailed by the person who reported what I've just told you. You should be aware that an official from Rome, since returned, came here on a secret mission. He informed me that he had a confidential brief from Count Ciano, Minister of Foreign Affairs, who has sent me a message that, while reminding me of his high esteem and affection for you, ordered me to speak to you in person. You should also know that Il Duce has ordered purges of all of our country's embassies and legations throughout the world, as well as in Italy. We are at the eye of the storm here, because Rome is aware that there are a large number of Russian refugees in Chinese cities, particularly Shanghai, and that many of them are Jews. As a result, this city is regarded as high risk, both politically and racially. Well, the official in question was given the task of investigating our own personnel, monitoring the presence of people who are Jewish or of Jewish origins and, at the same time, keeping an eye on how many Jews might be in contact with our offices in China. You can imagine his surprise when, making an inspection of the home of Olga Aleksandrova, a singing teacher invited to our parties because she's a self-styled "friend of Italy", he saw you entering her residence with a young Chinese woman. Naturally, you've been under surveillance since then. I received personal instructions from Count Ciano not to reveal the unpleasant affair, but to arrange for you to be transferred to Tianjin as soon as possible and to advise you to give up this unsuitable attachment. I don't think there's anything else for us to say, except to discuss your handover here in Shanghai.'

Out in the street, in a bid to tire himself out, the Venetian began wandering aimlessly along the Boulevard des Deux Républiques to the junction with Yu Ya Ching Road. He then turned north and headed towards the lodgings in Honan Road that had been placed at his disposal by the Italian Consulate and that he had not been using for some time, where Chee May, his faithful *amah* still did his washing and ironing.delivering it to Windsor Court, where he was now living. Then he headed towards the French Concession. Here the floral fragrances and bitter aroma of Gauloises mingled with Shanghai's usual scent of vinegar, incense and mould. Paris on the Whangpoo, Shanghai—the Paris of the East, thought the Venetian, crossing Avenue Edward VII and heading towards Bubbling Well Road.

The contrast between Nanking Road and the streets of the real China seemed to symbolise the difference between two mindsets. There was no clearly defined frontier between the two. Everyday he discovered new aspects of Shanghai, the international metropolis which some regarded as a perfect example of many nations working together for the common good, and that others saw as the world capital of vice, founded on a de facto system of slavery.

As he finally made his way towards Green Bay, he realised how much he loved Shanghai, the city where he had met her, the city he was now about to leave.

Green Bay had a spare hour before her husband came home, so she took a bath, washing her long black hair in a rosemary and nettle tisane, wrapping it in a white towelling turban, sitting like one of those bathing concubines in old paintings, her thoughts of the future floating like petals on water. The cooling bath made her shiver and brought her back to the present. Swathing herself in a bathrobe she walked over to the large mirror on one wall and dropped the gown. She thought it immodest to look at herself and blushed to think how often Lucky Omen's eyes continually examined her, following her every movement, but emboldened by the love she was experiencing, she stared at her face, the sweep of her neck and shoulders, the soft curves of her breasts, the sinuous movement of her pelvis, the graceful line of her legs. Finally, she slowly turned sideways and placed her hand on her stomach, gently caressing it.

'Tonight,' she promised herself 'as soon as Lucky Omen comes home, I'll tell him.' Then she covered herself with soft silk.

When her husband finally returned, she came to sit in front of him, a delicate figure framed by lacquered caskets and screens. Lucky Omen bent over and murmured as he sat down beside her, 'Do I have to tell you how beautiful you are?'

She blushed and placed her hand in his.

'Lucky Omen,' she said simply, without hesitation, 'We are to have a child.'

The announcement dropped on him like a stone on water. She ran into the kitchen and came back holding two goblets and champagne. The Venetian gazed at his young wife's delicate features through its golden filter. If he took Green Bay and a child to Italy, he thought, his ill-tempered, narrow-minded father would contemptuously call her and her family 'yellow faces.' His stepmother, full of her ridiculous middle-class prejudices, would wrinkle her nose and disapprove of their marriage for fear that their relatives and friends would do the same.

He fell silent. This chilled Green Bay and her eyes misted with sadness. She saw only surprise, bewilderment and then fear in his face. A flush crept over her face and tears welled in her eyes.

The Venetian sensed her pain and forced himself to move closer to her, but he felt as if his young wife had withdrawn from him and that he had not allayed her fears.

Only later, on that sultry summer night, did the Venetian finally tell Green Bay the situation. They discussed what he should do—rashly give up his career to stay with her, or should he leave immediately for Tianjin, as ordered? It was unthinkable to appeal directly to Count Ciano and ask him to intervene to obtain royal assent.

Green Bay listened lovingly to him and tried to come up with an immediate solution by offering to convert to Catholicism: she suggested that Lucky Omen pay a visit to Father Fontana to discuss this, rather than to Father Gherzi.

'Father Gherzi deals with real typhoons,' she said trying to inject a little humour, 'but Father Fontana has worked with our people for many years. Try and see him before you leave.'

The Venetian nodded. 'But first I should go to the Consulate and have a word with Confucius.'

The next morning, on being confronted by the young Italian, Confucius immediately realised this was a special situation. 'Honourable sir,' he said 'You want to speak to me about something important?'

'Not here. Let's meet at one o'clock on the pontoon of the Customs House, near the passengers' exit.'

They arrived together and walked to a little inn on the confluence of Suzhou Creek and the Whangpoo river, where they sat down at a small secluded table. The Venetian began nervously tracing with his chopsticks the crisscross grooves on the faded oilcloth in front of him.

'Confucius,' he began, 'we've known each other a long time

and I've always had the same high regard for you as does his Excellency Ciano . What I have to tell you is a demonstration of that high regard.'

The Chinese man listened impassively: only the slight blinking of his eyes, his black pupils barely visible between the oblique slits of his eyelids, showed he was paying attention.

'You ought to know,' continued the Italian, 'that a few months ago I married a daughter of your great country in a Chinese ceremony. A love match that is now also being blessed by a... forthcoming happy event.'

'Permit me to congratulate you. I am pleased that you have honoured my country with your choice—an act of love, and bravery.'

Confucius immediately fell silent again and listened as the Venetian told him about his meeting with the Consul.

'Luckily for me,' he concluded 'no one has mentioned the marriage. They mustn't find out—if anyone were to discover that I'd married without royal assent, I think I'd be immediately suspended from service and put on the first steamer to Italy.'

The Venetian watched the Chinese man sitting opposite for some sign of what he was thinking. After a long pause, Confucius said: 'Permit me to congratulate you again. The Miao family is of noble, honourable lineage and your wife, Green Bay, is a worthy descendent.'

'How did you know my wife is called Green Bay? I've never mentioned her name.'

Confucius' eyes narrowed. 'My apologies,' he said, 'but didn't Consul Parisi tell you that he appointed me the Roman official's interpreter to help him question anyone who might be able to provide useful information. After seeing you go into the Russian woman's house, we both went back to the young Chinese lady's apartment at Windsor Court and kept watch. When you came out, the official ordered me to follow you. After seeing you go to your office, I went back to your official lodgings in Honan Road, and told your *amah* that I had an appointment with you. Chee May was surprised that you hadn't mentioned it to her. I pretended my impatience at waiting. She suggested you were at your wife's address. "Why are you calling her his wife?" I asked her. "She'll be just the same as many other women; if she were your daughter, you'd slap her face!" But she protested: "No, it's true! I've seen the wedding photographs. The woman is from Hangzhou and has many relatives." I told her not to gossip, then left. But I thought it best to return and threaten her, on pain of losing her job, to never talk of those photos again. I too, have held my tongue.'

The Venetian shuddered at the thought that he might have found himself, as if under arrest, on board the gunboat commanded by his classmates, the very same who had asked Green Bay to dance at the Cathay.

'So, if you hadn't protected me, I'd be on the next steamer to Italy, without my wife, waiting to be placed in some humiliating post! Why did you risk compromising yourself for my sake?'

'I have the same respect for you as I did for Count Ciano when he was here. I would have done anything for him, so why not for you, his friend? Anyway, I'm outraged by Western hypocrisy towards China. Their "morality" allows them to find an obliging "Shanghai girl", or a beautiful Chinese woman to keep them company every now and then. But when the relationship turns into something that is not only destined to last, but to develop into marriage, then it's taboo! But you got married, and with a Chinese ceremony. You couldn't have given a clearer demonstration of your love for your wife and your respect for my country. But sadly, I couldn't warn you —and what good would it have done?... May I ask what you are going to do now?'

'Save what I can,' replied the Venetian.

He decided he would visit Father Fontana immediately, as suggested by Green Bay. The Salesian priest had years of experience with young mixed couples.

When he arrived at the Salesian Institute, the director, Father Fontana, was surrounded by some thirty noisy children with shaved heads jumping and somersaulting around him. They all looked identical in their cloth pinafores patterned with small white and red flowers, and their black cloth slippers. A young Chinese girl authoritatively stepped to the front of the group and led them towards the entrance of a small building. The Venetian was aware of the same cheerful industriousness that he had noticed on other visits.

Father Fontana was a thin, pale, rather timid man renowned throughout the city for his ability to source funds for the Institute's children, and the poor. But the local people, who had never needed to seek his help, regarded him as an evil man, accusing him of spreading disease, regarding him as a hated Westerner laying down the law and protecting his own interests.

Father Fontana immediately recognised him and came over to greet him. The Venetian found it hard to recognise the missionary. His face, with the shadow of an unkempt beard, looked gaunt and furrowed by chronic fever, but he spoke proudly and at length about the Institute.

'They are good, obedient students. Clever—their manual dexterity has been handed down by generations of skilled craftsmen. They have a "collective soul" too. They can switch from apathy to flashes of rebelliousness.'

The missionary continued to walk around the Institute giving explanations and relating facts without asking the reason for the young Italian's latest visit. It was the Venetian who broached the subject.

'Father Fontana,' he asked without preamble, 'what is your view of mixed marriages?'

'It can be a distressing problem. Such people approach us when there's some kind of difficulty, though there is a framework in place for them to marry in Shanghai, if they want to. Sadly, many obstacles stand in their way—religion, to begin with. If the two youngsters are both Catholic, the moral problem doesn't... er...didn't arise...'

'What do you mean?'

Uncomfortable, Father Fontana replied: 'As you know, in Italy there is a great deal of German propaganda. I understand that the authorities do not want what they shamelessly call the "contamination" of the race. This deplorable discrimination has already hit the Jews. Now priests have been officially advised to make sure that the young couples who come to us to marry are of the same faith and race, before we publish the banns.'

'Of course, the banns,' repeated the Venetian who had forgotten all about this.

'Naturally. They have to be published—only in exceptional cases can the authorities—you Embassy people—intervene to speed up the procedure. But things are very complicated at present because your embassy has now decreed that only in exceptional cases will they grant the necessary consent for an Italian citizen to marry a Chinese one. Mixed marriages are no longer tolerated. Our concern is, of course, religion. For us, it's important that both the bride and groom share the Catholic faith, but the Concordat of 1929 also commands us to work with your Embassy.'

How damned ironic, thought the Venetian, furious. Not only is every possible avenue closed to me, but I must put up with being accused of supporting this hostility towards mixed marriages!

After taking his leave with a Piedmontese '*Cerea*', Father Fontana returned to his countless tasks, muttering: 'And they send one of their lot to make sure that we've understood they don't want any more mixed marriages! Oh well, back to God's work!'

12

On his way back from the Salesian Institute, the Venetian had time to go back to the office and meet briefly with the Consul concerning the following day's handover of his position. The colleague who was taking his place was still in Nanking, delaying his transfer to Tianjin. The wheels had now been set in motion and his replacement, whom he did not know, was expected the following day.

Arriving early at Windsor Court, the Venetian ran up the flight of stairs, too impatient to wait for the lift. When Green Bay opened the door, he flung his arms around her and held her tightly, torn between his happiness at seeing her and his anger.

'They can't treat me like this. They can't interfere in my private life and hurt someone who has done nothing wrong.'

'Is it permanent—the transfer?'

'The Consul has no intention of disobeying orders from Rome.'

'I could at least go somewhere to be closer to you. Beijing, perhaps. It's a big city—I could live somewhere where no one will recognise me!'

'Later, perhaps, but for now you must go to your family in Hangzhou. Our child must be born in a place where he has everything he needs. Then you can join me in Beijing later with the baby and an *amah*. Meantime, I'll get a house ready for you. We just have to be patient. Have you asked Olga for the name of her gynaecologist?'

'Yes, I've made an appointment for tomorrow. His surgery is in the town centre, at the junction of Nanking Road and the Bund. His name is Rappaport—he's Jewish. He fled two years ago and he's already built up a clientele in the Concessions.'

The next morning, he found out that, due to unexpected commitments, his successor would not arrive in Shanghai before the evening, so he took advantage of this delay to sort through the documents he had amassed during the course of his mission in China. They contained information of a particularly sensitive nature which could give rise to all manner of dangerous situations in the event of an alliance with Germany, though in the secret services no agent knew his counterpart in the same theatre of operations. Reports were passed to the communications expert who coded the despatches for forwarding via diplomatic channels or radio broadcasts; it was down to the agent who had carried out the enquiries and written the reports to ensure the safekeeping of any copies of information.

The Venetian did not know who to trust with the documents. He could not rely on Consul Parisi. He was even less inclined to deposit the box containing copies of his reports and direct communications with Ciano in the Consulate's safe. So he emptied the contents of the box into a sturdy canvas bag of the sort generally used for envelopes in the diplomatic post bag. He placed this at the bottom of a cardboard box then filled it with copies of meteorological communications received by the Consulate from the Zikawei Observatory, and sealed it with strips of gummed paper. He then telephoned Father Gherzi as a matter of urgency. An hour later, he was with him.

'Father,' he began immediately, without standing on ceremony, 'the situation in Europe is coming to a head. What happens there is bound to have repercussions here. I must leave for Tianjin tomorrow, and I won't be back for a long time. The political situation will probably create staff turnovers in our Consulate here in Shanghai, so I'd like to safeguard some documents, to prevent them from... how shall I put it, falling into the wrong hands. The consequences could be serious. I'd like to ask you to keep this packet in a safe place and not to give it to anyone. If one of your brethren is curious and asks what it contains, you can tell them they're meteorological charts and maps returned by the Legations in line with the usual agreements.'

Caught off guard, Father Gherzi did not object, believing it simpler to agree to this mysterious request from a fellow countryman. The box was stowed at the bottom of a cupboard along with various papers.

On his way back from the observatory, the Venetian went to the corner of Nanking Road and the Bund, watching people emerging from the building's four lifts, until he spotted Green Bay.

She greeted him with a joyful smile, blushing to see her husband under such circumstances.

'What did the doctor say?' he asked.

'He said everything is perfectly normal and there's nothing to worry about. He also said that he wants to see me again in six weeks and to telephone him if there are any problems. He added that I must eat well and that I must walk a lot. Our little Venetian must learn to go everywhere on foot.'

'Then let's start immediately and walk somewhere for something to eat. I'll lay odds that you're hungry now you're eating for two, and I still haven't had any lunch.'

They continued chatting light-heartedly. Neither of them wanted to broach the more serious subjects that hung in the air between them. They walked past the majestic entrance of the Hong Kong and Shanghai Bank, guarded by two enormous bronze lions.

'They're not roaring,' said Green Bay.

'And why not?'

'They only roar when a virgin walks by!' she answered with a laugh.

That evening, listening to the radio, the Venetian learnt that German troops now occupied the Low Countries and had reached the English channel. Hundreds of thousands of English and French soldiers were surrounded in Dunkerque and the English Government was devising a large-scale plan to evacuate them from the continent. Mussolini, whose exact intentions were as yet unknown, was quoted as saying: 'It is humiliating to remain with our hands folded while others write history.'

13

It was time for the Venetian to leave. The taxi slowly made its way along the crowded quay in the port where the *Qingdao* was moored, until it came to a police cordon near it, which prevented the hundreds of beggars and paupers milling about on the wharf from pilfering any goods. The Venetian presented his travel documents and entered a shed in the enclosure where he found the agency representative and two customs guards, who again checked his tickets and documents. He was then escorted outside where two *coolies* had unloaded his luggage from the taxi. The guards drew blue chalk symbols on each piece and ordered the porters to take them to the hold. The agency representative introduced himself to the young Italian and asked the new passenger to follow him onto the ship.

The *Qingdao* was used to transport merchandise and a limited number of passengers. It belonged to the China Navigation Company, a subsidiary of Butterfield & Swire, one of whose officials, by the name of Carter, the Venetian knew well. The officials were all English, the crew members being Chinese. The standard of service was excellent and every cabin had a *boy*, a cabin steward who wore a floor-length white tunic and a black felt skullcap and shoes.

On board, he was introduced to his *boy*.

'Can do valise, Master?' he asked in pidgin English.

The Venetian was shown to his cabin and the *boy* immediately began unpacking and putting away the Italian's clothes and personal items. When the Venetian went back to the cabin to change for dinner, he found his *boy* by the door waiting for him, grinning broadly. The cabin was in perfect order. On the bedside table, the photograph of Green Bay welcomed him with a smile.

The passengers' living quarters were on the upper deck. They had one lounge stretching the length of the ship, where they spent all their time at sea. When they stopped at a port, they would stand on deck watching the cargo being unloaded or admiring the coastal panorama and the islands. At mealtimes, summoned to table by a resounding stroke on the gong, they sat at a single rectangular table with the captain at the head.

The journey passed without incident. The Zikawei Observatory had signalled the presence of a seasonal incoming typhoon. The *Qingdao* could have found shelter in the port of the same name, only six hours away, but the typhoon headed for the vicinity of Haichow and dissipated along the line of demarcation between the provinces of Jiangsu and Shandong.

Once safely at his destination, the Venetian hurriedly took his leave, impatient to disembark and go straight to the Consulate to find out the latest international political developments. The only available news on board had been bulletins sent by the short-wave transmitters of various countries that were only broadcasting what they wanted their listeners to know. The Legations, on the other hand, received the truth in coded messages sent by the respective Ministries of Foreign Affairs. At the Italian Concession, the Venetian learned that in Rome, Il Duce was about to declare war on England and France.

In Shanghai, diplomacy had prevented Green Bay from saying goodbye to her husband on board ship. Someone of a weaker nature might have sunk into depression, but Green Bay was able to accept life's ups and downs calmly. She had been happy, and now she was alone: she accepted both. The love she had experienced with the Venetian had resulted in a child, and that child had to be born in Hangzhou. So, as summer was drawing to a close, Green Bay travelled to Hangzhou to pay her family another visit. Everyone was waiting for her at the station. Her mother, Splendid Gem, was as straight-backed and resplendent as usual. She looked intently at her daughter who, lowering her eyes, said, 'Yes—I'm carrying your first foreign grandson.'

They climbed into the car and drove to the house on the hilltop. Waiting there were Magnolia and Fragrance, who uttered little cries of joy as they gazed at her gently rounding belly.

Green Bay, buoyed up by the miracle she was carrying inside her, surrounded by her family's love, managed to feel more confident that she would be reunited with her husband.

Her mother, who always worried that her daughter would lose her good looks, kept talking about her complexion.

'The city dust is ruining your face,' she said. 'You don't look as I remember you. I cannot alleviate your sadness, but I do have a special cream made of almonds and crushed pearls recommended by my friends that will restore your complexion.'

Her unruffled presence, which always helped the family face any situation with serenity, made Green Bay's delivery easier.

But there was a surprise in store for everyone.

'It's a girl!' cried the midwife. 'A healthy, beautiful girl. She weighs almost nine pounds!'

I was born in the bloodiest period of the war in China. Chiang Kai-shek continued to send victory messages such as "The Communists will never cross the River Yangtze", but no one in the family listened to these broadcasts as they, and most others, had lost faith in him.

Though the Miao family could be thought of as modern, they preserved certain traditions as a sign of respect for ancient customs. Despite the crisis, Radiant Wisdom sent a red card to his friends announcing my birth and inviting them to a lavish banquet. Before this, relatives and friends also gave my mother, Green Bay, valuable gifts. A Cantonese cook was hired to prepare shark fins, crispy duck and other delicacies. Later, they celebrated my first month according to tradition, when many eggs were painted red, and every relative took one and placed it in the tub into which I had been lowered for the ceremonial bath. With this traditional gesture, they were wishing me prosperity, probably because the ideogram for the word "red" is similar to the one for "abundance". The guests also placed a personal gift in the water to win favour with the spirits. Then, in the house's second courtyard, incense was burned with paper money, a paper horse and a paper sedan chair. The next day, I was shaved and my hair was collected in a red silk handkerchief that was sewn to the pillow. One hundred days later, it was thrown in the river—a ritual that was supposed to guarantee great courage in life.

I was not named immediately because this was the exclusive right of my father; they simply called me *Bébé*. My grandfather, Radiant Wisdom, gave me the gift of one year to raise my rank in the family hierarchy. The Chinese are already one year old when they are born because they take the gestation period into consideration, so children can be two years old on the day of their first birthday. However, I was actually three, counting my grandfather's gift.

14

The Italian Legation in Beijing was not only the oldest, dating back to the time of the Boxers, 1901, but also the most imposing. As the story goes, it was decided to create a foreign diplomatic quarter in Beijing after the Boxer siege. The Italian delegate, Marquis Salvago Raggi, taking advantage of the absence of ministers from Belgium, France, Germany and Austria (who were still discussing the locations and dimensions of their respective Legations), employed a group of Italian sailors to trace out what he felt were suitable borders for the new domain. Inside this fence, he erected a sign with the words: "Legation of the Kingdom of Italy". A group of outraged ministers rushed to confront Salvago Raggi, accusing him of securing half of Beijing!

However, by 1928, when the diplomatic representatives were being sent to Nanking and Shanghai, Beijing was no longer the capital of China, and the diplomatic quarter—a cement and asphalt island with flag poles and radio masts—had become a ghost town. The documents and cipher books had been despatched to Nanking some time ago. There was no European representation and its former territoriality, the right of European citizens to be judged by European magistrates according to European law, was merely nominal. The German and Austrian Concessions had been the first to leave, and now the Italian colony's heyday had also come to an end. The Embassy had been closed, together with the houses earmarked for councillors and secretaries.

When the Venetian arrived, the Beijing plain was already the colour of summer, its green maize still without ears of corn. The soft blues and violets of the bleak mountains of northern China, traversed by the ancient Great Wall, formed its backdrop. It was like a stage set that might slide into the wings to make room for another. To find the right house for his reunion with my mother—and for his first sight of me—my father had turned to a Mr. Robinson, recommended to him by his Shanghai friend, Carter. Robinson, who had been a friend of both Ambassador Varé and Ciano, knew everything and everyone, and never tired of reminiscing about Beijing's glory days.

'I remember that anyone who entered the diplomatic service then,' he related, 'stayed there for a certain number of years, more or less without remuneration; after reaching a prestigious position, they had to use their own money to finance the entertainment expenses that etiquette demanded. Daniele Varé was forced to live anything but a quiet life and had to work very hard without receiving the recompense he deserved. But when there was less work, the officials introduced badminton and treasure hunts on horseback, to keep themselves busy. They say diplomats were somewhat eccentric, perhaps because they had to adapt to so many different countries. One of the most extrovert personalities was actually your Ciano, nicknamed "Chigi boy and dandy" by someone whose name I forget. His energy was boundless. He was famous for galloping along the walls of the Forbidden City, as well as for his passion for the fox-trot, beautiful women and practical jokes. Schoolboy pranks, of course, in which I was a willing accomplice when we became close friends and engaged in high jinks together. Mind you, he was also very capable and applied himself seriously to his work. He was following in the footsteps of famous predecessors like Carlo Sforza, Cerreti and Varé. Despite being very young, I think he was a worthy heir to this marvellous tradition of Italian talent and diplomatic skill in Beijing. I don't believe he became Minister of Foreign Affairs just because he married Lady Edda. I wonder how he's managing now. The situation is worsening between our countries, but if the worst comes to the worst, it won't be Ciano's doing. I remember him saying that anyone declaring war on "Perfidious Albion" would also have to take on America and that there's no way that Italy can allow itself to make an enemy of the United States. Millions of Italians live there and are loyal to the country of their birth. The money they send continues to be crucial for your budget, so a war would be ridiculous.'

My father nodded, thinking that this last statement was correct, though an unusual take on the situation. However, he had no desire to hear about Ciano's politics which he knew only too well, and when Robinson went on to comment on the complex interplay of alliances with Germany, my father interrupted, preferring to hear more about Robinson's personal reminiscences about Ciano.

'You were talking,' he said, 'about high jinks...'

Robinson drew deeply on his cigarette, smiling at his memories.

'Innocent schoolboy pranks, as I said. We were at a party in a suite on one of the top floors of the Hotel Wagons-Lits. My wife wasn't there, nor was Ciano's. The buffet supper had been served very late and the party continued long into the night. This was not unusual in those times, when there was the right mix of people in the room and the right blend of liqueur in their glasses. I suddenly realised I was virtually the only one left in the room, so I went next door where I could still hear voices. I saw Ciano conversing with our host. Noticing me, he called me over. I had one for the road and, as it was now early morning, announced my intention of going home. Ciano immediately took the trouble to offer me a lift and phoned the night porter to tell him to alert his driver. We said goodbye to our host and went out into the long, narrow, deserted corridor, the only sign of the human presence being the pairs of shoes outside the doors of the rooms. We set off towards the lift and I pushed the button. We were surprised to see that it was one of those new automatic lifts that did not require a lift boy at night. Ciano's eyes gleamed. 'Quick, the shoes,' he said, 'let's take them!'

He disappeared down the passage, gathering as many pairs as he could carry in his arms. I followed suit. We threw them all into the lift, then we entered, went down a floor, repeated the operation and so on—for three or four floors, filling the lift with shoes. Ciano stopped the lift at the first floor, and we walked down the stairs to the lobby. From the bench near the entrance, the porter watched us come down. We casually bade him good night, left the hotel and climbed into the car, where we burst out laughing. We didn't stop all along Rue Hatamen, picturing the faces of the hotel guests when they returned to the hotel, perhaps a little tipsy, and called the lift to find it filled with shoes. Then we imagined the dismayed managers waking the floor boys who were supposed to shine the guests' shoes at first light. It would have been quite a job for them to try and pair up the shoes, let alone line them up so that each of the furious guests—including our host—could find his own! Good times!'

'Life in Beijing isn't like that anymore, that's for sure!' said my father. 'I have to go back there in a few weeks to live for an indefinite period. Do you know if it's easy to find a house there?'

'The situation is good—many of the foreign residents left Beijing when war broke out in Europe. Now, I know of a Frenchman, Jean Vauban, who lived in China for many years and who left his apartment to move to New Caledonia. I saw him again a few days ago when he came back to collect his boarding card. He was leaving on one of our ships bound for Hong Kong, the first leg of his journey. I have his address here in my pocket diary... I know it was in the Rue des Legations... Here it is.'

'Thank you... Delighted to have made your acquaintance, Mr. Robinson. Even though our countries are at war, you'll always be welcome in my house in Beijing. You'll know where to find me!'

'Goodbye, old boy! Good luck—to you both!' he replied, in English. Sly old fox, thought my father (as, no doubt, did Robinson) as he walked away.

Jean Vauban's house on the Rue des Legations, the best-known thoroughfare in Beijing, proved to be an excellent suggestion. The proprietor was a French scholar fond of

Chinese culture. Before leaving, he had lovingly restored the ceramic tiles and repainted the entire house. It was a characteristic square residence hidden behind a security wall. The inner garden was planted with white lilacs and jasmine known as "seven mile fragrance". At its centre stood a tall plum tree. All the rooms had been laid out according to the rules of geomancy, the science that ensures every human structure is in a correct cosmic position with relation to the natural world, so that it can benefit from the peace and prosperity created by the "energy" circling the universe. The large living-room was in the south, while in the west lay the bedroom with its central large *kang*, a bed made of bricks with heating underneath for the chilly Beijing nights. The house had a modern bathroom and the kitchen, which boasted a French-made iron stove, was adjacent to the room occupied by the cook, who came with the house. He had served the Frenchman for twenty years and had become a fine cordon bleu chef. He could make excellent soufflés as well as preparing spicy mouth-watering specialities from Sichuan, his native province.

Pleased with his choice, my father wondered what Green Bay—and I—would make of it all.

15

Beijing was a masterpiece of mathematical poetry built by the Imperial Geomancers using vertical and horizontal lines, right angles and acute corners, in such a way that all the streets, gates and doors formed an energy field radiating out to every part of China from its epicentre in the imperial palaces.

Here, my parents enjoyed what would prove to be their last truly happy time together. After their long separation, and stay in Hangzhou, Green Bay was now standing in the house's inner courtyard, which was illuminated by a ray of sunshine, as she held me up in her arms as if to show me how beautiful were the house and garden.

'What a wonderful house,' she exclaimed, smiling affectionately at her husband. She walked over to the plum tree and saw that it had already fruited and was losing its leaves. 'The person who lived in this house must have been someone special. Just looking at it makes me feel happy,' she added, smiling at the pleased cook, standing behind the new Italian tenant.

My mother soon began to finish the job of furnishing the house: buying furniture became a fascinating history lesson for her, a way of travelling through time. It intrigued her to visit stores like the Little Shop on the ground floor of the Peking Hotel, which was owned by Charlotte Horsman, Ciano's regular German dance partner. Green Bay regarded every new purchase as a homage to a lovingly preserved tradition, even though the old world was already partially in tatters. As well as a flourishing centre of antiques, Beijing was also the city of silk. There were opulent stores where the faint rustle of fabric could even be heard in the entrance courtyards. The sales assistants stood behind long counters unrolling the silk in a single movement, their nails trimmed specially to avoid damaging it.

The Chinese authorities did everything in their power to obtain the luxuries they denied themselves, believing them indispensable to Western diplomats. Various pavilions belonging to the temples on the Western Hills had also been placed at their disposal.

China's majestic historical and cultural heritage was mysteriously present in Beijing, a city very different to Shanghai. Thousands of men through the ages had described the surroundings that my mother admired with such pride. The distances she covered on foot seemed nothing to her, because she was walking to see surviving ancient structures.

One day, a seemingly trivial, incident revealed a sad truth to her. She ventured onto Morrison Street, the busiest street in the centre where crowds flocked to the large stores. She stopped in front of a window full of musical instruments, through which she could just make out a gleaming pianoforte inside, and on impulse, she walked into the shop and went over to the impressive Steinway. Looking up from the pianoforte, her eyes met the gaze of the sales assistant. Instantly, they both realised they shared a passion for Western music.

'May I look?' asked Green Bay, hesitantly. 'I mean, may I sit down there?' she corrected herself timidly, pointing to the rectangular inlaid ebony piano stool in front of the keyboard.

'Please do,' replied the young man 'but don't only look!'

'Ah, but I play badly,' she replied, laughing. 'I'm not trained, I only play to accompany myself when I sing.'

The sales assistant's urging overrode her timid fears and, after gazing long and hard at the keyboard as if trying to refamiliarise herself with the notes, she absent-mindedly picked out some simple arpeggios.

'Why not sing something?' suggested the sales assistant.

Green Bay looked up, trying to remember a simple melody, and, at that moment, she realised how long it was since she had last sung. She sensed, with an unexpected feeling of disappointment, almost bitterness, that not only had her singing ability diminished, but that her new family had now replaced this passion, the main reason for her love of Italy. She thanked the young man and left the shop.

In June 1940, after barely four months in Beijing, the news from Italy was becoming ever more alarming. My father came home from work one day, in dismay. 'Trouble is brewing,' he said. 'When I went into the office this afternoon, you could cut the air with a knife. Everyone was there! Zappi, the Consul from Tianjin, Captain Del Greco and Tavanti, the ship's lieutenant—even Di Noy, the manager of the Grand Hotel was present, whispering with the pilot, Riva. Every member of staff on duty was out in the corridor, talking about a message that had just come in and had been decoded. Ciano had handed a declaration of war to the Ambassadors of France and Great Britain. Mussolini will announce it to the nation shortly. It will be a tragedy, believe me. I think we should have our daughter baptised in a Catholic Church as soon as possible to ensure her safety.'

Another war, thought my mother, and with what consequences for China, already ravaged for so long by war and invasion, despite the fact that representatives of the warring nations had lived peacefully side by side? And what consequences will it have for us?

'Alright,' she said aloud, 'our daughter can be baptised as you wish. I'll tell my father and mother—they won't stand in our way, though a few of our relatives may grumble. For 500,000 years, we Chinese have incorporated other religious beliefs. No one is criticised if one day they're Buddhist and the next Taoist. Our daughter will be able to practise both Catholic and Buddhist religions, if she so wishes.'

They decided to visit the Frenchman, Abbot Bollard at the Church of St. Michel, renowned in the foreign community of Beijing for his dislike of the Japanese because of the atrocities they carried out on Chinese soil. My father had thought it wise to place me in the safety of a French mission because both Chinese and Japanese authorities recognised the Catholic missions as extraterritorial zones, and so they were safe. Also, the French had succeeded in monopolising nearly all the Catholic missions, due to substantial financial help from the Government in Paris and effective Consular support. Mussolini's Government had done nothing to undermine this amicable status quo: the dictator had even earmarked a sum of money for foreign missions in the state budget because he regarded missionaries as champions of the Italian spirit, colonisers of a sort.

I was christened Rose Marie—not a single name, but one with two parts—half for my mother, and half for my father. My parents had wanted to evoke memories of a carefree time when they had only just met and the bands in the big hotels on the Bund were playing the film's signature song sung by Jeanette McDonald and Nelson Eddy. My godmother was Joanne, the wife of a Belgian diplomat.

Abbot Bollard, after first solemnly making an expansive sign of the cross in the air to the kneeling congregation, invited the couple to follow him into the sacristy where he gave them, along with the certificate of baptism, a letter for Father Corcouf at the Ningbo mission—a night's journey by ferry from Shanghai.

The ensuing months were filled with fear and anxiety. Foreigners, particularly the Italians, were worried about the course the war was taking. My father had not received any direct communication from Ciano since the spring of 1939 when they had met in Italy, and his main aim was to work out how to get back to Shanghai as quickly as possible. A new official from the Fascist party, one Poletti, had arrived at the Consulate with a brief to develop propagandist initiatives with the press and local associations. In view of all the changes that had taken place and the unexpected worsening of events, my father felt it should not be impossible to gloss over the "scandal" of his relationship with a young Chinese woman, so he skilfully schemed to obtain a transfer.

But events moved faster than he did. Generalissimo Chiang

Kai-shek had ceded Northern China to the Japanese. Abandoning Beijing and Tianjin, he moved to Shanghai with the pride of his army, the 88th Division, expertly trained to goose-step by German military advisers. It looked like the war would last a long time. The Japanese were demolishing the West's apparent superiority. They closed the Concessions in Beijing and Tianjin and, except for a few low-ranking officials, the diplomatic corps hurriedly retreated to Japan, and from there to America and Europe. Others, like the Venetian, were immediately transferred to Nanking and Shanghai.

A special train was organised by the diplomatic authorities for the transfer. The convoy had complete diplomatic immunity and carried a cross-section of almost all the countries at war represented by their officials as well as, in many cases, their families and domestic staff. The train had a special carriage for servants, which was an unexpected stroke of luck for the Venetian. He succeeded in convincing Joanne and Simon Dupont to say, when the time came to leave, that my *amah* had been their servant for many years and that Green Bay and I were the *amah*'s daughter and granddaughter. The two women and little girl ended up quartered with the Belgian couple: so my mother, forced by political "reasons" to conceal her identity and deny her marriage, was able to travel on the same train as her husband, albeit in a different carriage.

16

By the time they arrived, Shanghai was completely surrounded by Japanese soldiers and an attack was imminent following the action taken by their aircraft in the Pacific against the American fleet in Pearl Harbor. For propaganda purposes, the Japanese also seemed impatient to declare that Shanghai had fallen.

Just before dawn on 8th December 1941, the Italian navy gunboat, *Carlotto*, had unexpectedly weighed anchor, and its place had been taken by a Japanese torpedo-boat destroyer. As always, thousands of *sampans* and junks were moored along the Bund, a floating city of mice and men, still shrouded in darkness, while rusted, flaking ferries were gathered in tight groups, as if helping each other to stay afloat.

Already the sun was rising behind the gloomy outline of the factories in Pudong, its rays spreading over the waters of the Whangpoo and illuminating the blocky forms of the American and English gunboats, the USS *Wake* and HMS *Petrel*. A thread of smoke from their funnels showed that they were about to weigh anchor. Some movement could be glimpsed on the Japanese torpedo-boat destroyer and a signal lamp was sending Morse code messages along the river towards the Hongkew quarter, where the growing light revealed the *Itzumo*, moored opposite the Japanese Consulate. Two transport launches with marines on board pulled away from the ship, and began heading for the *Wake* and *Petrel*.

Suddenly, a great roar was heard, creating a shockwave that carried a heavy pall of grey smoke from the middle of the river. Alarmed by the explosion, my father ran to the Palace

Hotel in the Bund just in time to see the *Petrel* sink. Incredulous, he watched burning fragments tumble from the sky, while other small explosions ripped through the ship. Then the entire hotel building itself seemed to sway with the deafening approach of aircraft engines.

'The *Itzumo* has sunk the *Petrel* and is now attacking the American ship!' cried the dismayed foreigners gathered in the hotel lounge.

The city was deserted. Various *sampans* arrived to gather up the dead and wounded. Burned and lacerated bodies, some still bleeding, lay in heaps. Trucks full of Japanese soldiers drove past. A battalion of Japanese marines advanced along the Bund. A platoon headed by an officer holding a Mauser pistol, ran up the stairs of the English Consulate.

A few hours later, the Japanese armies paraded in front of Western banks and offices, and herded thousands of civilians of all nationalities towards the dock to witness the flag-raising ceremony on the USS *Wake*: the Japanese flag was now fluttering from its mast in the chilly December breeze.

The International Concession was in its death throes. Two years ago, my father had warned Rome about the gradual decline of all privileged positions in China, and now the fall of the Concession, his home for six years, hit him like the loss of another country. He remembered how proud he and other Westerners had been of the Concession where they lived in gilded exile, governed and guarded by their own people. All the foreigners were united by their shared Western homeland and their absence from their own countries. Their ships on the Whangpoo saluted each other at dawn; the different national anthems were sung in brotherly harmony. On special occasions, the San Marco battalions paraded together with the Seaforth Highlanders and the American Leathernecks. As far as they were concerned, the Shanghai Club was the best club in Europe—they talked business over gin and tonics, and met there almost every evening for official dinners. It was difficult to feel hostile to people of other nationalities who were safeguarding the privileges of that small patch of land. Now everything had gone up in smoke with the *Petrel.* It was the end of an era.

The Japanese spread through the International Concessions. Thousands of foreigners were trapped. Only a few lucky individuals managed to board ships with the diplomatic and consular authorities and make their way to Central America, then Europe. The routes to the West were blocked by the lightning Japanese occupation of the English ports of Hong Kong and Singapore. The Japonese requisitioned radios and cars, sacked and occupied abandoned houses. They were everywhere, shouting incomprehensible orders and threatening passers-by with rifles equipped with bayonets.

With the exception of their Italian and German allies, the foreigners trapped in and around Shanghai had been given 24 hours to pack their clothes and personal items, with enough food and water for the transfer to Longhua on the outskirts of Shanghai—the site of a concentration camp, called a "Confinement Centre" by the authorities. They had to assemble at dawn on the following day in the small square facing the Anglican Church and were only allowed to bring everyday items: a mug, a bowl, cutlery, articles for personal hygiene and provisions for three days. When World War One had started, the German citizens living in Shanghai had been repatriated by the British authorities, who made them march along Nanking Road—the long thoroughfare that crossed the city centre and ended near the embarkation point. The current German Consul took his revenge by convincing their Japanese allies to do the same with foreigners from the Allied Powers. The prisoners were ordered to advance and, carrying their hurriedly packed, heavy bags, they began marching, four by four, escorted by the Japanese soldiers: weighed down by their baggage, they were paraded along Nanking Road, which was lined by a mocking crowd. The English tried to sing *It's a long way to Tipperary,* but were immediately stopped by the furious reaction of the escort. The prisoners marched slowly in groups of different nationalities: English, American, French, Belgian, Dutch, Russian, Hungarian, and unarmed Foreign Legion. They walked past Bubbling Well Road and from his house where he now sheltered, my father glimpsed Olga and Igor in the middle of the long line. Two suitcases were strapped to their shoulders and they had a pair of shoes tied with laces and a pair of Wellington boots, hanging from their necks. Igor had two blankets over his shoulders and, like Olga, was wearing several layers of clothes. Olga also carried a sturdy bag which probably contained her husband's precious metals and gems.

Not all contact between the Italians in Shanghai and their friends imprisoned at Longhua was severed: the prisoners received encouraging notes pushed through the mesh fence surrounding the camp, brought by beggars who carried these messages across the soya bean and millet fields, and who then were used by the prisoners to send replies back to Shanghai.

However, it was not long before the Italians in Shanghai also began to feel they were no longer safe. Relations between the Germans and Italians became strained. The Germans talked resentfully about various unsuccessful Italian exploits in Greece and Africa

So Italian hearts were gladdened by the Germans' unexpected humiliation when Richard Sorge's arrest confirmed rumours that had persisted about the presence of a spy inside the German Embassy. In Italian diplomatic circles, criticism had been levelled at Ambassador Ott for obvious leaks from his chancellery. Richard Sorge, German on his father's side and Russian on his mother's, was regarded by the Germans as an unrivalled expert on problems in the Far East and the entire Pacific area. With the advent of Hitler and Nazism, he immediately became a card-holder of the National Socialist Party, getting himself sent first to Japan as a correspondent of the *Frankfurter Zeitung*, then to China. He began living in Shanghai, where he kept the Russians informed about the decisions and movements of the Germans and their allies, the Japanese. Meissinger placed a great deal of trust in him and showed him reports and inter-ministerial telegrams whose contents, soon after, winged their way to Moscow. Sorge met his collaborators—taken from the rank and file of Chinese Communists— in Shanghai's dancehalls. He used the Russian hostesses as unwitting allies by ordering them to distract the

133

Japanese so that he could meet his men in greater safety. He was also a skilled radio engineer. Each of his broadcasts always came from a different place, even from his office in the Embassy. He made the radio transmitters himself and some were so small that, when dismantled, they fitted easily into a briefcase. In May 1941, he wired Moscow with news of Hitler's decision to mass 180 divisions along the Russian frontier and launch an attack on 20th June. He also informed the Russians that the Japanese had chosen the route through Southern China to attack Hong Kong and Singapore. This information enabled the Russians to transfer all their divisions from the Chinese frontier further West and face the German threat. Sorge was so careful in running his operations that he was regarded as above suspicion. He managed to compare and supplement his information with data from the Italian and Japanese allies received by his Embassy. In the end, rivalry between two of his agents alerted Japanese counterespionage. Sorge was arrested and sentenced to death. Meissinger, head of the Gestapo in China and a colleague and friend of the spy, was dismissed, and Ambassador Ott was transferred to Tianjin.

Although the war had now been raging for years and the country had once again been hit by a serious famine, my mother's family, although forced to give up its prestigious position, was still living in tranquillity. My grandfather, Radiant Wisdom, and his family, no longer saw themselves as followers of Chiang Kai-shek. The portrait of him gazing into the distance, his gloved hand on the hilt of a sabre, no longer hung on the wall behind my grandfather's writing desk. These views were now shared by an entire class of Chinese citizens. However, the Western press continued to speak of Chiang Kai-shek in overblown terms, repeatedly stating that he held the future of China "in his white-gloved hands."

Shanghai also continued to be abandoned by Italians fleeing to safety. Although I was kept safe in the care of the French mission in Ningbo, my mother left me at my grandparents' house on the Hill of Distant Fragrance, in the heat of summer.

There, with my Chinese relatives, my unusual wavy hair was a talking point. Watching me grow up, my grandfather, Radiant Wisdom, raised his eyebrows and said: 'We certainly won't have any difficulty marrying her off.' As far as he was concerned, the only future for me was marriage.

I had to learn to adapt to the two different cultures represented by the mission and my Chinese grandparents' house, continually shuttling back and forth between the Chinese and the European worlds, between the Catholic and the Buddhist religions.

My Chinese family had to sell precious vases because the house needed repainting, the furniture in the rooms had to be repaired and, in some cases, the worn, faded silk upholstery had to be replaced.

In the gardens, cabbages, pumpkins, and string beans were grown in the place of peonies, orchids and chrysanthemums. The absence of caretakers meant there were no more goldfish with bulging eyes in the ponds. Wooden pens with hens and cages of rabbits stood in the shady areas of the courtyards. As if to justify himself, my grandfather, Radiant Wisdom, consoled himself by repeating: 'We have enough to eat,' or, 'These are only temporary hardships.'

Naturally, everyone living under his roof pretended not to be aware of the situation. He often thought about his daughter, Green Bay, in Shanghai; a strange pride prevented him from telling her the truth about their "temporary" financial difficulties and, in fact, he took pains to send her a little something every now and then to help her overcome the difficulties created by the occupation.

Although the mulberry trees had been decimated by the bombing, the family watched the customary incense-offering ceremony held every spring in honour of the God of Mulberry trees and the Goddess of Silkworms.

In a private temple, my grandmother, Splendid Gem, worshipped Buddha. She was often there, head bowed, telling the sandalwood rosary, murmuring *'oh mi to fa,'* until all 108 sacred beads had been recited. Often, in the middle of the night, she would also murmur long litanies behind her bed drapes, for her "revolutionary" son.

Many students, intellectuals and professionals had left the big city to take part in the resistance movement against Japan and had entered secret Communist organisations. Every well-off family had at least one member who had become a militant Communist out of patriotism. My uncle had left university and enlisted. He was only 20 when he entered the party and he never talked to the family about his new allegiances, inventing various excuses to explain his frequent absences. Initially his group carried out support missions, which included carrying messages, transporting supplies, collecting provisions and clothing for the resistance, or keeping close watch on the movements of the Japanese troops and passing the information on to the headquarters. But the hostile Japanese forces did not remain inactive and stepped up their drive to destroy all secret resistance organisations. Many young people were rounded up, tortured, and often murdered. This would have been my uncle's fate if quite a few people had not given evidence in his favour, stating that he was a local farmer whose only concern was his work. They signed their statements by placing a red thumb print at the foot of a document. Although they were running a grave risk because the Japanese would shoot anyone who gave false statements under oath, these statements were believed. My uncle was freed and took refuge with relatives who lived in another district.

As Mao Zedong's sphere of influence increased along with the area occupied by his troops, Chiang Kai-shek treacherously attacked his allies and massacred all those he managed to capture. Even his powerful Western allies were shocked and angry at his brutality. To escape the massacre, my uncle fled with other fugitives along the "stone path" in a lorry, an old banger that needed frequent stops to avoid overheating the engine. During the journey, the lorry ran into road blocks set up by Chiang Kai-shek's soldiers, and was thoroughly checked. The fugitives managed to avoid arousing the commanding officer's suspicions and continued their journey in stages. After a week, they stopped in a village where a woman in military uniform was waiting for them: 'You can get out, this is a liberated village,' she assured them, escorting them to a house on a deserted street, where they were given a hot meal. Suddenly, they heard the sound of firecrackers popping. The woman in uniform jumped to her feet, screaming: 'Machine-guns! We're under attack!' They could hear firing and bewildered shouting as everyone rushed out of the house and came face to face with machine guns held by Chiang Kai-shek's soldiers. My uncle escaped the massacre, but was captured with a few other survivors. They were all imprisoned in an abandoned air-raid shelter that also held other prisoners, including many high-ranking resistance fighters. A man who survived those days told our family that he had been under arrest for four weeks before he was interrogated. The prison was damp and my uncle soon fell seriously ill. A doctor was requested, but no one came. His condition became so bad that his companions had to take turns spoon-feeding him with the little food they had. He suffocated to death during a terrible coughing fit. My family only found out about his death when his former companions managed to deliver the urn holding his ashes. My grandfather, Radiant Wisdom, merely said: 'We must do our best to resign ourselves to life, in times of sadness or joy, because every experience forms part of the rich tapestry of life allotted to us by fate.'

17

The confusion caused by the fall of Fascism on 8th September 1943 had immediate repercussions in China. The treaty of alliance between Italy and Japan had already become strained by late July, when adverse military events had undermined Mussolini's position, but on that fateful day in September, when Italy withdrew from hostilities against the Allies, the country was immediately considered hostile by Japan. Only Mussolini's subsequent liberation by the Germans and the constitution of the Salò Republic on 23rd September 1943, lessened the severity with which the Rising Sun repeatedly attacked Italian interests in China. Italians could only avoid reprisals by declaring they were still Fascist and signing a document of collaboration, although nothing prevented the Japanese confiscation of the Legation, ships, arms and munitions.

Italian diplomats were allowed to leave in line with international conventions: they boarded the *Teiko Maru*, a Japanese troop transport ship, and were taken to Japan. It was strange for many of them to be back on a ship which had already taken them from Europe to Shanghai. The ship, which had flown a French flag then, had been called the *D'Artagnan* and had been the pride and joy of the Compagnie Messageries Maritimes on the Far East route. In 1942, it had sunk in the Whangpoo river following a fire and had then been salvaged and restored to service by the Japanese, who changed its name. But its fate was sealed: in 1944, it ended up at the bottom of the Pacific, torpedoed by an American submarine.

On this grey November morning, my father watched from the Bund as the *Teiko Maru* cast off its moorings, and was pushed out by the tugs, then veered round, pointing its prow towards the river mouth. He made his way towards Honan Road and from there to Bubbling Well Road to see my mother. He had a gloomy feeling that this might be their last meeting. The Japanese were scouring the city using lists supplied by informers whose safety had been guaranteed in return. The wanted men and women were to be sent to one of the internment camps that had sprung up in those parts of China controlled by the Japanese. To avoid this my father merely had to sign the document of collaboration. He had thought long and hard about this and was prepared to do so. It would not surprise the Japanese, because he was known to them as a loyal Fascist.

However, not far from my mother's house, he heard Confucius calling him. He turned round in surprise and was guided by the Chinese man into the entrance of a building. 'Someone,' whispered Confucius, 'has told the Japanese that you're very close to Minister Ciano, or that you were his special observer in China. Now they know he has been arrested by Il Duce, I'd advise you not to sign the document of collaboration. As far as they're concerned, you are now an enemy of the man who treacherously arrested his own son-in-law. If you sign, you'll also be suspected of disloyalty and cowardice towards someone you've served personally, and the Japanese regard nothing more ignoble than disloyalty.'

Bewildered, my father thanked him and headed home. As soon as he came through the door, my mother immediately said tearfully: 'The Japanese came looking for you. They've been given your name. They know you didn't leave on that ship today.' A few minutes later, they opened the door to two Japanese officers and a Chinese man in civilian clothes. After checking his papers, they ordered him, under penalty of being arrested and shot, to come alone to the Gongping Road Wharf the next morning, with one suitcase and enough food for 48 hours. My father realised that Confucius had been wise: the document of collaboration would not have given him the slightest guarantee of protection and might have been used against him. The Japanese soldiers were known for their spite and cunning and could attack at the most unexpected times.

The next day, a resigned Green Bay accompanied her husband in the pouring rain, past Suzhou Creek. They were separated near Gongping Road Wharf by a cordon of soldiers who were not allowing anyone through if they were not on their long list of names. While the Venetian was waiting his turn to board one of the lighters moored there, he heard a voice calling him: 'Here, Master Italy, take this! It might come in useful.' Before he had even recognised Zhang's voice, he found an envelope containing a folded ten-dollar note in his overcoat pocket and a water bottle that later proved invaluable, in his hand. In a flash Zhang had disappeared among the submissive line of prisoners, prodded and guided on his way by bayonets.

For a long time my mother stood there, sheltering under the cornice of a shop, with many other silent, weeping women. The Japanese soldiers, after addressing a few incomprehensible sentences to the small, drenched group of women gathered there, took up their positions on various lorries and disappeared into the light mist shrouding the port. The owner of a launch returning to his mooring from the direction taken by the lighter carrying the prisoners, informed my mother that the boat was being towed to Woosung, at the mouth of the Whangpoo, where the river boat *Victoria* was waiting. The boat had already taken some other prisoners on board the day before and was now ready to sail back upriver. A stop in Chinkiang was scheduled, then it would sail for Yangchow, on the Grand Canal. My mther treasured this news. At least she knew where her husband was being taken. If she went to Suzhou, where she could count on Ludmila's hospitality, she would be nearer Yangchow.

After a journey of almost six hours, my father saw through one of the ship's portholes that they were near Yangchow, which was where the prisoners disembarked. When they arrived at the internment camp, they were enthusiastically welcomed by about 200 internees. The guards took all their money and valuables. The camp was the hospital of the Baptist mission which was still under construction and all the

140

prisoners were put into small rooms—men, women and children together.

The internment camp was within an extensive agricultural zone and the Japanese had no reason to deprive the prisoners of food. Rice, vegetables, sweet potatoes and cereals were grown in the fertile countryside around Yangchow, and the camp canteen not only served pork, but also donkey and buffalo. Water, on the contrary, was scarce. It was drawn from the Grand Canal, then transported on carts in vats. As a result, it was strictly rationed and this shortage hit internees very hard during the summer. There was also no coal, so the prisoners themselves had to gather sticks and dried rushes for cooking on the stoves they had built. They were allowed to write one letter a week, but none of the Venetian's letters ever reached Green Bay. No newspapers found their way into the camp, so the prisoners were completely cut off from the rest of the world.

Worried by the lack of news, Green Bay decided to go and look for her husband. She threw some clothes into a travel bag and telephoned Confucius, asking him to inform her family in Hangzhou of her absence. She ran to the station and arrived in Suzhou that afternoon, after a journey interrupted by repeated checks by Japanese soldiers.

Ludmila was happy to see her young friend again and optimistic about the possibility of getting close to Yangchow; Suzhou had remained a relatively peaceful city and was not considered a danger by Japanese commanders, so the garrison was small and patrols few and far between. Nonetheless, Ludmila acted as if she were in a state of siege, afraid that, as a Russian refugee, she would share Olga and Igor's fate. The hardships of her past had left a legacy of fear. As always, she spent her days in the voluminous rattan armchair on the veranda, which stood on piles driven into the bottom of the canal. From there she watched the boats busily plying back and forth on the water, but kept out of sight of passers-by because she no longer trusted anyone. 'You could be betrayed for a small barrel of rice by someone who has bowed to you in greeting,' she often said.

Early in the morning, my mother, disguising herself in the blue cloth dress of a peasant woman, mingled with the peasants. They showed her the quickest way to Yangchow: she had to reach the Yangtze, in the north, find the embarkation point for crossing the wide river, then cut inland, bringing her to the northern stretch of the Grand Canal where Yangchow was situated. It was a journey of about 60 miles, but she did not lose heart, despite the lack of regular transport.

After various stops with peasant families, she arrived in Yangchow on the afternoon of the next day, and immediately set about trying to find the internment camp. Once again she relied on information from the peasants, discovering that there was a flourishing trade between the local population, the Japanese soldiers guarding the camp, and the prisoners. During the day, the peasants were allowed to bring their wares to the camp fences, where goods were openly traded. Security measures were rudimentary because a Westerner imprisoned in China could never hope to escape unrecognised. The peasants had not only told her where the camp was, but had also suggested the best way to get close to it. But she was anxious that she would not find her husband, and if she did, she doubted that she could talk to him without arousing suspicion.

Drawing closer to the side of the enclosure indicated by a peasant, Green Bay hesitantly approached the barbed wire with a cluster of people. Her heart ached as she examined the prisoners crowding up against the other side of the fence. Suddenly she thought she glimpsed her husband and as he turned, she recognised him immediately. It was an incredible stroke of luck. She trembled, unable to believe her eyes. She was so taken aback at seeing him there in front of her that she was speechless for a few seconds. They stood there looking at each other in disbelief, riveted by the joy of seeing each other, and the agony of not being able to touch one another. She stared, unable to breathe for her tears. She dropped her basket, and the potatoes rolled into no-man's-land between the two barbed-wire fences. She took a step forward and heard the voice she loved say, without betraying the slightest emotion, a few short sentences: 'I'm dreaming, I can't believe my eyes. You're a very brave woman. No one else would have done what you've done.'

At that moment, a sentinel walked over to the barbed wire. The same impassive voice whispered to her to pretend she was crying because the potatoes had fallen onto the ground and she was unable to reach the ones that had rolled between the two fences. The soldier came over and, without looking her in the face, kicked the potatoes over to her and continued his slow patrol. My father drew closer again: 'How's our daughter?' he whispered.

'She's fine. She's cutting more teeth. I went to see her three weeks ago. The Japanese searched the mission but the priests hid her in time. With that wavy hair and her straight little nose, she stands out from the other girls,' Green Bay continued hurriedly. The sentinel was coming over again.

For the next few days, my mother turned up punctually at the camp and always found my father waiting for her, walking up and down with feigned indifference. He was becoming more and more worried about her: if the guards stopped her and discovered her identity, she was in danger of being shot. At their last meeting, he said: 'Listen to me, my darling. It's too dangerous to go on meeting where the other prisoners can see us. You have no idea how many of the prisoners here are prepared to betray someone in order to obtain favours from the guards.'

'I understand. I'll go back to Shanghai and think of something else. I'll come back again to find out how you are.'

He looked at her with profound tenderness, but he hid his feelings so as not to upset her further.

'Goodbye, dearest one. Don't worry about me. Remember, you're always with me in my thoughts.'

He watched her walking away. In her baggy peasant dress she looked even more delicate. His eyes followed her until he could not tell her apart from the peasants making their way back to the village. There were tears in his eyes. My father stood there, staring vacantly into the distance. He turned back to his prison, now a familiar landscape that he was almost afraid to leave.

18

The Chinese guerrillas laid traps behind the lines, cut off Japanese supplies, interrupted communications between Beijing and Tianjin, and blew up the road blocks. They had also stepped up their offensive in the provinces of Anhwei and Kiangsu and were now trying to push coastward, from Chinkiang and Yangchow, north of the Yangtze delta, to edge closer to Shanghai, where the Japanese, embroiled in their war against the Americans in the Pacific and the English in Burma, did not have enough reserves to neutralise guerrilla activities. This meant they were forced to scale down the number of guards in the internment camps in order to deploy them against the guerrillas. Many camps were combined in places that could easily be watched by fewer guards.

In what proved to be her last journey to the internment camp in Yangchow, my mother learned that most of the prisoners, particularly the youngest ones, had unexpectedly been transferred to the camp at Pudong, on the outskirts of Shanghai. In the smutty, clattering train that slowly took her back to Shanghai via Suzhou, she could not stop thinking about Ludmila, prematurely aged by her memories of hardship and the fresh fears fostered by her past.

As soon as she returned to Shanghai, she contacted Confucius, who knew about the camp in Pudong, housed in a group of buildings lining the northern stretch of the Whangpoo. He found her lodgings in the Chinese quarter of Chapei—her house on Bubbling Well Road had become too expensive and she had been forced to leave. Her family's situation in Hangzhou was not ideal and she certainly could no longer count on her husband's help, so it seemed that in future, she was going to be living in Shanghai.

At first my father was pleased to learn of the transfer to Pudong because of its proximity to Shanghai, but he soon realised that conditions were much worse there than at Yangchow. The camp stood in a desolate landscape dotted with sparse trees and shrubs shrouded in a thick blanket of soot. A lake of liquid sewage extended in every direction, stretching as far as the canteen building. The tall four-storey brick building where he was billeted had been declared unfit for use by the English twenty years ago, when it had been used as a depot by the British American Tobacco Company, and nothing had changed since. The camp needed to be completely refitted to make it habitable, so the prisoners did their best to rebuild the lavatories, showers, kitchens and canteens.

When the new inmates arrived at the camp, there was already a motley crew of prisoners from every walk of life. Many of them had friends outside the camp and were allowed to receive small gift parcels that often kept them from hunger and disease. As a result, there was a flourishing black market. The only view of part of Shanghai's port was from a window in room 13, on the top floor. In the two years my father spent imprisoned in Pudong, he often went up there to watch the junks loaded with cotton sailing across the port. From the same vantage point, he was also distressed to see the overturned bulk of the *Conte Verde*, lying on its side beside its mooring buoy. It had been immobilised at the outbreak of the war. After 8th September, the captain, learning that his ship was about to be seized by the Japanese and would share the same fate as the *D'Artagnan*, had ordered his crew to open the sea inlet valves along one side of the hull to sink it. The dismayed Japanese had found it lying, one night, on the muddy bottom of the Whangpoo, like a huge island partly blocking Shanghai's port activities. The captain and his crew were arrested and taken to the internment camp on Rubicond Road in the Japanese district of Hongkew, where the former ambassador of Italy, Marquis Talliani, was already imprisoned.

In the spring of 1945, there was a clear sense that the military situation had turned. There were rumours of heavy Japanese defeats in the Pacific, while the war was drawing to a close in Europe with the defeat of the Germans. Things had certainly become very difficult for the Japanese, now that the Allies could unleash all their military might on them. The Americans were drawing closer, conquering the islands that were only a few hours' flight from Japan and the Chinese coast.

Allied aircraft often managed to bomb the Japanese fleet blocking Shanghai's port activities. They also pushed further inland, where cities like Hangzhou and Suzhou were not spared. From the window of room 13, my father managed to watch the *Conte Verde* being salvaged. The Japanese engineers had attached long steel cables to the hull and after several months, had managed to right it. During the final stages of the rescue, an American Mitchell bomber flew over the zone observing the rescue effort without attempting to hold up the work of the salvage crews. My father wondered why the Americans did not bomb the ship: it would have been easy to hit an unmoving, defenceless target. Once righted, the hull was surrounded with large tanks that were sunk and attached to the sides. All the exits were sealed and then compressed air was pumped into the tanks which slowly began to float, lifting the massive bulk of the ship like huge lifebuoys. Then the water-scooping pumps set to work draining the hull of water. In the late spring of 1945 a fleet of tugs surrounded the ship and the flag of the Rising Sun fluttered from the mast above the Italian tricolour. My father couldn't understand why there was no sign of the solitary American plane, but he was not disappointed for long. It appeared in the sky when the ship had already been towed along the Whangpoo, and merely observed activities for a long time. When the *Conte Verde* reached Woosung, at the mouth of the river, more American planes suddenly appeared out of nowhere and, releasing four bombs, sank the ship right there, blocking the entire Whangpoo River, and access to Shanghai. The indomitable Japanese simply began salvaging the ship all over again and, ironically, finished the task just in time to allow the Allied warships access on the day the hostilities ceased. With a secretly assembled radio, my father also managed to keep track of the conclusive phases of the war. Apart from smuggling food parcels to my father, Confucius had supplied him with parts for his radio receiver using a system of loaves: a baker outside the camp baked round loaves and Confucius trained one of the *coolies* who loaded them onto the delivery truck for the camp, to give his loaf to my father, who always found something useful in it.

It was by listening to his radio that he heard about the atomic bombs dropped on Hiroshima and Nagasaki. That very day, after the second bombing, a plane flew low over Pudong dropping leaflets that confirmed the news and announced: 'Stay calm, don't leave the camp, we're coming to your aid.'

When Japan signed the unconditional surrender, the gates of the prison at Pudong were thrown open. Escorted by patrols of English and American marines, the civil police rounded up the Japanese garrison and imprisoned them in the same barracks that had housed the Western inmates on the first night. The Japanese were quite happy to be in custody, safe from reprisals by the Chinese nationalist troops who had now come out into the open. My father did not wait around to watch this reversal of fortunes; he made his way with a small group of former prisoners to the bank of the Whangpoo where they managed to persuade a boatman to take them to a quay near the mouth of Suzhou Creek.

The camp at Longhua had been liberated even earlier than the one at Pudong. As soon as she heard the news, my mother thought of Olga and Igor, who had been imprisoned there, and immediately called a rickshaw and sped along Avenue Joffre to 256 Kiangze Street. Racing up the stairs, she found the door ajar. Igor was alone, sitting on the worn armchair near the bed, wearing a filthy overcoat, despite the heat. His lips were pressed tightly shut, as if he had a secret. There was a deep furrow between his thick eyebrows, which looked even blacker in contrast to his shock of snow-white hair. Noticing the young Chinese woman, Igor looked up with a cheerless smile. There was no sign of Olga. Suddenly, Igor began crying uncontrollably, shaking with the effort of trying to suppress his sobs. He managed to look up again and, gazing intently at her, he said without preamble: 'That day, 18 of us died— Olga too. Killed... a crate of food, cigarettes... Crashed through the roof. Parachutes didn't open in time. The first time, the American planes were higher... No danger... but we were scared it might happen.'

Green Bay was no longer listening to Igor. The news stunned her and she merely looked at him, unable to stop the flow of his disjointed words.

'Several days... before our liberation, it started. Three American planes flew low over the camp. They veered round and came back almost immediately. What to do?—Throw ourselves onto the ground... Wave bright clothes at them? Suddenly, the planes dropped pallets—wooden, a parachute at each corner... Metal containers on these bases, packed with things—food, cigarettes, clothes, boots, soap, medicines. The first time, one of the parachutes didn't open... The pallet smashed to the ground, burst open. It fell on top of a group of men from B block, killing ten—a box of tinned meat killed Piet, the Dutchman near me—we were less than 100 yards away! These pallets, so many ended up outside the camp fence. Looted by the Chinese... They were starving. Broke down part of the enclosure fence. Got inside the camp. The Japanese guards panicked, took refuge with us, begged us for protection! So that day, when the planes arrived, we decided to stay inside! Olga was in the toilet, while I was at the window in the corridor. Everyone was looking up at the sky. Only two of the parachutes on the pallet from the last plane opened. The wooden base tipped over, the containers tore loose from the ropes... plummeted to earth like bombs. One... it fell right on top of the toilet. Olga took the brunt of it. She was killed with her best friend. No one can escape their fate.'

My mother was sobbing. As she comforted Igor, her thoughts turned to her husband. She realised the prisoners at Pudong must have abandoned camp, so she was frightened not to be able to see him there, in front of her. She left Igor's house, hoping that Confucius would know if anything had happened

149

to her husband. She found herself walking to the peaceful Temple of the City Gods, not far from the Yu Garden, to pray that Lucky Omen would come back safely to Shanghai and stay with her forever.

Usually, it seemed as if the temple's customary silence had been imposed on it by some mysterious power, forcing it to meditate on its centuries-old past. That day it echoed with the sound of drumbeats and zithers, and the metal triangles hanging from the entrance roof tinkled when struck by the believers on their way in. The temple was at its most atmospheric at times like this, when the congregation filed in behind the monks in their bright cassocks to the sound of ancient sutras intoned by the choir. For Green Bay, the temple would be at its most eloquent when the silence fell again. As she drew closer to the temple, the tinkling of the triangles became louder, the beating of the drums became faster and her weary steps were greeted by the deep, melancholy notes of the bronze bells. Kneeling on the large cushion in front of the altar, she paid homage to the Goddess with a deep *kow-tow*. Then she lit some sticks of incense and placed them among the lit candles in front of the Goddess of Mercy. After one last prayer, she walked out into the adjacent courtyard, and over to the monk squatting under a sloping roof hung with countless birdcages. My mother handed him a coin and he unhooked a cage containing a goldfinch. She walked to the centre of the courtyard and, as was customary, opened the little cage, releasing the bird from its captivity. In this way, she was respecting the ancient Buddhist tradition which accorded every creature the divine right of freedom.

19

Having left the camp at Pudong that morning, my father and his companions would have been almost indistinguishable from the crowds of the poor jostling along the city streets. They ran across the quay and the embankment beside the railway track. My father hurried off along the railway line towards the station, a jute bag with a few personal effects over his shoulder.

As he drew nearer, he realised he was in the vicinity of the Heron Fountain and he thought of Zhang. Luck was on his side. He found the inn open and his old associate busy inside. This was the first familiar face he had seen since he had gazed at Green Bay through the barbed wire at Yangchow.

Zhang gave him a warm welcome, then told him he was now the manager. The old proprietor had given him the job when he retired and he had turned the inn into a haunt for Japanese petty officers in search of company.

'Until a few days ago,' he said, 'business was booming, but things don't look so good now.'

'Don't worry, Zhang. There'll soon be so many Americans here that you won't know what to do with them. And they've certainly got cash!'

'I hope so. But you've only just got out of the camp. I'll call you a rickshaw immediately and, in the meantime, here's some money. You'll be wanting to see your loved ones now. But come back one day, Master Italy!'

When he arrived at Confucius' house, my father found only the Chinese man's wife and three inquisitive children. The woman remembered the Italian and told him in rudimentary pidgin English that her husband was out and that Green Bay now lived in a little apartment not far from their house. She told her oldest son to take him there, while the youngest, even before his mother had finished speaking, had slipped out and disappeared down the stairs to lead the way.

Five minutes later, my father found himself standing in front of a block of flats and saw the young boy had got there before him, so Green Bay knew he was coming. She ran downstairs trying to stay calm, her heart racing. Not wishing to lose control of her emotions and not wanting to be seen in the street, she stood waiting in the shady courtyard, barely daring to breathe. She did not hear his footsteps, but she saw his shadow coming closer and closer, until she made out his face in the light filtering through the open door. She still did not move, and it was only when his figure was sharply outlined against the light that she attempted to go and meet him, but her legs folded beneath her and she almost fell. Locked in each others arms,trembling,they gazed at each other incredulously. Time seemed to stand still.

'Lucky Omen, Lucky Omen,' she murmured, drawing back a little to examine his gaunt, weary features. 'You look exhausted,' she said. 'Come in straight away.'

Inside at last, Lucky Omen drew her close and they held one another for a long time, as if they could not bear to be separated. Green Bay's delicate fingers caressed him softly, fluttering like butterflies against his face and hands. They kissed, their hands impatiently exploring their bodies. Like sleepwalkers, they surrendered to the passion that had so long been denied them.

My father's happiness at his return was soon tinged with sadness when he learned of Olga's fate and Igor's grief. My mother told him Ludmila had also died.

'How did it happen?'

'Not long ago,' Green Bay told him 'in one of the air raids against the Japanese on the Yangtze. A plane hit a motorboat towing heavy lighters full of sand along the canal behind her house. The towing cable broke and one of the lighters continued its unstoppable course along the canal. It collided violently with the piles holding up the veranda, shattering them. The veranda collapsed and Ludmila, who was still sitting in her rattan armchair, was dragged into the canal, where she drowned, trapped under water by the rubble.'

'And I was imagining there was no more peaceful a place than Suzhou! After all she had suffered, the poor woman. She had already faced death so many times before finding a little peace and quiet in Suzhou. What has become of the house?'

'From the front, it looks as though someone is living there, but from behind, anyone sailing along the canal can see that it's been gutted. It's bound to end up in the hands of the authorities.'

Saddened, my father thought about how much the war had changed things and how much people had suffered. He realised this was a new era, but found he it hard to adjust to the new status quo, which had been forged on the anvil of war during his absence. He felt as though time had stood still while he was in prison. When he had been liberated, he had thought he would find people, customs and places unchanged. Instead, it was a different world, and he felt uncomfortable in it— apprehensive and worried, though he did not know why. He tried to banish these feelings, but it was impossible. Things had changed too much. He felt drained and tired.

Green Bay also seemed changed. She had been just as happy as he was at their reunion—their long separation had shown them how important they were to each other—but they had also become used to doing without the other.

He feared the fast-approaching time when he would have to choose between her and Italy. If he chose to stay, it would be a betrayal of his youthful ideals and lasting ambitions. The thought of never seeing her again, however, was unbearable. He began to think of a plan to smuggle her out with him, but soon realised it was not feasible—having her with him would cause all manner of problems for him. He had to resign himself to abandoning her, but as the time for giving her up grew nearer, he became increasingly worried about the impact this would have on both their lives. He would not have wanted to choose between her and his work, but he realised that his only course of action for the time being was to leave China.

Before he made any decisions, he asked to see his daughter.

'Has she grown so much? It'll be very strange for me to speak English to my wife, and French to my daughter. What a shame none of the French missionaries taught her Italian— or at least English!'

'If it makes you feel any better, I can assure you that her Chinese is perfect, even though she speaks with a strange Ningbo accent!' replied Green Bay. 'I also can't wait to see her.'

'We'll go straight after my visit to Father Gherzi. I won't rest until those documents and the copies of the reports I sent to Ciano have been destroyed. I wouldn't want them to tarnish his reputation. I must find a car to drive me to Zikawei. Maybe Confucius will be able to help us. What would I have done without that man? The bonds of friendship seem stronger in China than anywhere else. How does he manage now that our Consulate is closed?'

'He has a finger in many pies. He works with his cousin, a party big shot. He leads a modest life, but I know he never lacked for anything, even when things were at their worst.'

'He's probably a Communist sympathiser now. The party's policy is to make friends with everyone,' remarked the Venetian without much conviction.

Nothing surprised him about China anymore. Everyone seemed to lead multiple lives, changing their personality to suit the different roles they had to play. Like the spirits of legend, no one was who they really seemed. He felt that he, too, had undergone a metamorphosis. It was as if his face had been replaced by someone else's. He had arrived in China nine years ago, full of idealistic convictions, but he was no longer the same man, no longer master of his destiny. He nodded sadly when my mother said, 'You seem so disillusioned, Lucky Omen.'

154

20

In Zickawei, my father had the good fortune to find Father Gherzi immediately, but he paled when the Jesuit told him that he had no memory of any box of documents being entrusted to his care a few years before.

'Yes, I recognise you,' he said 'we've met before. You're from the Consulate, aren't you? Have the Fascist staff been re-elected again, despite the fall of Fascism in Italy? Who can make head or tale of any of this?'

The Venetian realised he owed Father Gherzi an explanation if he wanted the return of his documents.

'I understand your confusion, Father,' he replied. 'Our Consulate is currently closed and I don't know when Rome will be able to send new officials to reopen it. You must be wondering what I'm doing here.'

'Exactly. After 1943, the few people still at the Consulate were loyal members of the Fascist party and enjoyed the protection of the Japanese. When I needed to go to the Consulate during those two black years, I never saw you there. Now your visit has taken me by surprise. I might even have reason to doubt that you're Italian or that you really belong to the diplomatic service, as you had me believe on other occasions.'

After briefly explaining his situation, my father concluded: 'Now I must go back to Rome and clarify my position. But before I leave, I'd like those documents back so that I can destroy them. They're of no use to anyone now and can only cause harm. Believe me, they'll be immediately destroyed. Hiding them here probably saved my life, as well as protecting someone else's reputation. Your work is over, so I beg you, let me destroy them.'

Father Gherzi did not appear to be completely convinced, but he allowed himself to be swayed. Leaving the muggy August heat, he entered the monastic chill of the observatory and headed straight for the cupboard in the map room. The Venetian followed him with his heart in his mouth: if those documents had been discovered, revealing that he was an agent under the direct orders of a Fascist Minister, they could have made his position a hundred times worse.

Father Gherzi opened a door and motioned to his visitor to reclaim the box. The latter, blowing strongly to remove the dust, felt a chill when he saw a large hole in a corner of the box, but he was probably no more scared than the family of mice nesting inside.

'My dear Father,' he concluded 'I should have left the documents here a little longer. Perhaps the mice would have eaten them!'

He returned to Shanghai and settled for a time into the strange post-war atmosphere.

In the city centre, loudspeakers kept repeating "Freedom, Victory", although the masses did not understand. Tall, fair-haired American soldiers strolled among the crowds escorting a new generation of Shanghai girls chewing gum and made up like Hollywood actresses. The city was seething with activity. Almost everyone was dreaming up get-rich-quick plans, while the more modest merely hoped for an end to hunger and the chance to spend the winter in comfort. Forgers and smugglers emerged openly as spies and advisers working for the Intelligence Service or the American O.S.S., raking up everyone's past and making lists of the names of anyone who had been in contact with Wang Chin Wei's puppet rule in Nanking—the government created by the Japanese to oppose Chiang Kai-shek. Life was particularly difficult for the Italians in Shanghai, beset by accusations and suspicions about the relationship between the Fascist Government and Wang Chin Wei's short-lived government. It was hard to know how to adapt to the new situation. Chiang Kai-shek's men, who had recently arrived from Chongqing, exacted cruel revenge, and blackmailed whoever they could. The Anglo-Americans declared they could not interfere in any activities carried out by the Generalissimo, who was their long-standing ally. For some months, it had been impossible to find their former German Allies in Shanghai and the Italians felt increasingly isolated. Like the Japanese, they suffered under the burden of defeat and the mistakes made by their government.

Veterans of many victory parades, the Japanese troops now stood dejectedly on the wharves, waiting to board ships bound for their homeland. Battered old boats despatched from Japan drew alongside the riverbank and the defeated soldiers embarked, returning home with shame in their eyes, clutching small white wooden urns containing the ashes of fallen compatriots.

Being Italian in China at that time also meant feeling alone and abandoned. Nearly all the other foreigners had gone and anyone left was counting the days until they went home.

No one really knew what was happening in Italy that September, and Rome only sent vague replies to the telegrams dispatched by the former Ambassador Talliani. They were addressed to him in person, as there was still no diplomatic representation. The Swedish ambassador, Sven Alland, who had been given the task of protecting Italian interests, was unable to do so, hindered by requests from the Allied Authorities, and the accusations made by Chiang Kai-shek's men.

There was no available accommodation anywhere in Shanghai. The hotels had largely been requisitioned by the American authorities to house their officials and to allow the officers and marines from the American and English fleets to spend a few days ashore. In the first two months after the Japanese surrender, over 20,000 American sailors, marines, pilots and soldiers spent their leave in Shanghai. The effect on the local economy was incredible. Every soldier who came ashore had around 2,000 dollars to spend, contributing some 40 million dollars to the local economy, although it was still not enough to fill the abyss.

The few Italians who were staying in hotel rooms were driven out by the Military Police, in the name of the victors. Some found lodgings, resigning themselves to live with people from all nationalities in the barracks of the Russian refugees, many of whom had died during imprisonment.

Gradually the internment camps emptied and the inmates went their separate ways, some to Shanghai, some to Nanking, and some to Beijing or other big urban centres in China. The veterans from the camp at Longhua recounted how the unexpected disappearance of the Japanese guards had alerted them to the fact that they were about to be liberated. At first, they had not believed they were free. They looked out into the deserted street in front of them and no one knew where to go. They were afraid of the city where they were supposed to start reclaiming the life they had forgotten. They began to look for accommodation; most of their homes had disappeared or were occupied by different families who could not be evicted because they had been placed there by the new Chinese authorities.

As if acting on instinct, the surviving American, English and Australian citizens from the camp at Longhua would meet regularly in the bar and lounge of the Park Hotel. They were reluctant to leave China, despite two years spent in prison. They believed they would not be able to adapt to the restrictions, constraints and customs of their native countries. These were people who had arrived in China years before, and had become wealthy there. They were suffering from the *mal d'Oriente*, which was the reverse of homesickness. They were people who only knew enough Chinese to give orders to servants, who had never wanted anyone Chinese to be allowed entry to the Shanghai or Peking Clubs where they dined in dinner jackets once a week, as if they were at Claridges in London. Some of them kept saying, 'China is the only place we can live now.'

Traces of their presence remained only in the pidgin English spoken by their *boys*, but even this was not for long: the word "master" was soon replaced by the term *tongshi* (companion).

In Shanghai, the masses no longer denounced Japanese

brutality or Western arrogance, but the abuses committed by Chiang Kai-shek's nationalists. The city began to look increasingly desolate and deteriorated rapidly with the onset of winter. Inflation was soaring, which made it impossible for thousands of families to pay their rent. They were left with no other alternative than to live on the streets. The most enterprising, who were not hampered by elderly or ailing family members, attempted to travel to the areas they had left years ago in search of better lives in the big city.

21

Reunited after a two-year separation in difficult post-war conditions, my parents slowly tried unravelling the tangled threads of their feelings. At first, their happiness at being together again had caused them to forget about the war and its consequences, the uncertain future and their almost inevitable imminent separation, which my mother had silently accepted. However, as time passed, the problems worsened and the situation changed.

Their accommodation had discreetly been provided by Confucius and this made the young couple's situation even trickier. To avoid running any risks, my father was forced not to go out after sunset. Confucius had been very explicit about this.

'You must stay indoors,' he said. 'The nationalist patrols don't spare anyone.'

There was already talk about the imminent arrival of a ship sent by Rome to repatriate the remaining few Italian citizens, including the members of diplomatic corps who had either been forced to remain in China throughout the war or, like my father, had chosen to do so.

This situation was upsetting them both and the silences between them had never lasted so long. The days were filled with anxiety, disagreements, fears, and disappointments. They began to lose confidence: they never talked openly about the decision they had to make but, as often happens, events moved faster than anticipated.

One afternoon, they saw Confucius making for their apartment. It was pouring with rain and they were worried as soon as they saw him. Why would he be hurrying to see them in the middle of a downpour?

'I've received confirmation,' he said, as soon as he had come inside, 'that an Italian military ship will be here soon. This is your only chance to escape the nationalists. But it's only for you,' he added, nodding at my father 'not for your family.'

That night, my father woke, shuddering with the realisation that his nightmares were coming true. The time had come for him to leave China and be parted from those he loved. He got up, went over to the window and opened the grey curtains, letting the wan dawn light in, although it barely managed to dispel the shadows.

He sat down on the bed by Green Bay's side and lifted her head, coiling her black hair behind her with a slow movement of his wrist. Then he leaned over and kissed her temples and the corners of her oriental eyes.

'You're so beautiful. You could have a better life if you weren't held back by a man who is struggling to keep his head above water.'

They embraced passionately, but neither love-making nor words were any comfort now. They lay side by side until the noises of the new day brought them back to reality. Green Bay slowly moved away from him and pushing aside the mosquito net, put her feet on the ground and stood up. Looking at him, she said: 'I have a feeling that this is our last day together, so let's try and make it last as long as possible. Talk to me. It's worse if we don't talk.'

'I don't want to upset you.'

After a pause, she said, 'Have you forgotten? We have a daughter.'

This unexpected reference took him by surprise: he was thrown by the realisation that he had not thought about her.

Understanding his dismay, my mother held out her arms to him. 'Hold me,' she said.

He held her lovingly, gently, as if she were a fragile Ming vase. He told her how much he loved her, promising he would return as soon as the dust had settled, or he would do his utmost to have her join him in Italy. He said the separation would definitely last no longer than a year, but in his heart of hearts, he knew it would be impossible for a Chinese woman to leave the country, unless she escaped illegally; and with a little girl in tow it would be even harder.

Green Bay was prepared to tackle all kinds of danger and hardship to follow him, but she sensed his fears and uncertainties. 'Do you really believe that Rome will let us be together one day?' was her final desperate question.

'Let's try and be patient, flexible.'

My mother realised from those words that he no longer had the boldness of spirit that had often led him to throw himself into situations without thinking of the cost; it was as if he had lost the daring that had prompted him to fall in love with her. He had changed—become cautious, sensible. Their love was fading and in danger of flickering out. Green Bay's relationship with the West had proved to be as much trouble for her as it had been for China.

For the last time, the young couple looked out of the window at Shanghai's sea of irregular roofs. Almost all were damaged by bombs and covered with broken tiles and sheets of corrugated iron held in place by precariously balanced heavy objects. It was a depressing sight, almost an omen of an uncertain future built on shaky foundations. He broke the silence.

'It makes me feel very humble and proud knowing you love me so much. I feel unhappy, guilty about it. I never wanted to hurt you by telling you that I have to leave. But you asked me to tell you the truth. The nationalist secret police want to arrest me, although I'm not sure why. I know that our gunboat, the *Eritrea*, is taking the last few Italians to safety. Yesterday our Ambassador secretly boarded the ship and, after it leaves, no Italian will be able to remain here legally. You can see I have no choice. Either I take the only way out open to me, or I force you to flee with me and perhaps meet a tragic end. That mustn't happen—to you or to our Rose Marie.'

'Please don't worry. I don't blame you,' she said resolutely. 'You've never killed anyone Chinese or betrayed my country. You were just a victim of events bigger than you, started on

162

the other side of the world.'

'Not my fault, but I now belong to a country that's done for. Mussolini has been hanged and the king has fled Rome. The Allies are laughing at us. I'm Italian and I'm a wanted man.'

How my mother had grown to hate the world of men with their bayonets, bombardments, barbed wire and bullets, who drag women into their cruel games.

'We've reached the end of the road, then?'

'Don't say that,' he replied. 'I'll come back, I promise. I love you too much. You'll see, fate will bring us together again and these difficult times will be a thing of the past. We've already surmounted so many difficulties and been happy again.'

His voice was flat, passionless. He no longer sounded like that witty, gallant young man whom she had known and loved nine years ago.

'We're not playing that amusing game in front of Olga's house, all those years ago. Bringing fate into this is a way of giving up. Sometimes you remind me of my father, you've obviously absorbed Chinese ways. You've lost part of your identity. And you don't recognise me either. We've swapped some of the traits that made us love each other. You have taught me to fight and now I must fight for all three of us, because I don't want to entrust our lives, our happiness to what you call "fate". You've taught me to take control of my life. You've opened up new horizons to me and I don't intend to give this up.'

This was a voice she had never used before—the voice of a woman in pain and who was prepared to fight. Every word she said made him feel more upset, conscience-stricken. He felt lost, disconnected from the past, from the future, from reality. Restless and disillusioned, she was forced to examine the most important events in her life and ask herself what had been the fruit of circumstance and what had been the result of choice. Struggling against feelings of bitterness, she went downstairs into the back garden, a small oasis between the peeling walls of the surrounding houses. The bushes were covered in flowers. She knelt down and picked some stems to fill the vases with the last of the flowers. Walking slowly back upstairs, she thought how some years of her life had been like bouquets of bright days, others like rooms filled with shadows.

She went back into the house feeling calmer. She prepared the Venetian a cup of Lapsang Soochang. The smoky fragrance of the tea reminded her of the day they had first met, of the time when they were the only people in the world. Now they knew the rest of the world existed. He took the cup in silence. It was his last taste of China, for soon after, they heard someone rapping urgently on the door with their bare knuckles. It was Confucius who had come to warn him to leave immediately. He had a vested interest in the Venetian leaving as soon as possible, as he could be suspected of being too friendly with the foreigner; if the nationalist secret police found out, this would compromise his new activities.

'You're on the list of people under suspicion,' he said. 'In the archives, I found notes and memos that mention your name. The Americans have completed the picture with their reports. They place particular emphasis on the statement issued to the press in 1941, announcing that Galeazzo Ciano was the first to recognise the authority of Wang Chin Wei.'

My father listened in disbelief. He had never had any direct contact with Wang Chin Wei's puppet government in Nanking. He had met the man once, when Wang Chin Wei had asked to stay in the Italian Concession in Tianjin, in search of a brief respite from Japanese pressure on him to succeed. My father had been instructed to accede to his request and welcome him in the name of the Italian Government. Confucius finished by telling him that the new Consul Farace wanted him to embark immediately. He had to avoid arrest and the ensuing publicity at all costs. Confucius would not be swayed, repeating that he had only a few hours left to leave China. The Venetian was tortured by the fact that there was only one charge against him, and a fairly weak one at that, which should be easy to disprove. He might have decided to turn himself in but for Confucius' insistence.

Helped by Green Bay, he packed hurriedly for the journey. They did not speak: events had moved so quickly and unexpectedly that their separation felt unreal.

After barely an hour, a sailor wearing engineer's overalls arrived with a package containing a pair of dirty, faded overalls for my father. The sailor explained that they were both to board a launch used for maintenance work.

The car sped away, weaving between cars and rickshaws. Green Bay tried to follow in a taxi, but lost them in the traffic. The Venetian had the impression that he could still hear her voice, until he climbed out at the far end of the Bund. He stood there, gazing at the *Eritrea* motionless in the mud of the Whangpoo, with its drab, limp Italian flag. He wondered if the gunboat was the same one that had managed to steal, three years ago, past the English barricades and ambushes, to take refuge in Shanghai. This ship had become a symbol for all Italians in China, and everyone had wondered how its captain, Jannucci, had managed to avoid the traps set by the enemy. Now it seemed that the *Eritrea* was trying to become one with the river.

After slipping on board, the Venetian was taken to the bridge where he met the Captain, Del Giudice.

'You're just in time. We'll be leaving any time now. I'll have you shown to your cabin. We're overcrowded and you'll have to take turns to rest. Excuse me, the radio operator is calling me.'

The engines were already throbbing and the vibrations were so strong that the cabin door was swinging on its hinges.

'The engines are clapped out,' said the officer. 'Heaven help us if we hit rough seas. They were repaired three times on the way here. There's not much else I can do.'

My father took one last look at the city, remembering the icy morning nine years ago when he gazed out from the *Conte Verde* at the impressive buildings lining the Bund, a symbol of the Western powers who thought they were lording it in a country that always managed to evict foreigners. He had almost succeeded in being accepted by China through his love for a Chinese woman, but he had been sent packing in the end, condemned to suffer a longing for China that would haunt him for the rest of his life.

As the tall buildings along the Bund dwindled before his eyes, he turned his gaze downstream towards Pudong, his prison for almost two years. The vibrations increased and the ship made its way along the winding river, leaving behind the marshes and reed beds, the abandoned, half-ruined factories of the colonies, and the tiny fishing communities. The *Eritrea* was leaving Shanghai for good and his thoughts returned to the country where he had spent almost ten years of his life. It seemed like a lifetime.

He could feel the engines pulsing in his bones, making it difficult to think. The sea pounded against the sides of the ship and the engines slowed at times, then picked up again with renewed energy.

The sea began to get very choppy when they were in sight of Hong Kong. The gunboat advanced with difficulty, the engines running as if on will alone.

A distant typhoon trembled in the air and the Venetian wondered if Father Gherzi's observatory had issued a warning.

22

My father's sudden departure for Italy marked the end of my father and mother's marriage and gave rise to various rumours. My mother took to her bed, grief-stricken and inconsolable. Anything that reminded her of her husband upset her further. My worried grandmother, Splendid Gem, asked the aunt who was a Buddhist nun in Suzhou, for help. The intercession rite celebrated by her was intended to help Green Bay recover from her depression and ensure her husband's return. For some time, she seemed calmer.

Resigned to the fact that Lucky Omen had gone for good, my grandparents' family also had a Buddhist "funeral service" held in his memory. All the members of the family prayed according to Chinese tradition for the dead man's three souls: one was symbolised by the coffin; one was hidden among the Ancestors' tablets; the other would roam the Underworld for 49 days. To placate the three souls and bring them peace, the family recited psalms and burned incense. And every spring, for the Ching Ming festival—the festival of the dead—my grandfather, Radiant Wisdom, would express his grief along with the rest of the family by standing before the portrait hanging on a wall in the Room of Ancestors and exclaim: 'Lucky Omen, oh foreign son!' The other family members present would then chant a collective lament, repeating the exclamation and calling the "deceased" by name. This portrait was not actually a good likeness: it was the work of a local artist who had heavy-handedly altered my father's features and the shading to make his face more dignified and solemn— at least in his opinion. The picture was placed with the wooden tablets of the Miao family's ancestors. The whole family was now convinced that Lucky Omen was dead. My grandmother, Splendid Gem, would take me, her foreign granddaughter, by the hand and we would both bow three times and she would light small incense sticks which were placed in a little censer in front of the portrait. The Miao family was not so traditional as to preserve the custom of kneeling in front of the tablets, so they gave a deep bow instead.

I prayed without wondering if the prayer would wend its way to the God of the Catholic missionaries at Ningbo, or to that of my mother's Buddhist family. I often asked Green Bay, whom I called *maman,* with a marked French accent, 'What's praying for? Why does God allow bad things to happen?' I asked my grandmother the same question, substituting the word Buddha for God, and her equally embarrassed attempt at a reply did nothing to alleviate my confusion.

I had an inquisitive spirit and a great deal of determination. I never let a subject drop and I stubbornly continued to the bitter end, until I was sure there was nothing left to know. I worshipped my absent father and I kept a large photo of him in my room. Gazing at it, I would often ask *maman* accusingly: 'Why isn't he here?'

My mother received one last letter from Lucky Omen in which he told her: 'My beloved, it will be hard for me to write to you for a while. If something happens to me, you will know. Remember that I'll always love you.'

Often beset by anxiety, she asked her mother what she should do, but Splendid Gem merely answered stoically, 'Nothing, just wait. If we act, we're just asking for trouble. It's just another typhoon. We must wait for it to pass.' This ancient traditional wisdom unexpectedly helped Green Bay to develop a sense of resignation. Her parents were very happy at her increased filial obedience and her reconciliation with the family. In Confucian ethics, there is nothing worse than a lack of filial piety. The venerable sage still exerted an influence on the Chinese like my mother, who regarded themselves as

Westernised in many respects. But Green Bay's feelings for Lucky Omen remained unchanged, and the mere mention of his name was enough to upset her.

Three years after Lucky Omen's departure and his funeral service, my grandfather, Radiant Wisdom, sent for a matchmaker. Green Bay was his only daughter and the family's influence would ensure that she would make a good match, despite the fact that she was now considered "second choice". In fact, the husband Radiant Wisdom soon found for her was also regarded as a good match. He was an old-fashioned gentleman of good character from Ningbo who had been married twice before; his first wife had died and his second had been repudiated and sent back to her family some time before. He also had a concubine, but Radiant Wisdom made his future son-in-law promise that she would be sent away if he married Green Bay.

Time had undoubtedly eased my mother's distress. The Italian experience had enriched her by introducing her to another culture and opening up new horizons that she remembered fondly, even if she was now preparing to bind herself once more to her own land. The years had been kind to her and when she married the gentleman from Ningbo, she looked much younger than her thirty years.

After the death of my grandfather, Radiant Wisdom, the Miao family sold the house on the Hill of Distant Fragrance. My family's wealth was no longer what it had once been, but my mother and her brother managed to cover the cost of my studies in Shanghai and took turns to come and see me at the *Couvent de Saint Joseph* where I had been placed. They would take me to visit the city where I admired the vestiges of Shanghai's past glory.

Now my grandfather, Radiant Wisdom, is laid to rest on the hill near his father, Accumulated Virtue, his mother, Spring Orchid, and his brother, True Wood. I saw him for the last time at the Dragon Boat festival, the ancient festival celebrated on the river by the Miao people. My grandfather always rose early for this festival in order to reach the boat which was ready to set sail for its mooring near the Maple Tree Bridge.

I'll always remember my Chinese childhood and my Chinese relatives. Eight years after the end of the war, the Italian Consulate granted me a visa to enter Italy. In 1953 I disembarked in Naples, alone, after seventy days at sea. The Chinese chapter of my life was over.

PART TWO

1

At the *Couvent de Saint Joseph* in Shanghai, where I had lived for seven years and where I had been educated, my departure had been the talk of all my friends. The preparations for my journey to Italy had seemed exciting. The nuns had obtained a suitcase big enough for everything I needed for my journey, as well as many small gifts from my friends.

Mère Sainte-Scolastique had given me a pair of pink sunglasses to wear when crossing the Red Sea, because she said the sun was stronger there than anywhere else. I could not wait to use them, and I continually checked the ship's itinerary on the map.

The day of my departure came. I watched the old ship slowly pull away from the dock, then veer round and head out to sea. I stood there, watching the ship's white wake—a ribbon that linked me to my country—until it dissolved in the dark of evening. I stayed there, motionless and bewildered, my icy hands clenching the rough railing incrusted with rust and dried salt.

The wife of Consul Rossi had escorted me on board the old Greek ship. She would not stop talking, giving me endless advice in French, which she then repeated in English. She also told me I should not worry because there were many other people on board and that someone would be there to meet me when I arrived. I did not listen to her. I felt so lost, so overwhelmed by sadness, that I did not look at her either. Suddenly I could not hear her any more, and I realised she must already have gone ashore.

I felt that I would never go back to China. Mu-Mu, Amah,

and the long summers in Kong-qiao were gone forever. The only love I had ever known had to be locked away in a small corner of my heart to make room for a far-off, unknown country whose language I did not even speak.

On board, however, I soon became the ship's mascot. As I was alone, everyone felt duty-bound to comfort me, advise me, and protect me. Many of the women gave me sweets or biscuits—they were all very kind to me. There were people from other countries. When we left Shanghai, we naturally moved into our ethnic groups: the Jews who wanted to return to Israel; the Russian women, nearly all of whom were married to diplomats, businessmen and professionals, who were going to start a new life in Europe after fleeing Russia across China; the Austrians; finally, the Italians—the largest group, to which I belonged.

Pasquale Decrescenzo, a barber who used to live in Tianjin, was going back to Naples to live with his mother. He was always surrounded by young women. I thought he was older than he really was, because I was still a young girl and I noticed his receding hairline. I did not understand what the other women saw in him. Perhaps they liked him because he sang beautifully: he would warble sentimental songs, drawing out the notes like the singers of the past, sending his admirers into raptures. He was also a great chatterbox and friendly with everyone. One day he managed to catch a large tuna fish by dangling a hook in the sea, so he was able to treat his fellow countrymen to an unexpected dinner. He was rather stout and was keen on keeping fit. He exercised every day but, as he soon tired of doing it on his own, he organised an exercise class at the stern of the ship that was only attended by women, of course. I tried to avoid his classes with the excuse that I did not own a bathing costume, even less a pair of shorts. He gave me an old white pillowcase, and told me to make myself a pair of short trousers by cutting two slits for my legs on either side, then threading string through the hem of the opening. He said I was too flat-chested, so he persuaded me to take part in his class to develop my bust.

The best-looking of the girls surrounding him was Mila, a

young Jewish brunette who always wore bright red lipstick. From the Russian group, I remember Mrs Silenzi who was married to a Roman. They had a four-year-old girl, Nanda, whom I looked after occasionally, in exchange for chocolates and biscuits. Mrs Silenzi was a beautiful, elegant woman: she drew the slender arch of her eyebrows with a pencil and wore a long string of pearls. Once she told me that she would have gladly adopted me if circumstances had allowed: I did not understand what she meant by "circumstances". I thought she was talking about an illness.

There was also an ugly, disagreeable man with ginger hair, pale freckled skin, and a hooked nose. I kept bumping into him in the most unexpected places. He would smile oddly at me, and once he grabbed hold of my arm and pulled me close, but I managed to wriggle away. From then on, I went everywhere with my playmate, Bengy. His name was really Benito: his father (who had died in the war in the China sea) had an Italian surname—Esposito. His mother was Russian, though, so Bengy was in the Russian group, although he spent a lot of time with the Italians, particularly as his mother and aunts were all bound for Naples.

I made friends among the passengers, but I was very lonely, and scrupulously followed the nuns' advice. They had told me that no one would take care of me or my clothes, so I had to look after myself, and do my own washing. The soap I had been given at the convent did not lather well, even though I scrubbed very hard. I did not realise it was because the water from the tap was mixed with sea water. One day, I was so busy doing my washing that I did not realise I was late for lunch. I ran downstairs to the dining room, and entered to a chorus and applause: my travelling companions greeted me with the old song: "Oh! Rose Marie, I love you". I was out of breath, my clothes were soaking wet, and the passengers were singing and making fun of me, but I still remember the incident with affection because it made me feel less alone.

In seventy days at sea, I had seen Singapore, the Indian Ocean, sailed around Africa and crossed the equator twice. We travelled to Durban and Cape Town, but I never saw the

Red Sea, and I never wore my pink sunglasses. The captain had sailed round Africa to avoid going through the Suez Canal and undergoing inspections by the English authorities. When he arrived in Naples he was reported for breaking the rules and ended up in prison. His ship, the *Captain Marcos* was stuck in port.

The long voyage and everyone's kindness went some way towards helping me forget my sadness: I felt like some heroine on a great adventure. At night though, my misery returned. Before I went to sleep, I replayed my memories of China and got into the habit of praying. For many years, from that time onwards, I would pray that there would be no more wars, floods, or epidemics in China, and I would say to God, 'Please see to it that Mu-Mu, Amah, and my Chang uncles and aunts don't suffer under the new regime.' My long list of demands continued obsessively; my prayers had become an insurance policy for everyone I loved.

It was not always calm sailing: every now and then there was a storm and I did not go down to dinner. On those occasions, I was sorely missed by a red-haired Jewish young man, who sat next to me at mealtimes and never left his mother's side. Unlike me, he was often hungry. I would leave nearly all my food on my plate, particularly the hard-boiled eggs they served us in the morning. When he realised this, he asked if he could have mine—how his eyes shone every time those eggs were served! He and his mother invariably nodded their thanks. To his great delight, at dinner I asked him if he wanted my portion of mutton too. To save him from embarrassment I added that I could not eat it because I felt seasick.

As soon as the ship docked in the port of Naples, the other passengers went their different ways, leaving me on my own. I was not yet 14 and had no idea where to go. Before leaving Shanghai, I had been assured that I would be met by a "foreign" relative when I arrived in Italy, but there was no one there that afternoon. I was taken to the police station, where I stayed until 3am, exhausted by the lateness of the hour and depressed by this inexplicable situation. I was disappointed not to meet the "foreign" relative I'd been promised, and I felt smothered by all the strange men around me.

At the police station, a man who spoke a little French asked me if I wanted something to eat or drink. Wordless, I shook my head, but he had them bring me a bread stick filled with pink meat that had white spots: I found out later this was mortadella. Just the sight of it made me feel full. In China, I had been used to small pieces of food. How far away China seemed and yet I had only left on the old ship two months ago. I felt seasick again when they gave me that huge and unfamiliar loaf filled with mortadella at the police station. As it was very late, they took me to the *Suore Spagnole* hostel for women university students, to spend the night.

The next morning, they came to take me back to the police station.

Walking through the streets of Naples was like being in Ningbo: crouds of people were heading in all directions without appearing to be going anywhere in particular; there was a strong smell of food in the streets and although the smells were different, they were just as strong; the lively shouts were the same, so were the children racing here and there—and there were just as many pedlars in the streets in Naples as there were in Ningbo. I remember the flat-bread man, the good luck man, and particularly the scribe with his four valuable implements—brush, inkstone, tablet, and paper—waiting for a customer to request a few lines of text. Near him stood the man with the little yellow bird that picked out with its beak small rolls of paper predicting the future. Noodles dried in the sun like skeins of silk on large frames, not far from the man selling steaming soup to cold customers. But nothing drew me as much as *da ping*, the round flat-bread sprinkled with sesame that I loved. It had a natural, fragrant aroma similar to the smell of freshly baked Western bread. It was piping hot and mouth-watering when it came out of the large, cylindrical charcoal oven. As soon as I caught a whiff, I would speed up, dragging my poor Amah, who would follow wearily on her painful bound feet, making her way through people rummaging through their clothes and hair for lice.

One day, happily holding the bread we had just bought, which I would have devoured then and there if Amah had allowed me, I suddenly felt a forceful wrench and whirled round in astonishment to find my bread was gone and a man was running away with it, pursued by Amah who was shouting and threatening to call the guards. Her anger and her unnaturally small feet made her run along in fits and starts, like a clockwork toy going around in circles. No one batted an eyelid: there was nothing out of the ordinary about this incident. Meanwhile, the thief had returned to his group of friends leaning against the wall, basking in the sun and waiting for the next opportunity to acquire something to eat.

I was very shaken. It had never occurred to me that an adult might snatch bread from a child's mouth, even if he was starving. When I came across a crowd of dirty beggars covered in sores, I had learned not to look at them, nor to ask myself why they were so poor; they were just part of the familiar scene in the streets of Ningbo, like the pedlars, the scribe, and the other characters from all walks of life. But on that occasion, for the first time, I felt unexpectedly sad. I felt a deep sense of pity that softened my initial rage, and I was embarrassed that Amah was making so much fuss and continuing to grumble behind me: 'No harm done, but you should have kept it close to your chest, instead of letting it dangle from your hand. Well, you've learned your lesson.'

I had learned my lesson: everyone suffers from hunger and everyone finds different ways to ensure they have enough to eat. I remember one pedlar who wore a straw hat and rope sandals, and carried a long bamboo cane over his bony shoulders. A wicker basket was suspended from either end of the cane by a strong piece of string. He swayed towards the market square, slowing down every so often to regain his balance. To even out the weight, he would lean towards one side then another, like a pair of scales. The flexibility of his gait and the instruments of his trade—bamboo, string, rush containers, wicker baskets—symbolised the flexibility of the

177

peasants who bend but do not break in the face of adversity, righting themselves like bamboo canes after the storm has passed. This particular pedlar would search for a place on the pavement in the square where he could sit down and set out his baskets. While the others preferred to stay near each other, he chose a spot some distance from them. As early as six in the morning, the streets were full of pedlars, but his wares were different—miraculous tablets that were antidotes to snakebites. His two baskets contained snakes that were used with heart-stopping showmanship to demonstrate the effectiveness of his product. Cautiously, he would open one basket then the other. This was a difficult task, because as soon as he raised one lid, a snake's head would immediately emerge, followed by two, three, or four more heads of these reptiles trying to escape. Confident as an eel fisherman, one at a time, he would pick up the grey snakes, each over three feet long, and with calm and skill, he would shut them back in the basket. But soon another snake's head pressed against the lid and managed to lift it, so he would patiently close it again. He was like someone struggling to shut a suitcase that was too full: when he pressed down on one side, the clothes popped out of the other.

People stopped, as I did, more to enjoy his snake handling than to buy his tablets. I'm afraid he did not do a great deal of business, and I never knew if the snakes were really poisonous, but he took his job very seriously, providing detailed explanations about the tablets' effectiveness. Every so often, he would give a practical demonstration: he would hold the snake's head in his hand, and make it bite his arm; then he would pick up the red tablet, as big as a lacquered medallion, moisten it then rub it over the bite. His arms were covered with round, red marks from the tablets but no one wanted to test the effectiveness of his antidote, despite his urging.

He stayed in his corner of the square until the sun went down. Then he would gather his wares, close the baskets, and fasten them to the strings hanging from either end of the sturdy bamboo pole. While still sitting crossed-legged, he would arrange the pole over his shoulders, then rise to his feet holding the ropes with his hands, slowly and powerfully straightening his legs. His bulging muscles revealed the effort it took to move without overturning the baskets. Everyone would have been in serious trouble if the snakes had escaped. They were common in the countryside, hanging from the roofs of huts coiled round a beam, or camouflaged among the rocks of low walls lining the lanes. I tried to imagine how and where the old snake man kept them when he got home. They certainly could not have stayed in those baskets.

I spent quite a few mornings at the police station in Naples, after being fetched from the nuns' hostel, while the police carried out their investigation and continued to ask me in French if I knew where I was meant to go. I always showed them the letter written in Italian I had with me, as well as my Chinese passport signed by Consul Rossi. I began to become accustomed to the presence of the police superintendent at his desk every morning in the middle of the bare room. There was just one picture on the wall, but no crucifix with an olive branch, which would have been familiar to me because I had seen it in the bare rooms of the missions I had visited in China.

The police superintendent did not stop talking, and gesticulating to emphasise his words. I sat on a bench opposite him, feeling completely exposed and defenceless, without even the support of a wall behind me. I kept my head and eyes lowered, staring at the tiled floor. I did not understand a thing he said, but he continued to direct his words at me, as if I understood him. I sensed he was also talking about me, otherwise he would not have got me there, morning after morning.

Every now and then, I furtively raised my eyes as he continued to talk to his colleagues, trying to piece something together from his gestures and his expression, but it was impossible. His eyes often met mine as I "spied" on him: they were sincere, kind eyes that smiled at me, as if wanting to convey that he was not cross with me, even if I was causing him and his colleagues so much trouble. Then I felt I was

179

looking at Kon-Kon, whose unsmiling expression had made me feel safe, and I was comforted by that thought.

Kon-Kon was the doctor in the village of Kong-qiao, which means "arched bridge". A man widely regarded as a leader and a sage dressed all in white like a missionary, he wore an explorer's hat to shield him from the sun. Every summer his family, the Changs, looked after me, because they were distant relatives. Having grown up alone in convents and missions, living with them helped me understand what it meant to be part of a real family.

Kon-Kon had five children, whom I called my "aunts and uncles", as a sign of respect, according to custom. When young, he had lived in France, so he now corrected my French homework. He was strict, and his voice was harsh when he told me off. I was very much in awe of him, as was all of his family: he could only be disturbed when absolutely necessary. He had a long staff that was as tall as he, on which he leaned when negotiating the slippery paths between the rice fields to the village of Kong-qiao.

We reached the village by walking round immense cultivated rice fields that turned silver when the sun was high, becoming as dazzling as the wind-rippled sea. Scattered pagodas wreathed in a quivering, incandescent heat haze could be seen in the distance. From time to time, we would come across a boy driving ducks along the riverbank, where there was often a woman crouched on a stone slab beating laundry, or plucking a chicken.

Boatmen propelled rafts with long poles, followed by cormorants searching with their beaks for fish. The hoarse croaking of thousands of hidden frogs and the creaking of the large wooden irrigation wheel turned by a water buffalo, could be heard—if they were not drowned out by the noise of the ducks flapping their wings in fright at the appearance of strangers. Buffalos lay motionless in the marshes as if made of stone: only the sudden lashing of their mud-caked tails showed they were alive and tormented by flies.

Then a large dark patch loomed before us, its edges blurred

by the heat, and we had arrived on the outskirts of Kong-qiao, its entrance framed by the "arched bridge". We walked faster, and I ran up the steps to the highest point of the bridge from where I could look down over the village with its beautiful blue roofs.

Gazing towards the large square, I could make out various scenes, as in a Flemish painting. In one corner, there was the watermelon seller, virtually hidden behind his wares. In another, noodles were drying on a harp-shaped frame. Leaning against a wall, a group of women were gesticulating, sitting among the hens and vegetables. The sound of a man shouting mingled with the cackling of the flock of geese that he kept tied together by the legs. At the centre of the square, there was a dark crowd of people in a courtyard, like a swarm of ants. The crowd parted at Kon-Kon's appearance, then immediately closed round him again; a red lacquered stool was reserved for the doctor—the stool of health.

Kon-Kon would sit down. A long line of mothers immediately formed in front of him, bringing children with distended stomachs, and heads yellow as pumpkins. There were also many old men with sore eyes who wearily brushed away the flies that clustered around their inflamed eyelids.

Kon-Kon never wrote out prescriptions because the peasants could not read them. He questioned the sick people who visited him, then told them to take some medicinal herbs, or to come back for another check-up.

I spent many summers in Kon-Kon's house. I arrived with the swallows that made their nests in the thick wooden rafters of the typical uptilted Chinese roof. In the mornings, I often followed "Second Aunt", one of Kon-Kon's daughters, to the river to rinse out laundry or wash rice. In the afternoons, when we were hot and thirsty, the watermelon seller's shout rang out even louder to attract the children.

Those simple, happy holidays in Kong-qiao became a ritual, for my stays there were like a cycle of nature reflecting the return of the swallows, and I was sure I would spend all the summers of my life in the village of the "arched bridge". I had no idea that my life was about to change beyond all imagining.

One day, after writing in ink on a strange lined sheet of paper with wide margins, the police superintendent began looking around for something on his desk, while blowing on the still wet ink. In no time I found the blotting paper for him and put it on his document. Amazed and delighted by my speed, he praised me loudly, his voice echoing in his empty room; he kept saying how intelligent I was because I already "understood Italian", and he told everyone who came into his office.

I felt happier after that and not so shy. I began to look at him more often and would also smile shyly at him. He tried to make himself understood more clearly; I listened, but still could not understand a great deal.

One morning he put me in the care of a young uniformed officer with a police dog. He gave me to understand that I had to stay with this man at all times. I took the instruction literally and for the month I spent in Naples, I followed the officer and his dog around like a shadow: if he stood up, so did I; if he stopped, I did the same. I must have been more obedient than his German shepherd. The young police officer was clearly amused by this. I thought I understood what he was saying to people around him: 'Just wait and see how she copies me as soon as I get up,' and everyone laughed when I hurriedly stood up as soon as he left his chair.

I was not overly impressed at people laughing behind my back. I was beginning to understand that my safety was at issue and that he was my only point of reference; if he went away, I was lost.

I established a scale of values. I tried to discard all my "petty" fears and just deal with the ones I felt could not be avoided; then I learned to cope with those as well and put them behind me.

The newspapers in Naples printed dramatic headlines: 'Girl escapes alone from China in search of Italian relative.' The journalists embellished my story and many Neapolitan families offered to adopt me. I was terrified by the idea of being adopted, perhaps because my life had almost always been lived outside a real family circle.

One day, the police superintendent handed me over to a man in civilian clothes, who accompanied me on a train to northern Italy; the fear of being adopted was receding, but I was being taken to face other unknowns, other fears.

2

At Naples station, I saw a real train for the first time. I had always travelled from place to place by boat or ship because there were not many roads in China, and those were always in a bad condition, whereas the tributaries of the Yellow River and the Yangtze reached every part of China, linking towns and villages.

Helped by my escort, I climbed up the high wooden steps of the carriage. In China, I had dreamed of travelling by train, but now, sitting on the wooden seat in silence, I felt only sad and anxious. So many images and memories flashed through my mind. I thought lovingly about my mother, Green Bay. I did not feel bitter at her sending me away—she must have had to give up things she loved deeply due to the levelling effect of the new regime, and she may even have been forced to become a blue-clad factory worker, demeaning the beauty she had inherited from her ancestors. I thought about my grandmother, too, and about the nuns and my friends at the convent, but I mainly thought about Mu-Mu and Amah.

I called her "Mu-Mu", a diminutive of *mujin* meaning "mother", which was like calling her "mum". She was a Chinese Catholic nun who had taken me in at the French mission when I was only a few months old. I had left her when I left China.

The first time I saw her, I was in my father's arms. He and my mother gave me to her when they decided it was advisable to put me into the care of a Catholic mission because of the war in China.

Mu-Mu was one of the few people who knew my parents;

184

perhaps she was the only person who knew my entire history. She was the one who put me out to nurse with a Chinese *amah*, who stayed at my side longer than the usual seven years.

The daughter of an official at the court of the last emperor of China, Mu-Mu was of noble descent and one of her aunts was an attendant to the Mother Empress. She received a monthly stipend from her family that she gave to the mission, spending some of it on me as well. She spoke Mandarin, the language of the educated Chinese class, and also French. She was the one who liaised with the Ningbo authorities about the administration of the mission.

In order to repay her affection, I would memorise long poems in a language I still did not know. I would repeat: '*Une figure doucement attentive... Marie...*,' and the sound of those French words created a picture in my mind, which I then translated into Chinese. I would painstakingly learn poems for the mission's various festivals, which Mu-Mu proudly made me declaim. She also taught me to dance, mime and recite episodes from the Gospel.

In my parents' absence, she was the one who filled my childhood with love. However, when Mao Zedong's army reached the gates of Shanghai, it seemed prudent to send the daughter of an Italian away. Mu-Mu was very sad at the thought of my departure, but tried to hide her feelings to avoid frightening me. She simply gave me some essential advice and tried to play down the situation. She also gave me a photo of my father, as well as one of my mother. That was when my parents, who had practically been non-existent for me, suddenly began to figure in my thoughts.

Although she tried to hide it, Mu-Mu became increasingly quiet; our games and our laughter almost disappeared. She knew I would have to take a long journey, alone, to a country on the other side of the world, where I might not have anyone close to me.

I sensed her anxiety and tried to hide my own, as she did. To comfort her, I said: 'If the moon we see in China is the same as the one in Italy, every evening we'll be able to meet by looking at it'; I made her promise that she would look at the moon to communicate with me. Mu-Mu smiled in reply, gazing outwards.

I still think of her and China, when I look at the full moon, or when the Moon Festival takes place in the eighth lunar month, when people in China gather together in the evening, to recite and to play the flute in honour of the moon, and to eat soft moon cakes.

When I remember Mu-Mu, I also remember the nurse who tended me, my Amah.

Until the age of fifteen, when she married, Amah had lived in her courtyard—known as a "heavenly well", *tian jin* in Chinese—in a village near Chonqing in the region of Sichuan, at the heart of the country, which she called "the belly of China"—a fertile, humid region, that gleamed as if soaked in oil.

Her father owned farmland where he grew watermelons and a little rice. He was to receive more fields in exchange for giving his daughter's hand in marriage to a weaver from Ningbo.

When she was five, her mother bandaged her feet to prevent them growing in order to make them daintier, according to the ancient Chinese rules of beauty. Tightly bandaged at all times, they became the palest part of her body and they only ever saw the light of day when they were given their daily wash in a basin of salt water. They were then tightly bound again in white bandages and slipped into tiny black cloth shoes, made by Amah herself. Those plump, round feet made me think of two little pinkish, tailless pigs. The Chinese call them *jin lian*, "golden lotus".

Widowed very young, Amah paid an annual visit to the Cemetery of the Ancestors in Ningbo on the anniversary of her husband's death, to pray at his tomb and tell him what had happened to her since her last visit. She would kneel down with her feet and her palms together, close her eyes and bow her head until her forehead touched the ground. She would remain there, bent and motionless as a round stone among the sparse bushes surrounded by tombs, while I waited for her to finish praying. It had also become a ritual for me.

There was nothing tragic about this ritual: the Chinese accept death as part of the natural cycle of life, just as people accept they have to retire at a certain age. I often heard Amah speak calmly about her future death to her only son, Great Rectitude, of whom she was very proud because he could declaim most of the Chinese sages from memory and, unlike her, had learned to read and write. She began looking after me when I was only four months old and she breastfed me for over a year, perhaps longer, as was the custom of the people.

I was alarmed by the idea that Amah might die one day so I would study her ears when she was not looking—the Chinese believe that big ears are a sign of longevity. They were really large in proportion to her face, just like those of a Buddha, and that made me feel calmer. However, I did promise her that when she died, I would give her all the rituals she deserved: I would buy her the kind of black coffin that wealthy people have; I would put on a white tunic as a sign of mourning and I would weep copious tears for her; I would also commemorate her with the joyful ritual of decorating the Buddha's altar with fruit and sweetmeats so that she could enjoy peace and plenty—at least in the afterlife. Amah seemed very grateful for these demonstrations of affection. We were very close and she could sense what I needed; she did not have to be told.

During the bombing, thinking to protect me, she would run like a madwoman from one side of the room to the other carrying me in her arms, trying to get as far away as possible from the sound of the aeroplanes. In summer, she would bathe me two or three times a day in the wooden tub, washing me with a transparent green oval cake of soap that smelled of trees. She would rinse my hair with a herbal infusion to make it shinier and blacker and put two velvet flowers behind my ears. She told me that I should point at the *maozi*, "the little hat", when I wanted to go out.

When I was ill, she would amuse me by giving me turtles that I put in a little bowl enamelled with red flowers. Then, to "reward me" for getting better, she would take me to see the jugglers, and the fireworks, which are a real passion for the

Chinese, who produce wonderful, ephemeral designs made of light and shaped like bunches of grapes or dragons.

In summer, we would both stretch out on a straw mat above the large water cistern to keep cool: we would look at the stars and Amah would tell me legends until I fell asleep.

I still remember the one about the Milky Way. The Sky Goddess, she told me, drew the Milky Way onto the sky with her silver hairpin to punish an idle married couple by separating them in two different constellations. The couple could only meet on the seventh day of the seventh moon. Then little birds formed a bridge between the two constellations for their brief tryst—if it rained on that day, their meeting was postponed for another seven years.

But it was not only the legends that were magical; I also believed there was magic in her *xiangzi*, her camphor wood trunk that was full of brightly coloured buttons, little stuffed dolls, ribbons, pieces of embroidered silk, beaded and embroidered slippers as well as many combs decorated with inlays of mother-of-pearl and velvet flowers and hairpieces to adorn her chignon.

Dear Amah, I will always remember her. Now, despite having ears as big as a Buddha's, she will have died of old age. I hope Great Rectitude gave her the fitting funeral she wanted. I had promised her I would do it, but circumstances took me too far away to keep my promise.

It was the height of spring. After leaving Naples, the train ate up the miles as I watched the rolling countryside speed past. At this time of year in China, Amah and I used to tie paper flowers and silk ribbons to the boughs of the trees to propitiate the Goddess of Flowers and ensure a good season.

This was the first time I had missed the ritual, and the lush countryside and blossoming trees were no comfort. The contrast between the riotous spring landscape and my frozen interior was too stark: I was suspended between my unknown future and a past which was my only reality, but which had now been rendered meaningless. I did not know the language to communicate with my escort, and besides, I had no desire to talk.

That long, silent journey gave me time to think. I tried to comfort myself by remembering what I had once been told by a soothsayer. He had studied the lines of my face and my hand, calculated the distance between my eyebrows, and looked at my earlobes. He concluded that the curve of my lips would ensure that I never went hungry; from other signs, he saw I had hard paths to travel but time would put things right.

The memory of those words always comforted me. Neither the Buddhism that my grandmother, Splendid Gem, had tried to instil in me, nor the Catholicism of the French missionaries made me feel any calmer at the time. Only the soothsayer's words gave me heart. I was not religious, even if I had not rejected the religion in which I had been instructed by Monsieur Corcouf, my "Great Helmsman", an honorific title that acknowledged the way he turned my life around.

After fleeing Beijing because of the Japanese occupation, Louis Corcouf had become the head of the Catholic mission in Ningbo. After many years spent in China, he had almost become Chinese, not just because he spoke the language perfectly, but because of the way he gesticulated and the way he walked, which was influenced by his habit of wearing cloth shoes. Even his features had become Chinese, particularly his prominent cheekbones, his taut, yellowish skin, and his eyes, which were little more than slits behind the lenses of his spectacles. When he spoke his native tongue and pronounced the French "r" with his Adam's apple running up and down his thin, scraggy neck like a billiard ball, his real origins were obvious—the Chinese find it very difficult to pronounce the rolling French "r".

I still remember the song about him: "Ko-Ko loves the little children like a father and we children welcome him and wish him long life." In Chinese baby talk, "Ko-Ko" means "father", but later I called him Monsieur Corcouf, French-style, which he preferred. From a distance, all the girls in the choir singing this song looked the same. We had our hair cut in a square fringe and we waved a paper peony, a good-luck flower, to welcome the Jesuit father. But my voice stood out from the other children's voices. At the mission, they wondered how a slip of a girl could have such a stentorian voice. I was already clearly a contralto.

Under the shade of a tall magnolia tree in his garden, he told me bible stories, and explained extracts from the Gospels. He took care of my religious education and gave me my First Communion. He also played a decisive role in another aspect of my life: aware that the Governor of Ningbo wanted to marry me and that my mother was inclined to "sell" me to him as his concubine, his fifth "wife", and wanting to protect me from the dangers of a country in which Mao Zedong was growing increasingly powerful, Monsieur Corcouf decided to speed up my departure.

Monsieur Corcouf's actions reflected his conscience as a Catholic and as a priest, but on the long silent journey north, I thought that many of my inner fears might also have stemmed from him.

In Naples, I had refused to be adopted because, despite being alone, I did not want to belong to anyone. I made my choice, which may have been wrong, because I ended up in an orphanage, but it seemed easier to be one of many than to be part of a family who would expect my love, when I now felt too old to be able to replace the memory of Mu-Mu and Amah in my heart.

So the first leg of my "Long March" was in a train, a locomotive taking me to places that were completely different from those I had known before, places where I would be an object of curiosity because, being half-Chinese and half-Italian, I did not really belong to either country. I was to be regarded as "different" in Italy too.

This time I did not have the traditional Chinese fan to hide behind; I was out in the open, with a history I had to forget in order to make room for a new life that would inevitably bear the stamp of my Chinese experiences.

3

In Shanghai, I was educated, and learned to speak three languages—English, French, and Chinese, my mother tongue —at the *Couvent de Saint Joseph* (Convent of Saint Joseph).

It was the most exclusive European school in Shanghai.I wore the number 56 stitched onto my uniform and beret and was one of the many European and Eurasian girls studying at the convent, the seat of the *Auxiliatrices du Purgatoire*. After a short stay at the Ningbo School of Heavenly Sciences. This was where I was educated until the day I left for Italy.

The girls at the convent were of many races and nationalities—English, French, Portuguese, Italian, Russian, Korean, and Eurasian; Shanghai was regarded as the most cosmopolitan city in the whole of China, if not Asia. Although most people spoke Chinese, the official language was English. English was spoken at the convent too, although the nuns insisted on replying in French since their religious order was French. We studied both languages there, though. All the major Western countries had their own consulate in Shanghai where Western influences prevailed; so my first encounter with the West was in Shanghai, and it was a harsh, aggressive encounter because of the war.

The wartime atmosphere of hostility was aggravated by the climate—bitterly cold in winter, and stiflingly hot in summer. I remember that my cheeks were always reddened and chapped by the wind in the freezing weather, even though I tried to protect them with glycerine, as Amah had taught me. Chilblains on my feet were a real torture too, particularly when we had to walk in the hard leather shoes that the nuns managed to obtain for us through a charitable organisation.

In summer, the water was rationed and the trickle of tap water was not safe to drink; I often saw tiny worms floating in it. You had to dissolve a disinfectant tablet in a glass of water, then wait for a good half hour before it was safe to drink. It was not unusual to be terribly thirsty in those tough wartime years.

The French school's rules and regulations were just as harsh as the climate and conditions. The nuns were extremely strict and lived up to the name of their order; living there was sheer purgatory. I had my palm rapped with a ruler for the slightest misdemeanour. Unfortunately, I frequently managed to mislay my uniform beret and, unfortunately, it was always the strictest nun who found it. She was also the one who shamed me by tying my shoes behind my back so that all my friends could see the holes in the soles caused by my incessant running and jumping.

But life at the convent was hard for all the girls. We had to get up very early and wash and dress in complete silence. Food was rationed and often barely edible, which was true of all these institutions during the war. The younger, less confident girls were also bullied by the bigger girls, who, for example, kept the best roller skates for themselves—roller skating was our only source of amusement at the convent, and we younger ones would end up with the broken skates with no laces, so I tried tying them to my feet with rags instead.

At night, there were air raids. Because of the curfew, we had to make our way downstairs in the dark from the third-floor dormitory to the ground floor. The falling bombs rattled the large glass windows. The nuns, who seemed impervious to the din and the danger, told their rosaries.

Two-tone sirens gave the first alarm. If they continued to sound eight or ten times, that meant heavy bombing and immediately afterwards you could hear the deep, threatening rumble of approaching aircraft. I slept in my shoes, tying the laces with double knots to avoid tripping up in the dark when I had to run downstairs.

Nevertheless, despite the constant tension of those years of blackout and terror, I derived a great deal of satisfaction from my studies. Every term I won medals for being top of the class in some subject or other, and I proudly wore them pinned to my uniform.

I remember winning the competition for penmanship. The prize was a papier-mâché doll with glass eyes held in place by a small hook; it was not easy to put them back in their sockets when the hook gave way, blinding the doll.

My friendship with Jeannette Souza, a Portuguese girl, and Thérèse Kim, a Korean, made the aggression of the war years and the harshness of life at boarding school easier to bear. The former shared the sweets brought by her relatives on their Sunday visits; the latter, like all the Korean girls excelled in sports,was extremely good-natured.

Then it was 1945, and the bombing of Hiroshima put an end to the war and the nightly terror of the air-raid sirens. One day, some men dressed in black came to the convent. They were Chinese and were carrying out a census. I did not know that they marked the beginning of a new era for China, because, in the early stages, I left for Italy.

The orphanage in Acqui Terme, where I was sent by the Neapolitan authorities after I had refused adoption, was run by the Sisters of St Vincent, the same religious order I had known at the Ningbo mission. Although I had been hoping that the atmosphere would be familiar, it was very different. The girls in this institution were taught needlework including pin tucks, smocking and plenty of embroidery, and they embroidered sheets and tablecloths for the bourgeoisie of Acqui in exchange for small amounts of money paid into their savings accounts. Only a few girls thought to be intelligent were sent to a state school near the orphanage. Luckily, they thought I was "intelligent" because I could speak three languages.

Every morning, a nun walked me from the orphanage in Acqui Terme to the gate of the Giovanni Pascoli secondary school, and she was there waiting for me when classes were over. We always walked back along an avenue of plane trees. It was rare that Sister Vincenzina did not come to collect me, but when she was not there for some reason, it gave me a wonderful sense of freedom to walk along that avenue of trees all by myself. Going to school meant that I did not have to stay confined within the walls of the orphanage like the Chinese countrywomen within the precincts of their "heavenly well". My foreign habits caused many small problems and misunderstandings.

It was hard to explain how I felt. The grubbiness of the refectory and the tin plates and cutlery just made matters worse. In the end, I would only eat bread and pasta, so I put on weight and suffered from the complex of being a fat girl whose looks were not improved by the shapeless school uniform and pigtails.

Every evening before bed, I unplaited and brushed my hair. The girls asked me why I did this and I replied that I had done it in China, where I was always being told that my thick, wavy, shiny hair was beautiful. Now, with it tightly braided into pigtails, I often suffered from headaches and looked like an Easter egg.

I did not want to look in the mirror any more, and I felt a deep sense of shame when the girls from the orphanage had to take part in religious parades and the occasional funeral procession, and people whispered as I walked past, 'Look at the little Chinese girl.' The situation worsened after I was given the part of Pikekai in a play. With a pigtail hanging from my hat, I had to sing: "I'm from Shanghai, from poor China who abandons her babies." Ironically, Pikekai was a boy, not a girl.

Yet in China, too, as a child I had also been made to feel like a foreigner, being half-European on my father's side. The children I played with would point at me and call me *wai-guo-ren* or "foreigner". Those Chinese children were quick at everything, even running barefoot among the bushes and along pebbly paths. I envied them and tried to imitate them by taking

194

off my shoes, but I always lagged behind because my feet hurt and they laughed at me. I could not run like them because I was different—I was of mixed race, as anyone could see from my straight nose and wavy hair.

Hair has always played a vital role in the history of China as a symbol of belonging to a social class or political movement. After the establishment of the Republic of China in 1911, the year that saw the fall of the Manchu dynasty, the wearing of pigtails, compulsory under the Manchu, also fell out of fashion, although some boys still wore the pigtail in rural areas. One boy used to spy on us secretly and watch us playing without daring to show his face. As soon as he realised we had spotted him, he would run off, like someone used to fleeing persecution, so fast that all we could see was his very long pigtail frantically bouncing up and down. For this reason, no one knew what he looked like but he was called "the devil's son with the tail".

Despite the discrimination I faced as a "foreigner" in China, I did learn some of the Chinese children's rural pastimes, such as "cutting the grass" in order to tickle crickets and make them sing. You picked a blade of grass and split the end lengthways to form strands with which you tickled the crickets, once they had been caught and shut in special little cages. I also learnt that the female "plays the piano", producing a particular vibration. The female cricket can be distinguished from the male, which is larger, by the fact that she has three stingers at the rear instead of two. I also learnt how to dig through the earth in search of worms. We would fix them to small hooks, then lie down along the river bank and try to catch crayfish.

The girls of my age taught me to paint my toenails and fingernails with a mixture of salt and orange pollen collected from flowers that only bloom on summer nights. I painted this concoction on my nails, then wrapped them in long leaves. I had to spend the night with my hands and feet outside the bed so that the compress stayed in place; and I kept waking up to check that the colour was setting.

One evening, I remember following a group of boys for the

lantern procession through the countryside. The lanterns were all different colours, shapes and sizes. Some represented animals, others mythical creatures, and some were geometrical in shape. Some were made of paper, some of silk. The boys holding them looked like bonzes in prayer. The moonlight chased us along the paths, illuminating the small shrines at crossroads in which a seated Buddha watched us with his customary benevolent smile.

I had trailed after the children in Kong-qiao, who played with me because I was Kon-Kon's "granddaughter", but none of them was a real friend to me because I was different. In China, Eurasian people are seen as a fusion of two hemispheres, East and West: they are caught between these two worlds, continually torn between two poles, the principles of Yin and Yang.

I still could not say, after journeying from East to West, which was my guiding principle.

I found this conflict particularly difficult during my years at the orphanage in Acqui. The sunny disposition that had kept me going throughout my years in China soon turned to melancholy.

My experiences at boarding school also left me feeling unsettled and seething with rebellious thoughts. I longed to attain serenity at any price, despite everything, as if by doing so I could take revenge for what had happened to me.

I spent six years in that institution.

Six years is a very long time.

4

'Brigadoi'... 'Here!'
'Rapetti'... 'Here!'
'Corrado'... 'Here!'
'Bonsignore'... 'Here!'.

Bonsignore was the girl I sat next to at the Giovanni Pascoli secondary school in Acqui. My name was not included in the roll call though, because I was just listening in on lessons: the school still had not obtained permission from the Director of Education to enrol me, so it did not have the same obligations towards me as the school in Ningbo.

Despite the bitter cold, as a child I had to walk several miles every morning to attend the writing school in Ningbo. I had to walk down the long Street of the Seven Lanterns, then cross the Gate of the Flowering Cherry Trees, wrapped in padded cotton from head to foot so that I did not arrive frozen at the School of Heavenly Sciences. I left the house with my cheeks shining with glycerine, a brass hand warmer filled with embers in my gloved hands and a scarf around my neck, mouth and shoulders. I was fond of that scarf, because it was made from the fur of my cat, Mao, which had been crushed to death by a bag of rice when hunting mice in the attic.

With Mao duly tanned and wrapped around my neck, I came into the freezing classroom. There was one brick stove in the middle, but every pupil had a brass foot-warmer. I wrote with mitts on my hands and my grey cat over my shoulders.

The first thing a Chinese schoolmistress teaches girls to do is prepare ink. The school provided the inkstone, which had a cavity for holding water on one side, in which I dipped the tablet of black China ink, then rubbed it in a circle with a particular rhythm to obtain a black, viscous liquid. It took a

197

great deal of practice to obtain the correct thickness. Then we had to learn to hold the brush completely straight and firm with three fingers of our right hand. To demonstrate the correct grip and the right degree of pressure from our fingers, the schoolmistress made us hold a pigeon's egg in the palm of our hand. We dipped the tip of the brush into the freshly prepared ink, then began to draw hooked, curved and sweeping lines.

We had to practise diligently to ensure that the characters were executed correctly, following exact rules for the direction and order of every brush-stroke—from top to bottom, left to right, first this, then that. Finally, when every character was executed correctly, we began to "depict" the words, then to grasp the balance of every character, every ideogram. We used special exercise books with transparent squared sheets laid over pages showing the ideograms, which we then traced. While we learned to draw the characters, we also learned their meaning. Every perfectly executed curve, line or stroke revealed the harmony of Chinese script. In contrast, I thought the spoken language was shrill and syncopated. Due to the wide variety of dialects in so many regions, the written word is the common denominator in China. I learned to speak the dialect of Ningbo first, then of Shanghai, but the written word did not change.

As a Eurasian, the writing school was a way for me to integrate more effectively with the Chinese. In a year, I had learned to write about one hundred ideograms, although I was well aware that I would have to practise for many more years to reach the quota of around one thousand characters necessary for a well-educated person.

I applied myself with enthusiasm. The schoolmistress seemed happy with me and circled in red the characters I had executed well. So I was understandably upset when the French mission told me that I had to leave the School of Heavenly Sciences in Ningbo and move to Shanghai to attend the *Couvent de Saint Joseph*, which was more suitable for young European girls.

I sulked for a long time, to no avail—although I could not

be upset with anyone in particular because I did not know who was to blame. Amah immediately realised I was in a temper; I was pouting and hanging my head like a disappointed child. She kept teasing me, using a saying often directed at sulky Chinese children: 'Put those lips away or someone will hang a bottle from them.' I did not want to talk to Amah either or hold her hand, and she kept asking me why I was in such a bad temper. For a long time, I refused to reply; then, eventually, I dropped a hint: I stuck out my little finger from my closed fist, a gesture used by Chinese children to show they are unhappy about something. After that first signal, Amah managed to coax from me a few mumbled words, then phrases, and finally the real reason for my unhappiness. She admitted I had good reason to be upset. She understood me completely.

I was six years old when I left the School of Heavenly Sciences in Ningbo forever.

In Acqui, pupils were already beginning to write essays in class: "Troubles are like cherries, they come in twos", or "The loss of a loved one". For the essay on cherries, which I had never eaten, I drew my inspiration from the arbutus berries that Amah used to buy me on the streets of Ningbo. However, the essay on the death of a loved one put me in a quandary. In the first instance, I could not talk about the presumed death of my father, because I was not even sure he was dead and anyway, I did not know enough about him to make up a story. Then I knew that my mother, Green Bay, was alive and still young, and I was sure that not even the Buddha would want my grandmother, Splendid Gem. I did not like her, I did not want her to hold me. When I was little, I used to pull her hair, though when I was older, during her rare visits, I tried to be nice, if not affectionate.

My grandmother was a devout Buddhist. She never forgot the Buddhist festivals and she burned incense for Buddha, and for various minor gods. She passively bowed to their will, particularly when it came to her problems, of which, in her opinion, she had many, and to which she always reacted theatrically. She made a terrible fuss to Buddha because my

199

birth had been very difficult; and on the occasions she visited, she always made a point of telling me how many prayers she had said for me and how she had stayed on her knees for two days and two nights, praying for the gods to ease the birth.

When we came across shrines with Buddhist images in country lanes, she always stopped, murmuring prayers and bowing three times. To my great annoyance, she ordered me to do the same, as if we were standing before the Buddha in flesh and blood.

She complained constantly. Her attention-seeking tears and dramatic gestures were very Mediterranean in some respects. My mother would quietly and respectfully listen to her long list of complaints—it was the only way to keep her quiet. Once her performance was over, she would dry her tears and her mood would change.

At home, she bred silkworms on long wooden tables. I hated watching those fat, white grubs squirming on the mulberry leaves—I thought they were disgusting; and the butterflies that came out of their cocoons were small and insignificant, like moths. They were certainly not as brightly coloured as the butterflies I saw fluttering in the summer fields.

I never managed to get close to my grandmother, and any hope of reaching a mutual understanding was shattered after the incident on the ship.

She had been asked to accompany me from Shanghai to Ningbo. We had reserved a cabin with two bunks and she was given money to pay for the tickets. As soon as we boarded, I saw her whispering to the cabin steward; then she told me to hide when the ticket inspector came. When she heard him knocking, she thrust me behind the bunk. When asked whether she was alone, she murmured innocently with an expression of convincing sincerity, "*Yi ghe ren*", "Yes".

Being shoved behind the bunk like a parcel was an insult to my dignity and I never forgave her for pocketing the money for my bunk. I forgot—or perhaps I was too young to know—that my grandparents' family had recently experienced severe financial setbacks.

Excluding my father, mother and grandmother, the only available relative I could "kill off" in my essay was my grandfather, Radiant Wisdom, who had been ill and very close to death. So I wrote about the long river journey I had taken with my mother to say farewell to my seriously ill Chinese grandfather.

First, we looked for a shop where we could buy the white cloth for the outfits we would have to wear if my grandfather's condition proved hopeless. White has remained the colour of mourning in China, as it used to be in other Eastern countries; death is not sad—it is the start of a new life.

There were no roads from Ningbo to the area where my grandfather lived: the towns and villages dotted along the rivers are almost never accessible by land, so we had to go by river, and the boat that made the twice-weekly journey was not running that day—it was tied to the quay, deserted. We had to find a boatman prepared to take us, and to negotiate a price. The journey seemed interminable; I thought we would never arrive in time to say goodbye to old Radiant Wisdom. I tried to remember what he looked like and what I knew about him, but I did not know enough. It felt as if he did not have a past. I did not remember the timbre of his voice because he did not speak. Perhaps the wars, the taxes and the economic disasters had taken their toll.

He always seemed detached and held himself aloof from everything and everybody. His only contribution to family life took the form of vague nods or gestures. He was depressed and probably very lonely. He was always looking out at the horizon, gazing into the distance like a nomad from one of the tribes that had inhabited the Yunnan, the land of his ancestors. He was always lying on his side, smoking opium, either to forget his failures or simply to avoid speaking, and he became more and more like his pipe—gnarled, long and stiff.

I only have one clear memory of him; he was standing erect, holding me in his arms to watch a military parade. I waved my paper peony at the soldiers and he looked at me with the trace of a smile in his narrow eyes.

201

When we arrived after our interminable journey, my grandfather, instead of being dead as we had feared, had virtually recovered; he was just thinner than he had been the last time I had seen him at the military parade. The inveterate opium smoker was lying on the mat, but there was no sign of his long pipe. His faded green uniform of a nationalist soldier was hanging in the wardrobe; he may not have worn it since the day of the parade.

After my story about my grandfather's "death", the schoolmistress wrote 'Well done! Very vivid! Keep it up!' on my essay in her sprawling hand. Then one day, she announced loudly that I was now legitimately enrolled in the school and, on that occasion, she called out my name—my father's surname—"Minella!", in the roll call. My classmates were as surprised as I was and they all turned to look at me. I blushed at finding myself the centre of attention. The regular insertion of that name in the roll call sounded like a warning: from then on, I would have to work hard and stop reading my friends' comics during lessons.

Although I managed quite well with numbers and mathematical sums, I found geometry very hard, because I did not understand the explanations and only had a rusty old compass with which I could not even draw a semicircle: it would scratch the paper too deeply and grind to a stop, ruining the problem before I had solved it. All my friends had a rectangular or square black box containing a compass, semicircle and other things I did not know how to use. I also found the problems very difficult: how many minutes does it take for a tap to fill a container of given dimensions if the water is flowing at a given speed? Fortunately the janitor, Golo, was very good at these problems. When he discovered how hard I found them, he suggested I make the excuse that I was going to the toilet, then bring the problem out of the classroom into the corridor where he sat. In a few minutes, he gave me back the sheet with the problem solved.

But despite everyone's help, I felt as if I would never be able to reach the standard of my school friends. They had been born and bred in Italy, they had attended primary school regularly and had a family life at home, where they could study in peace. I had to go back to the orphanage and apply myself to needlework, like the other girls. So I was at the bottom of the class and I felt ashamed when I thought back to the many prizes I had won when studying at the *Couvent de Saint Joseph*.

For two years school was tough, to say the least. When things began to improve, I was already fifteen and half.

5

After three years at secondary school, I had reached the sixth-form college. I still walked along the avenue of plane trees where I caught the attention of a boy, Ugo. There was something other than the usual curiosity in his eyes. I remember him being tall and fair-haired, and he looked kind. The white duffel coat he wore was too short; so were his jackets, which made him look even taller and thinner. Although I was sixteen and half, I still wore a uniform made by the nuns, and white ankle socks rolled down over mannish black shoes with a low, square heel. When Ugo first looked at me, I felt embarrassed and more awkward than usual. My friends at college all wore transparent stockings and high-heeled shoes. One of them wore her belt so tight, to enhance her bust, that she could barely breathe. Others dyed their hair blonde, or wore lipstick and French perfume. Some had love affairs, others were engaged.

Making the most of the rare occasions when I was on my own, Ugo came over and, with a self-assurance that paralysed me and made me blush, told me I was really pretty and that he liked me because I was different from the other girls. As he went on to tell me about himself, I thought about what he had said. He was flattering me, of course, but his words also suggested to me for the first time, that I could use the fact that I was different to my advantage, instead of letting it making me unhappy. Ugo helped me to realise, without spelling it out, that beauty was not merely a matter of nice clothes, make-up and high heels, but was to do with something else. I imagined it might be what I saw in his eyes. Of course

I did not have nice clothes like the other girls, or their freedom to talk to strangers. I had never even gone for a walk alone with a boy. Besides, in China, you are taught not to show your emotions. When I was a little girl, I was never kissed—it was not the custom. When people meet, they greet each other by brushing cheeks so that they can smell the other person's "fragrance".

I had a vague idea of love. After all, I learned about it in books I secretly read, or from magazines, or at the cinema; my friends' love affairs, the stories they told me, provided material for my daydreams. But I experienced love indirectly, interpreting their stories in my own way. I knew enough to analyse and observe situations. I saw the complicated feelings it aroused. I thought I knew everything: how love started, how it developed, how it ended. The rituals at the start of a love affair were always the same: the looks, the notes, the flowers, and the words.

I had also come across love stories, both happy and unhappy, in China as well. There was the story of Norina, who was in love with her confessor. I had always thought that she was devout to the point of being over-religious because she went to confession so often and stayed so long in church. I thought she was praying; but she was daydreaming.

It was her diary that gave her away—a nun found it. The first part was coded and incomprehensible. Then there were lengthy accounts of vague feelings. Finally, she described how thrilled she felt when she met her confessor's eyes; she wrote about what she thought he felt for her, and about sins never committed, only imagined. For two pages she despaired, promising to give it all up, become a nun and go to work in Dr Schweitzer's leper hospital.

When she used to bump into the confessor, she would blush, as if he knew about her flights of fancy, but no one, least of all him, had even noticed. If her diary had not been found, her love and her repentance would have remained her secret. I really do not know how she had mislaid it, because she always carried it with her. To our great amazement, no action was taken against Norina—it was the confessor who was sent away.

He was guilty of looking like Gregory Peck, and the nuns thought it would be wise to appoint a confessor who was not so handsome.

Of course, my own "sentimental education" included shared and imaginary loves. We were all in love with the short-sighted Professor of Philosophy and his "interesting" spectacles; and we were all in love with William Holden in *Love is a Many-Splendored Thing*. But that film had special significance for me. Jennifer Jones, the heroine, played the part of a Eurasian woman and her love story unfolded in China. The film brought me closer to the China that had become so distant to me. The film's theme music made me feel nostalgic and sad every time I heard it.

After seeing that film, hearing Ugo's compliments, and living so many love stories at one remove, I began to apply Nivea cream, wear make-up and pat myself dry with talc. I still did not use face powder, but I did use Lux soap, the one used by "nine out of ten film stars". I had come to a decision: I wanted to be beautiful.

Two years later, with the enthusiasm of an eighteen-year-old who was extremely thin due to deliberately skipping so many meals, I set off to see life and conquer it. I had finished college and, relishing my newfound freedom, I thought how lucky I was—in China, I would already have been married for four years, with children.

The freedom was exhilarating at first, but it soon became a source of anxiety. I realised I was standing in a space that was too large for me to choose which way to go. I could not find my bearings. I decided to go one way then another. There were no landmarks. Until then, my life had always been decided by other people. My birth, my childhood in China, my move from one civilisation to another were events over which I had not had any control. I was also used to living within the narrow confines of courtyards, of being "caged"—first, in the mission in Ningbo, then in the school in Shanghai, and finally in the Italian orphanage. Now I was being forced to leave my cage, but my wings had been clipped—they were like Chinese women's feet that had been bound for too long. My wings were so small that they could not bear the weight of my dreams of freedom, my desire to live life to the full. I did not feel capable of facing up to life. I had no experience of the world outside my cage. I could not make a choice because I did not know what to choose.

My freedom was not unlimited, of course. The tutelary judge had appointed a guardian for me. I turned to him. But all he could do was advise me to find a husband; women—he said—should get married and have children. The idea of finding a husband frightened me. I ended up envying Chinese brides, who do not have to choose. It was easier to be chosen than to choose.

One day, Italia, one of the girls at the orphanage, enquired: 'Haven't you ever asked what happened to your father?' I looked at her in surprise and replied: 'But he's dead!' What else was there to say?

She knew she had dropped a pebble in the water, so she made herself scarce, aware that she had upset me. Then she returned to the subject on another occasion: 'One of the nuns said your father is alive and married with two sons.' This news surprised me, but I kept quiet. She looked at me and said: 'Aren't you curious? If I were you, I'd go looking for him.' And she started telling me how she would go about it and suggesting what I should do. She even worked out what my father and I would say when we met: I spoke my part, then she spoke my father's. According to her script, he would have explained everything and taken me away with him.

Italia seemed to know a great deal about it. I, on the contrary, knew very little about my parents or my Italian family. I did know that news of my birth had reached my father's family months after the event. Word arrived accompanied by a photograph that did nothing to soften my "Foreign Grandfather"; he flew into a rage about the existence of a Chinese baby granddaughter and threatened to disinherit his son. He never changed his mind.

My "Foreign Grandmother" died before I was born, so my father could expect nothing more from his family. My "Foreign

Great-Aunt" reacted completely differently. Moved by the photograph, she repeatedly contacted the Italian Consulate in Shanghai in order to get me to Italy; but the war hindered her efforts and she died before she had achieved anything.

My parents had always been strangers to me. At the mission, I was told one day, that my father was on a ship that had been bombed in the port of Shanghai, and that he was missing. Then they said he was dead and they made me pray for him. I never knew if they had been given this information by mistake or, when my father was forced to flee after the war to Italy, they thought it would be wiser and "simpler" to tell me that he was dead.

Now I was being told that my father was living in Italy with a wife and children. My unexpected arrival on the scene would no doubt cause problems for his family—no one had known he had a Chinese daughter; it had not even occurred to him that the mission in Ningbo might one day send me to Italy. That may have been why he had not replied to the letter sent by the nuns from China, or maybe he did not receive it. All I know is that he was not in Naples when my ship came into port, and it was three years before he started looking for me.

One day I received a summons. 'There's a man here to see you. He's in the other room. He says he's here on behalf of your aunt, your father's sister,' announced one of my friends. My aunt had already been in contact with the orphanage in Acqui.

A man came forward to meet me. How he stared at me! I was used to people staring at me, since I looked foreign in both China and in Italy. But it was unsettling being stared at by someone who could be my father. I tried to remember a photograph, the one Mu-Mu gave me before I left. Was this really my father? After what Italia had told me a few weeks earlier, I was not sure what to think.

He came over slowly, almost awkwardly; he did not smile immediately. I did not say anything. He nodded in greeting; I did not reply. He looked at me, waiting for me to say something, but I did not say a word. Then he said: 'I'm your father.' He added that he knew how I was doing at school because his sister had kept him informed. He was very ill at ease. He asked me how I was and added that I looked a great deal like my mother. Then he asked me if I would have lunch with him. I agreed.

Over lunch, he commented on the food, trying to get me to speak.

Suddenly he said: 'Aren't you going to say anything to me?'

What did I have to say to him? They had told me he was dead. I was not expecting him. I did not know him.

He carried on talking. He said I caused him all kinds of problems: he had two sons who were doing very well at school—the eldest had won a scholarship; he was married to a wife with a large number of relatives, which made things very complicated. He stopped and thought for a second. Then he began talking again. He said he had bought a car.

I listened closely to what he was saying, to every nuance, for some sign that might help me understand what he wanted. He seemed to want to say something. Perhaps it was difficult for him to say what I was expecting him to tell me. And he did not say it. He never said it. He just went on talking, telling me how much he missed the years he spent in China, in Tianjin, in Shanghai. That, it seemed, was all we had in common. Then he looked at me, waiting for me to say something. I said nothing. In true Chinese fashion, I did not tell him anything about myself. It was a habit of mine: I never asked anything and I never gave any explanations. He said something else, which I did not catch. I had stopped listening. He realised this and fell silent. He paid for the meal and walked me back to the orphanage. He stopped trying to make conversation; perhaps he realised that we would never talk to each other.

He said goodbye. I remember him being tall with brown hair. I watched him walk away, becoming smaller and smaller, the way someone shrinks to a dot among the people on a platform, as you watch from the window of a train pulling out of a station.

6

I grew up with two religions. Amah, my grandmother, Splendid Gem, and the people of my country taught me Buddhism; the missionaries taught me Catholicism. I thought the two religions were very alike, even if they had different roots. Both had their saints and demons; both had their arcane mysteries and dogmas.

As I remember, the sacred places of both religions smelled of incense, smoke, candles or flowers. Their rituals also seemed similar. They prayed, they decorated the altars, and they celebrated feast days. The bonzes, like the priests, wore tunics and a tonsure. They shared the same social ideal— "love thy neighbour". The Buddhists, like the Catholics, told their rosaries, taking the beads between their index finger and thumb and moving them round one at a time. The missionaries' rosary had five groups of ten beads, while the Buddhist rosary was a single circle of black stones.

At the orphanage in Acqui, I had four rosaries: a pink one, a blue one with beads shaped like grains of rice, a white mother-of-pearl one, and a small silver one, with round beads.

Once I stayed for a few days of spiritual exercises at an Italian villa that was as isolated as a Buddhist monastery. I took meditation walks, moving in crocodile formation with the other girls along paths bordered with flowers and bushes, which reminded me of the bonzes walking together round the fish pool.

I also remember being taken to a Buddhist monastery by my aunts to visit a distant relative, who was a nun. She had freely chosen the life of work and prayer she shared with the other bonzes, even though she was a woman. She wore a grey cassock over a pair of trousers, instead of the monks' long grey tunic.

The monastery was in open countryside, a long way from the houses dotted among the rice fields. Except for the green of the trees, the landscape was as colourless as the monks' faces—a complete contrast to the polychromatic interior of the pagoda opposite the monastery. Like almost all pagodas, this one had nine floors. In China, numbers have a meaning: the number three represents the three treasures—sons, wealth and prosperity—so nine has a sacred power.

The pagoda was in the form of a tower, making the rooms circular. Every floor was presided over by a deity watched over continuously by a seated bonze who recited monotonous litanies while telling a rosary and striking a wooden sphere. On the ground floor, shrouded in smoke from sticks of incense, a complacent-looking Buddha sat in the lotus position. On the next floor, gold and black lacquered shrines held images of brightly-coloured demons and fierce warriors with bloody swords. Climbing even higher, I was struck by the sight of two statues: one with a white head on a black body and the other with a black head on a white body. The contrast was striking and their proportions frightening. My aunt told me the legend of the two friends, who, after a swim in a river that bore them into the heavens, had been in such a hurry to put on the heads that they had removed before their swim, that they donned the wrong ones.

The air was heavy with a strong smell of incense. I just wanted to escape. I didn't want to hear the legend my aunts were telling me—I was longing for fresh air and daylight.

During the day, the monks dedicated themselves to working in the fields and helping the poor; in the evening, during prayers and meditation, they took turns to watch over their deity in the shadows. Only their shaved heads gleamed in the lamplight. Except for my relative, the nun, all the monks were completely shaven. They never looked at me when I walked past them. Only the abbot, who looked like someone who liked a laugh, joked with me. He wore a little crown on his head like a saint—an honour he had been given for praying in a cell for three years. My aunts told me that they had lowered water and food to him through a hole in the cell roof. But, in contrast to the hermit-like life he had lived for three years, there was nothing ascetic about him.

After leaving the pagoda, we went into the monastery where words, gestures, objects and food were all kept to the bare minimum. The refectory was furnished simply with a table at the centre, two benches, and a statue of Buddha at the rear of the rectangular room. My aunts and I joined our relative to eat a typical lunch of vegetables and rice. I enjoyed my plate of herbs and sour-smelling fermented cereals so much that my relative asked if I would like to stay for a few days. I accepted—partly through greed and partly through timidity.

In the evening, when it was time to say goodbye to my aunts, I was already regretting my rash decision, but I could not back out after being so enthusiastic. I began to feel frightened of what I had seen in the pagoda and of the silence that descended on the monastery.

On the first day, the mournful tolling of a bell could be heard at regular intervals as it was the fifteenth day of the Seventh Moon, when the Buddhists celebrate the "orphan spirits"—spirits who had gone missing, drowned or died far from their families and who had no one to honour their memory. The tolling of the large bronze bell was supposed to comfort them.

They had given me a top-floor room overlooking the treeless courtyard, where the monks walked round a square fish pond murmuring prayers, their eyes downcast. In the moonlight, their shadows lengthened and distorted. The dark patches on the moon made it look as if it was grimacing at me. There was a constant knocking from the room next to mine: a figure in a grey tunic stayed awake all night praying, obsessively repeating a sacred phrase in a low voice that was supposed to break his contact with the outside world, and with his own body.

I could not sleep. The monks seemed like spirits, not living

212

beings. I could not get used to the sound of their prayers, their rituals. Every evening, the sound of my neighbour's prayers filled me with fear.

Religion was a strong influence on my education. I was taught how to pray from a very early age, and I prayed a great deal. First, I prayed to Buddha, then to God. Sometimes I prayed to both, when I wanted something badly.

At the orphanage in Acqui, the day started with a mass, as it had in the convent in Shanghai. I followed it in Latin with the libretto, but I knew it by heart. Often my knees were red from praying on my knees for so long. I studied the catechism and the encyclicals. I still remember the *Rerum novarum*. I liked sacred music and I sang Gregorian chants in my deep voice. Singing helped me concentrate, because my mind always wandered during the unsung mass. I did not even manage to concentrate during the consecration. When the priest rang the bell, the sound reminded me of the tinkling of the little bells round the necks of the homing pigeons at the mission in China that announced their punctual appearance every morning at eleven o'clock.

They flew extremely high, higher than the kites I flew in the fields that dived and soared in the air, waving their long, twisting tails decorated with little flags. When the grey pigeons arrived, their dark silhouettes stood out against the white clouds. No one knew where they came from or where they went, and no one knew what was in the messages they carried tied to their legs. But, as I watched them, I dreamed of far-off countries and imagined the landscape they saw from up there: the winding curves of the river, the geometrical rice fields reflecting everything around like big mirrors, the blue-roofed villages, and perhaps me too, sitting in my "heavenly well". I would drop whatever I was doing at that moment to watch their flight, following them with my gaze until the tinkling of their bells died away. In the evening, their return was announced by the same pleasant tinkling; they were tired and not flying in such tight formation, but they were heading back to where they had set off from at eleven o'clock that morning.

I watched this remarkable sight every morning. It never lasted as long as I would have liked and it was the signal for me to head off to collect eggs in the hen house. I ran as fast as I could, in case some over-zealous missionary nun beat me to it. I liked the hens, they were beautiful and no two looked alike. There was the common brown hen, the white hen, the dwarf hen, and so on. They behaved differently too. Some fluttered down awkwardly from their perch, squawking hysterically as I rushed in; others arrogantly strutted away as I carried out my chore; and some just sat impassively on their eggs, cocking their heads and looking at me.

My heart would skip a beat when I spotted the eggs in the straw: they could almost have been real treasures. The more I found, the happier I was. Sometimes I found two in the same place. I thought I might find a golden egg the next time, like the ones in the long fairy stories the tailor told me. Spurred on by this hope, I collected the still-warm eggs every morning. I put them in my apron and carried them carefully to the missionary nun, the way I did with the baby girls. These were real newborn babies who were abandoned outside the mission doors and who were my childhood playthings—real newborn baby girls, as real as the eggs in the hen house. Only the golden egg in the tailor's fairytale was imaginary.

Again, as communion followed consecration in the Catholic service at the orphanage in Acqui, my thoughts began to wander. I thought about how I helped the missionary nuns make the communion wafers in China. Using a little ladle, I would pour the pale batter into the middle of the piping hot bottom plate. The top plate was then closed so that it fitted tightly onto the bottom plate. Using a knife, the missionary nun scraped away the batter squeezed out by the pressure from the edges and gave it to me to eat, still warm. It was delicious. Remembering this, I felt ashamed. Believing I had committed a sin, I would recite a Pater and three Ave Marias as a penance, endeavouring to stop my thoughts wandering. These were the same prayers that the confessor usually gave me as a penance after hearing my sins, which were always the same: I had been disobedient; I had told lies; I had coveted my neighbour's things. Sometimes I confessed to swallowing the water while I was cleaning my teeth and doing the same with the communion. At other times, I even doubted the Holy Spirit. Then the confessor gave me more Ave Marias to recite.

The Catholic religion often frightened me. It seemed to me that God wanted to punish anyone who could not understand his dogmas—as if it was a sin. Buddhism, on the other hand, never mentioned retribution and was not intimidating; it seemed more lenient and more understanding. I was often afraid of the devil. In the illustrations in the catechism, the devil was black and hairy, with two horns, a tail, and a trident in his hand. He also looked like that in the pictures I was shown at the mission in Ningbo. They told me the devil is everywhere, particularly where it is dark. This may be why I still keep the lights on at night, to this day.

I spent a lot of time thinking about Jesus. He said we should turn the other cheek—he never talked about revenge. I recalled that he only lost his temper once, when he drove the pedlars and moneychangers out of the temple.

As a child, I preferred the Madonna. I had a picture book that showed various aspects of her: she was always holding a baby boy and was often in Chinese dress. By happy coincidence, the Chinese ideogram for the word "kindness" takes the form of a woman with a baby. I would have liked her to be my mother. She always followed Saint Joseph and did whatever he wanted, like a docile, patient Chinese wife.

But as the years went by, my imagination was fired more by Jesus. The missionaries had told me many things about him. I was told that he walked on water, brought the dead back to life, and healed the sick. I liked his sense of social justice. I thought it was a shame that Jesus had never been to China: he could have shared out the world's natural disasters more fairly, instead of making them all happen in China.

Most of the population in China was involved in agriculture, so natural disasters hit the whole country very hard. The defence systems in the countryside were very primitive and the peasants were powerless in the face of these forces of nature. Oxen still turned massive wooden wheels that brought up water from the river to the farmlands.

Centuries of famine might seem the stuff of legend to anyone who has never lived in the Chinese countryside. When talking among themselves, the farmers would always brag about the number of bowls of rice they had managed to eat. Rice was their only food and anyone who had managed to eat more than one bowl would beam at the recollection.

With the arrival of the monsoons and heavy rains, the people who worked the fields were no longer sure how many bowls of rice they would be able to eat and the ancestral spectre of starvation loomed over them once more. Then again, the elderly described invasions of locusts appearing like a massive, dark, low-flying cloud that completely devoured the crops in the fields and destroyed months of work.

As to monsoons, I myself witnessed them on many occasions as gales brought torrential rain and flooding. I remember the chaos it caused to people who were always so methodical: they swore, or gave orders, running to put their livestock under cover, or carrying bags over their shoulders trying to save what they could; others were paralysed, watching gloomily, mesmerised by the terrible devastation, thinking about all their hard work being undone so quickly. But the gales continued, the pitiless rain beat down, blown sideways by the wind. The rivers swelled as far as the eye could see, flooding the fields and sweeping away the boats. You saw roofless houses, flurries of flying objects, trees carried away with the carcasses of livestock. It was like the end of the world.

In the cities, though, life went on. The rickshaw drivers were the hardest hit. They prepared for the heavy rains by putting on a cape of woven coconut palm leaves and a three-cornered hat. Rain or shine, like draught horses, coughing, puffing, and spitting, they raced along in their straw sandals. They were almost all malnourished and had tuberculosis. While waiting for customers, they squatted by their vehicles, eating a handful of cold rice with dried fish that they kept in a mess tin.

I often travelled by rickshaw in torrential rain. Although protected by a waxed cloth that came right up to my face, splashes of water still got in through the gaps, and I ended up being soaking wet. Through the gaps, all I could see was the man's back, which seemed to grow longer as he pulled. I could feel the splashes hitting the waxed cloth as they were thrown up by his feet pounding through the puddles. After the war, almost all rickshaws were replaced by bicycle-rickshaws. These were supposed to make things easier for the driver who now only had to pedal, but the weight was actually doubled; the new rickshaws were built to carry two people instead of one.

As a child, none of these Chinese problems seemed of the slightest interest to Jesus!

7

Fate had decreed that I would end up in an orphanage for war orphans and that I would be released after about six years, because of the upper age limit of 20. This unexpected change of status felt like a rebirth, liberating me from the ever-present sense of guilt that had been deeply instilled in me by Catholicism. Spending such crucial years in that sad place had made me prone to melancholy.

My twentieth birthday marked an important turning point in my life. My guardian had found me a job and starting work changed my life; it made me grow up, gave me financial security and took me from the small town of Acqui to the city of Genoa. It also introduced me to the world of men.

Up until then, I had only known women: I lived in a world of women. I have known women of different races and social classes and I have noticed that women's relationships are the same everywhere: at times mysterious and contradictory, they exist on an emotional level and are founded on nuance, collaboration, confidences, and mutual aid in times of weakness such as illness, disappointment, love affairs, or failure.

Apart from my mother's brothers, who were my real uncles, the men I knew well were "First Uncle" and "Second Uncle"—Kon-Kon's sons—and the brothers of "First Aunt", "Second Aunt", and "Third Aunt", whom I called my aunts and uncles as a sign of respect. They were all professors. Everyone was named according to their place in the family hierarchy. The eldest son was called Number One, the second eldest Number Two, and so on. The same rule applied to uncles and aunts, so that the rank of every family member was clearly defined.

Although "First Uncle" was a professor, he did not teach and I thought this was odd. He came and went unexpectedly, without telling anyone in the family. He was often lost in thought, staring into the distance; but sometimes I managed to monopolise his time and we played at "telephoning" each other from different rooms, holding to our ears bowls tied together with string. When he left, he said he would "telephone" me. I knew this was unlikely, but I nodded, letting him know how happy I would be if he did. His return was always greeted by a great commotion and merry-making; the whole family celebrated. The large square table was taken out into the open courtyard, where it was laden with snacks and a great many guests were invited.

I started to wonder about "First Uncle's" mysterious trips so, one day, I asked him point blank why he was leaving and where he was going. He immediately replied that he was going to visit his wife, Winter Light, my "New First Aunt". I was not satisfied with just a name. I wanted to know more, so I kept asking questions. I asked him why he had not brought her to pay her respects to Kon-Kon during the summer holidays. He replied that the summer was too hot and the light of the rice fields too strong for her eyes. Then I said he should change her name: if she were called "Summer Light" she would probably not be so fussy. I even felt jealous of this stranger.

What is more, my "uncles" were always discussing things I did not understand. I heard them whispering about people hidden in the mountains, women and men of different social and cultural origins. Were they talking about dangerous gangs? A plot? They never talked about the Japanese, perhaps because they were retreating. This was already the period of Mao Zedong's gradual rise to power.

If I unexpectedly walked in on one of these conversations, my "uncles" immediately changed the subject. When once I stood to one side and listened, they seemed to be chatting amongst themselves; then everyone fell silent and "First Uncle" walked out, saying loudly: 'I'll go immediately.'

I heard other things, always keeping out of sight. I knew

they did not want me to find out about certain events, but I was desperate to discover more. That was how I learned about the execution of a woman who had been arrested for transporting weapons. It all seemed very exciting to me, particularly the thought that Kon-Kon's family had no idea that I knew one of their secrets.

"First Uncle" left on another occasion, telling me that he had to visit Winter Light in the north. I then began to think that Winter Light was a spirit. I had heard tales that the world of the spirits was in the northern darkness. There, in the gloom, the spirits were more energetic. I was inquisitive and confused. During the preparations for his departure, the family fell silent, obviously worried about his activities, as if they were involved too; they ignored me. When everything was ready, the maidservants, Marvellous Jade and Marvellous Perfume went down to the river and loaded "First Uncle's" cloth bags onto the boat that silently carried him away. I did not see him again on that visit. I was left looking at the empty river, imagining great adventures.

I wanted to know everything and I knew very little. These were years of tremendous upheaval, and I was just a little girl. By 1945, the Japanese had left. Mao Zedong's Red Army, formed in the south, swept through China. Many women fought alongside the men, sleeping in caves dug with their bare hands and obeying the hard-and-fast rules of guerrilla warfare they had been taught by the organisation. Although intellectuals, teachers and students were the most deeply involved—they stayed in hiding and moved around continually to escape the persecution of Generalissimo Chiang Kai-shek's Secret Police—close-knit rural communities also supported the struggle.

I kept asking what had happened to "First Uncle". Had he fled the Secret Police without involving the family? Perhaps he had entered Shanghai triumphantly with Winter Light. But who was Winter Light? The New China?

My revolutionary uncle was my favourite in my Chinese family. I thought he was the most interesting, even if I was not able to appreciate his good looks properly, being too young.

I was influenced by his aura of heroism, and he was happy to play with me—when he was not engaged in revolutionary activities. Since I was a little girl, I have always appreciated feminine qualities in a man, and the clearest memory I have of Chinese men is the femininity of certain of their physical characteristics—their soft skin, slight build and small hands. Also there is something feminine about their language, which is composed of nuances, hints and allusions. They have subtle minds and are taught to approach women with great discretion. They do not rush things and their capacity for waiting creates huge emotional tension in a woman. Love is not an end in itself, but the climax of a lengthy ritual.

In Italy, work propelled me into the world of men. Mixing with my colleagues, I understood how men can make a woman happy or unhappy; I realised how vital they are to a woman's emotional and social stability. My male colleagues seemed protective of me. They taught me to realise that beauty and charm are powerful weapons in a woman's armoury. From them, I learned the art of seduction.

Work also earned me money. I began buying pretty clothes to make the most of my appearance. I was no longer complimented solely on my hair, but on my skin that was delicate, clear and soft, like most Chinese, from being washed in rainwater from childhood. I had lost weight and I showed off my slenderness by wearing silk. I learned to flaunt my "difference" rather than hide it; I straightened my wavy hair so that it was as smooth as that of Chinese women and wore it so that it drew attention to my Oriental almond-shaped eyes.

Good luck and instinct kept me away from men who might have harmed me. I used little tricks to protect myself. My best defence was relating the sad details of my life; it entertained them and stopped them trying anything on.

Gradually, I learned to fly with my small wings and I left my cage. I began to make choices. I did not care for mediocrity. I chose the best for myself, wanting to better myself and improve my prospects.

I bore the scars of a lonely childhood, of being torn between two civilisations, of being "foreign" wherever I went. I wanted to rebuild my life, to find myself. I spent my holidays visiting other countries, cities, and museums to broaden my knowledge. I read books to assimilate new ideas and new words. I became my own mother and adviser. I only mixed with people who would make me a better person and when that was not possible, I dropped them and made do with my own company.

I learned all about love in those years too, but religious and moral taboos kept me from sexual experimentation. I dreamed of a Prince Charming. I dreamed of becoming Wise Orchid, the Governor's first wife. I dreamed of her palace with its oak and camphor trees. I wanted to be as beautiful and versatile as she, always there for her husband. The China I had left behind took its revenge; I also dreamed of being a gentle, subservient Chinese wife making my husband feel more important than anything else, of hiding my feelings, of being perfect.

I was cautious and sensible. I did not allow myself to act rashly, although I would have liked to. I did not want to have my heart broken like so many of my friends. I preferred boys who were almost maternal in their behaviour. I did not like boys who were only interested in making conquests, which I thought absurd. I did not like showy gestures—embraces, kisses, any kind of fuss. They seemed aggressive to me.

I let boys take the initiative; I wanted them to be attentive. I enjoyed the waiting game. I discovered I could recognise people from the way they walked, or by their smell; I sensed their mood by the way they cleared their throat or laid their keys on the table. I detected the many nuances in a single look.

I remember Beppe, who liked brushing my long hair; Mauro, who was worried about my health and often took me to restaurants to make sure I was eating properly. I loved the tales Sandro told me, especially the one about the kangaroo that could not hop because it was lame. I still have the teddy that Carlo gave me for my birthday.

The slow strokes of the brush on my hair, the tales, the concern that I was not eating enough, the toys: these were all feminine, maternal gestures, which was what, deep down, I was searching for.

8

In the summer of 1962, the era of the Beatles, I went to "swinging London". I immediately felt at home. London reminded me of Shanghai: the 1930's mansions along the Bund, the wide streets, the parks, the cosmopolitan atmosphere.

I went into the Ho-Ho Chinese restaurant in Mayfair in a bid to recapture my long-lost youth. I wanted see the colours of China again, re-experience the flavours, smells and sounds. I wanted to hear Chinese spoken, even if I did not understand it because the waiters were Cantonese. It still sounded nice, like background music. I wanted to use *kuaizi*, the chopsticks I had used when I was a little girl.

I watched the waiters carrying past me an array of dishes, each more tempting than the last. Unable to resist, I ordered a wide variety of courses. The waiters looked at me oddly, as if they would have liked to question what I was ordering, but I wanted to try everything from starters to desserts. I tasted every dish. How could the waiters understand? They were the dishes of my childhood. They jogged my memory and proved that I had not forgotten China after so many years. The smells, the flavours and the tea were still the same. I felt so happy. I took little tastes here and there—what did it matter if I did not finish the courses? What was important was to finish the bowl of rice, without leaving a single grain, as I had been taught when I was a child. What was important was that I could still use chopsticks and that I did not drop anything.

In China, I used to have little red coral chopsticks with silver tops linked by a chain. They were a birthday present from an *ayi*, an aunt. They formed an attractive contrast against the ebony table inlaid with mother-of-pearl. The high-backed chair also had mother-of-pearl panels and Amah would put a cushion on the seat to make me higher.

Breakfast was a bowl of *congee*, rice porridge, with different chopped side dishes. For lunch, everything was cooked outdoors. Every day, the menu was different—Chinese cooking is so varied. At midday, on the table there was always a meat dish, a fish dish, a poultry dish and vegetables or *tofu*, served with steamed rice.

For *dim sum* snacks, I ate *paotze* and *chaotze*, and other dumplings stuffed with minced pork and vegetables or shrimps.

Dinner was the biggest meal. We often ate at a round table, which solved the problem of precedence in the interests of equality and made it possible to reach all the courses easily. Chinese cooking is a true art that obeys the rules of harmony and balance. A crispy or dry dish should be accompanied by one in a sauce, a sour dish by a sweet one, while a spicy dish acts as a foil for one with a delicate flavour. There is no real main dish, but a steady succession of different courses with four key characteristics: colour, aroma, flavour and composition. The men begin dinner by drinking rice wine, which they continue to drink throughout the meal, while the women sip jasmine tea, never neglecting the duties of hospitality. My seat was indicated by my red coral chopsticks, which I took with me when I travelled. I usually sat next to an *ayi*.

On important occasions, like New Year or other festivals, there were so many courses that I did not taste them all. The servants took away the barely touched dishes of one course and brought us 12 more steaming dishes, fresh from the wok. The lady of the house, out of politeness, would start the dinner by picking out the most tempting piece from each course with her own chopsticks and delicately placing it in the guest of honour's bowl. Dinner was eaten fairly quickly: we never waited between courses. Everyone quickly took what they liked best with their chopsticks. As a result, dinner was a very sociable occasion. The same thing happens in Chinese restaurants as well, where diners always order together. Often, my *ayi* would finish lunch with a game of *ma-jong*, flaunting their showy rings and long nails painted red, European style.

But while we enjoyed an endless succession of courses on our table, most of the population were starving to death. The peasants and poor people of the cities and countryside had to make do with a handful of rice with dried fish or vegetables. I was not really aware of the contrast, nor did I attach much importance to it, because I was used to the situation. I saw hungry people in the city streets, in the villages and in the French mission, where I enjoyed a privileged position as a paying guest.

That particular London restaurant was very busy. I noticed a group of young men of Chinese extraction with several young blonde women. They seemed to be having fun. I sensed they were looking at me—the Chinese always look at everyone and everything. Suddenly, one of the women in the group stood up and came over to my table. She told me her Chinese friends wanted to know what was my nationality. One of them said I was French, another could not make up his mind, and another was amazed to see me use chopsticks like them. I told her that I had always used chopsticks because my mother was Chinese and I had been born in Shanghai. Before I could continue, the young woman ran back to confer with the others and I heard a chorus of enthusiasm. The Chinese boys all stood up and invited me to join them. That group became an integral part of my life for many years to come. There were Agnes and Billings, Duncan, Jerry, Karl, and Mark. New girls appeared on the scene, but they were always blonde. During the time I spent in London, Mark was my constant companion. He was teased about it but he did not react, although he did blush. He was a man of few words and long silences, saying only: 'It's time to get ready,' or, 'It's late.' He always set the pace for me.

I had never met any Chinese boys before. When I went back

to Italy, Mark said goodbye as usual. He gave me his hand. He had Chinese hands: gentle, slender, firm hands with long fingers, the hands of a future surgeon. After I went back to Italy, he continued to write to me. He was my link with the group. One day he sent me a plane ticket because the group wanted me to spend Christmas with them. They lived in Chelsea, although Agnes and Billings lived in Belgravia. For two years I shuttled back and forth between London and Genoa. The boys graduated and started their own careers.

9

One evening, Marquis Vincenzo Invrea invited me to dinner at the home of one of his friends who had an apartment in the 15th-century Palazzo Negrone, in the Piazza Fontane Marose. The apartment was at the rear of the building, hidden behind the tops of trees that grew in the garden of that building and that of the Palazzo Pallavicini next door. Someone said the apartment building, with its arched windows and tiny panes of glass, had once been a cloister. It was hard to imagine there could be such a haven of greenery and peace so near to the square.

That evening, I wore an old rose silk suit, high heels and a pair of Mitsuko drop earrings. The men were elegant and courteous and gazed at me with interest; so did the women, one slightly suspiciously. I felt flattered. Being watched like that made me feel confident, even though there was no one of particular interest to me. I looked around, delighted by the beauty of the apartment, by its sophisticated interior design, red floor and subtle lighting.

I remember a fireplace in the middle of the room and, at the back, a library with a velvet divan. The bed was in a mirrored alcove. White roses cascaded through a window into the apartment. There was something to discover in every corner, even if it was only a clever lighting effect. I was lost in admiration and thought I could be happy if I had an apartment like it.

An elegant English gentleman walked over, handed me a glass of champagne and asked: 'Is the apartment to your liking?' I found out that he was the owner of the house and he invited me back many times after that.

It is the evening of 1st December, my wedding day. There are about 200 guests. The wedding reception is being held in the same building on Piazza Fontane Marose where my husband has his apartment. The reception rooms, lent for the occasion by the Marquis Negrone, are reached by a sweeping central staircase that leads up from the hall, where there is a black 18th-century sedan chair.

The guests walk from room to room admiring the frescoes on the cap vaults or the flower arrangements of two thousand white carnations from San Remo. Their perfume mingles with the fragrance of the gardenias scattered over the tables. For the occasion, 18th-century Genoese furniture has been arranged along the walls, which are adorned with antique tapestries and large gilded mirrors.

The master of ceremonies is Marquis Invrea, who was also one of our witnesses at the religious ceremony, which took place in the morning behind the sacristy of the Chiesa della Maddalena, in Vicolo della Maddalena, because my husband is Anglican and I am Catholic.

I cannot wait for dinner to be served, so that I can sit down. I have been standing on high heels all day and I am tired, but the cocktail reception seems to go on forever. My husband warned me that the English are never in a hurry to eat and there are a great many of them at the reception. While waiting, I mingle with our guests at his side, many of whom I have met only once; but I remember everyone's name and the gift each gave us. They are surprised and congratulate me.

Then the guests merge into a cheerful blur. I feel bewildered because the reception rooms of the apartment building have reminded me of the hall where, as a child, I celebrated New Year in Ningbo.

There is no set date for the Chinese New Year. Being linked to the lunar cycle, it varies from year to year, taking place around the middle of January or towards the end of February; it falls between two dates separated by about two months.

Traditionally, the years are paired with twelve animals and the cycle is naturally repeated every twelve years. Each animal has characteristics popularly attributed to people born under its influence, characteristics that are modified in part by the influence of the birth month.

There are long-drawn-out, brightly-coloured, noisy celebrations to welcome in the New Year. On New Year's Eve, the streets are full of revellers wearing their showiest clothes and children are dressed in ancient Chinese costumes with a mandarin's skullcap and padded silk tunic; the little girls tie red ribbons in their plaits as a symbol of fertility.

Paper lanterns bearing a large sign—a symbol of good fortune—are hung outside shops, together with silk banners printed with messages that wish everyone well. Firecrackers are detonated to drive away bad spirits and fireworks explode with loud bangs in the sky, creating winged dragons and other marvellous, whimsical shapes.

On this day in Ningbo,I can still remember a long line of men scurrying along under a large piece of canvas that represented a dragon, but actually looked more like a prehistoric millipede. The city echoed with music and noise. The soothsayers made a killing telling fortunes. The cooks in the booths and shops prepared mountains of delicacies. They made very long noodles on that day to wish long life to their customers, who ate them swiftly, sucking loudly to show their enjoyment. It always amazed me how the cooks managed to produce so many noodles with their bare hands, repeatedly dividing a ball of dough in half, then stretching it with an accordion-like movement to turn it into a many-stranded skein of dough. It looked more like juggling than cooking.

People were eating everywhere in the streets, where pedlars prepared steaming soups in portable ovens, which even the poor people who could not go into restaurants, were able to enjoy. Everything smelled so tempting that I kept tugging Amah's hand to make her stop so that I could try this or that.

The wealthy gave endless parties and even the poor made merry. Everyone wanted to celebrate, hoping for better times, whatever their social situation. The prevailing mood was one of festive optimism, fertile soil for cultivating everyone's hopes for the new year. The entire city stayed in party dress for a whole week. In well-to-do families, a number of round tables were laid with the best hand-painted china; relatives and friends were invited to eat, drink and be merry, transforming the New Year dinner into a sumptuous banquet with at least thirty-two courses. Exchanging presents was widespread and people always gave each other coins wrapped in red paper, folded like a greeting card. The coins had a square hole in the centre, a symbol of integrity, signifying that the recipient's character was "square" inside and "round" outside. I would bow three times to all my uncles and aunts and receive a great many little red packets in exchange. The guests finished dinner with the inevitable game of *ma-jong*, but by this time I would be half-asleep, dazed by the sights and sounds of so much revelry.

Marriage was my fourth cage. My husband immediately began to help me finish my apprenticeship—I was completely inexperienced. I did not know how to run a house because I had never lived in a real family. I soon understood that being young and beautiful was not enough to be a good wife. You also had to be a cook, a housekeeper, a dressmaker and a nurse.

I began doing household chores. The intricately engraved silverware had to be polished, the overflowing cupboards tidied, the cocktail-parties organised, and the guests entertained—and of course there was the cooking.

My first lunch was a disaster. All my husband said was, 'The cheese was good'. He read a book by P. G. Wodehouse all afternoon. The second lunch was even worse, because the fish was half cooked, though one guest said my jasmine coffee was excellent. My husband made no comment. Again he read Wodehouse for the rest of the day

So I decided to buy an Italian cookbook called *The Silver Spoon*—but I had limited success. After various endeavours, I asked Mina, my husband's elderly governess, to make some dishes before she left. I did not realise that my husband was not accustomed to reheated food.

After this, he decided to teach me to cook. I was upset by his impatience, which made me more afraid of making mistakes. I realised he was scrutinising everything I did: how I peeled an apple; how much salt I put in the food; how I held the cutlery; how I pronounced a certain word in English. Although he did not know it, I had nicknamed him Professor Higgins, after the character in Shaw's *Pygmalion*.

As if all that was not enough, I was forced to learn to swim because we went to Paraggi every week-end, and then to ski as in winter we went to the Sestrière.

As a child, I had not learned anything about all this—the Chinese culture does not teach girls and women about these things. It was an ordeal that gradually sapped my morale. When I lost my temper, I would call my husband a "colonialist", because I was sure his behaviour was the result of the years he had spent as an officer in India.

I felt oppressed by these continual daily lessons that eventually stopped me from relaxing at all in my new cage. I realised that a husband, house and social status could easily be undermined by a poorly prepared meal, a crookedly sewn button on a cuff, or a light that had not been switched on. I realised that a couple's stability is extremely fragile, not only when there is a difference in age, experience, and culture, but also because we are all different and it is difficult to manoeuvre in a space as small as a marriage.

All it took was a slight lapse of concentration to cause a misunderstanding and create a rift. In the end, I wanted him to be at work, so I could make mistakes without him spying on me and making remarks about my actions.

When he was not there, as if to spite him, I would take out my chopsticks and eat as I had done when I was a child; I would also drink tea with my meal, Chinese-style. I spent hours at the window gazing at the roofs and the trees over the roofs. I felt like a little girl again, in Kon-Kon's house.

Down below, in front of the low quadrangular old house, I remember a wide, enclosed, rectangular space formed of courtyards, and surrounded by low boundary walls. This low wall stopped anyone approaching the door in a straight line and protected the house from evil spirits that, according to popular belief, only move in straight lines and are unable to follow a curve. In the middle of the central courtyard was a square pool filled with goldfish with bulging eyes. A weeping willow trailed its branches in a brook that slowly trickled along one side. It was like a Chinese scroll painted on silk or rice paper.

I stood there for a long time, gazing at the boundless rice fields on the far side of the river. It was like looking at a bright sea of light. A Chinese proverb says: "Faced with the immensity of the sea we forget our own mother." Enveloped in an immense, comforting silence, the rice fields filled my mind with images and colours, and I immersed myself in their brilliance.

A temple was silhouetted against the light on the horizon near the outline of a colourless pagoda. The herons' flight and the beating of the wild ducks' wings occasionally interrupted this tranquil silence, which allowed me to gaze without a thought in my mind.

The dark shapes of peasants hurrying between the rice fields rippled by the occasional breeze, tempered the white light with their black figures. A branch of the tall willow trailed in the clear water of the river. Another branch grazed the pointed roof, brushing against the window out of which I was leaning; its shadow caressed me slowly, like a fan.

A pair of mandarin ducks cut across the brook, swimming close and perfectly parallel, as if propelled by a single force towards a single destination: if one of them were to die, the other would too, of a broken heart. They are the symbol of everlasting love.

The crystals of the wind-chimes, the "little Chinese bells", began to tinkle more insistently. The breeze stiffened, causing swollen, pearly clouds to scud across the sky, heralding an August storm. Suddenly dust and bits of straw rose in the air, forming spiral vortexes that interrupted my peaceful thoughts. I closed the window and turned my back on nature.

The window continued to be important to me in my first years of marriage in Genoa. In the early years of living with my husband, tea seemed to be all we had in common. We both liked sipping it slowly, while sitting down. When I was alone in the house, though, I felt free to go over to the window and chat, like an old woman, to one of our neighbours, Bruno, who shared the same delightful garden. Bruno had come back from a business trip to Vienna and was living with a friend in the same apartment block as me. He was a sophisticated man about town who taught me about style. He even helped me choose what to wear for various occasions, how to prepare elaborate sandwiches and dress the table with elegant ornaments. I was a quick learner and made a great deal of progress, acquiring a new confidence.

But I continued to feel trapped in my cage, struggling with domestic problems, while my husband spent those first three years avoiding the same problems by taking refuge in books. Our first years of marriage were the Wodehouse years—he would only read books by that author, and he had them all, in first editions. Then came the Evelyn Waugh years, followed by the Aldous Huxley years, always in the first editions he collected. All he did was read, while I tried to solve thousands of problems.

But there were also distractions, and most importantly, there was the sea. Every now and then, we went to the Yacht Club. I spent many hours on the sailing boat of a couple of friends, on short cruises along the two Ligurian coasts. This gave me a chance to experience the thrills of sailing and the skill needed to ensure a safe, peaceful journey. But I am not a good sailor and I preferred the cruises along the Amalfi coast, or other longer cruises to the Balearic islands, along the Spanish coast or in Corsica on much smaller boats. The long silences and endless hours that slipped by when sailing reminded me of similar silences and long hours spent travelling from one place to another in China, when I was a child. You cannot rush things in China, or on a sailing boat.

Given that there was almost no rail transport and that the

streets were little more than mule drivers' tracks, impassable when flooded, water was the element that dictated the pace of life in cities, towns and villages in China. It has been said that there is a greater variety of boats in China than in any other country in the world. The Chinese are an "amphibian" nation; millions of Chinese people live on boats, not all of them seaworthy or capable of dealing with river currents. They are true floating houses, lashed to one another like large islands that often form an entire neighbourhood. As in all neighbourhoods, every family wants to excel at something. So there were brightly coloured masses of flowers in many areas of this shaky mass of boats, where the owner had transformed his deck into a gaily-coloured garden of chrysanthemums or dahlias, depending on the season. And there is always someone who wants to keep up with the neighbours, so the islands of flowers spread.

I remember boats shaped like birds in gaudy colours, others shaped like fish, and yet more decorated with cheerful lanterns that were lit for festivals at nightfall, so that their gentle rocking added to the reflections in the constantly moving waters of the port.

For festivals and celebrations, I remember boats depicting dragons with nostrils spouting flames and two red tongues protruding from their mouths.

Some boats were escorted by smaller boats with armed troops on board because they were carrying cargoes of precious minerals or valuable silks. Others were extremely fragile, like shells, and were used for fishing with cormorants—the birds repeatedly dived into the water, surfacing with a fish in their beak that they could not swallow because the fisherman had placed a tight ring around their necks. Many boats were used as gaming houses or restaurants. There was something to suit every taste and pocket.

As a child I was desperate to venture onto one of those amphibious restaurants, just for the fun of eating on a boat, but Amah was too much of a landlubber to go on board. With her painful, bandaged feet, she was terrified of taking a boat trip, even one that was necessary.

I do not remember ever seeing two boats the same during my childhood. There were outboard and inboard motorboats, boats with oars, or one, two or three sails; boats that glided silently on the water propelled by long poles manoeuvred laboriously by the boatmen, who walked from prow to stern, then back again, lazily dragging the pole in the water and making the most of the time it took to catch their breath. But the most vivid images of my Chinese childhood are linked to the memory of the teeming masses who made the boats their home: families who had been afloat for many generations and who rarely stepped onto dry land. Many of them live and die on their boats; for them, the land is too firm.

10

Having moved to Milan from Genoa because of my husband's job, I decided to work in the fashion industry.

It may have been inevitable that the "silk route" would lead me to fashion. From childhood, my skin had smelled of silk. My eiderdowns, shoes, and clothes were all made of silk. I played with the silk reels hidden in Amah's trunk. I even liked the stories that the tailor told me.

As a child, I was more interested in the tailor than in the clothes he made me: he told me all kinds of tales to make me stand still while he was taking my measurements or during a fitting. He was a Chinese tailor who had been summoned to the mission by Sister Pauline, who had decided not to dress me in Chinese style like the other girls. She had given him a French fashion magazine from which to copy styles, so that the tailor could make me look more European.

He came every season. He could not read the instructions in French, but then he could not read his own language either. He had to make the clothes just from looking at them, but he was very good at reconstructing fashions so far-removed from his own culture. Sister Pauline said he was a first-class copier, but I am sure she would have preferred a French tailor, if she could have found one.

Rather than sitting on a chair to sew, the tailor sat on the table with his feet on a bench. His tape measure hung round his neck and his spectacles were perched on the tip of his nose and held in place by a silk cord tied round his head. His swollen lower lip was always wet: he kept moistening his finger on it to dampen the thread before threading the needle—in

China, they use such short needlefuls!

Pairs of scissors, reels of thread, pincushions and scraps of fabric were scattered everywhere in a creative chaos that was a complete change for what was usually such a neat room.

I would rush to help him find the things he continually mislaid, so that he would not break off from telling me a story to which I was listening with bated breath. His slow, miraculous tales lasted for hours. I would get pins and needles in my legs because of sitting still for too long on the stool at his feet. He always wore black cloth slippers with light-coloured soles that he made himself from scraps of fabric.

He had a gift for suspense. He told me stories in instalments, always stopping at the most exciting or most beautiful point. I had to give him some coins to make him continue for a little longer. He would accept them after looking around suspiciously and saying, 'Don't tell a soul.'

I made him tell me the most entertaining stories over and over again. Like most children, I became annoyed when I realised he was changing details because he did not remember them and was making them up. I corrected these inaccuracies: only the first version seemed true to me, and I liked to think that his stories were true.

As well as fairy tales, the tailor also told me about popular beliefs relating to clothes, which were just as fascinating and mysterious as his tales. The Chinese believe that clothes have a profound influence on the wearer. A garment transforms the soul, inspiring pleasure, pride or satisfaction. When a Chinese girl became engaged, the clothes in her trousseau had to be made and embroidered by young, healthy, happy women, so that their hands would transmit eternal youth and longevity to the wearer of the garments.

Burial clothes also have traditions that apply to both women and men. They are made when a person reaches adulthood and are kept lovingly as a talisman throughout their life. Grave clothes are actually regarded as a symbol of longevity and are worn on birthdays and festivals.

The French-style clothes that I was given at the mission by frivolous Sister Pauline, all looked the same. The only small variations were in the smock-stitch embroidery and the colour of the fabric. They always had a small scalloped collar, a fitted bodice and a full skirt tied with a bow at the back. I was ashamed of my skinny legs as I thought they made me look like a little heron. I preferred trousers. Also Amah preferred me in Chinese dress; like Sister Pauline, she was a jingoist.

So the "silk route" brought me to fashion. At the time, there was only haute couture, so I arrived at the Milan couturier's workroom trying to look as Chinese as possible. The models were very tall compared to me. I had to compete with them and make up for my lack of inches by being different. So I endeavoured to look more Oriental, more like Hiroko, the famous Japanese model who worked for Pierre Cardin. I styled my hair like hers, straightening it and giving myself a square fringe, which was how I had worn my hair when I was a little girl.

The reaction of the couturiers, as I had hoped, was very positive: they told me that I looked like Hiroko and asked me to model for them. I liked the work: I was well paid and I did not have to be away from my home in Milan very often. Being much smaller than the other models, the couturiers decided that I should model on my own. Then they discovered I was photogenic, so I also modelled clothes for fashion photographs. The customers reacted favourably because they were at last seeing a model who was the same height as they were.

In the fashion house, standing in front of the mirror for fittings while the *première* carried out alterations, I learned to identify what was wrong not only with the clothes, but also what was wrong with me. This taught me to camouflage my bad points and emphasise my good ones.

The first fashion show was at the Palazzo Pitti. I still have magazine cuttings with the photographs of me alone on the dais in the White Room. In Rome, the catwalk parades of the leading designers were held at the Hotel Excelsior.

During those years, I found that I enjoyed living in Milan. Milan had welcomed me without a hint of rejection. I lived in the city centre and often took the long way home so that I could walk along the streets lined with Patrician houses and aristocratic mansions. Behind the main gates lay dressed stone courtyards with delightful gardens.

When I hurried past, I could tell they were there by the perfume of the lime trees, horse chestnuts or magnolias (depending on the season), or by the fresh smell of recently watered gardens. The courtyards and gardens are Milan's "heavenly wells", where a lucky few lead hidden lives.

There is no river in Milan, which was a disappointment as I was used to rivers in Kong-qiao, Ningbo and Shanghai. However, the few remaining canals resembled the manmade Chinese waterways linking the town centres with the rivers, and irrigating the surrounding farmland where rice was grown. I discovered that the canals headed towards the Ticino river and that there were rice fields a couple of miles from the last few houses in Milan. I had not imagined that I would end up so close to a familiar landscape! And when the rice fields were next to farmhouses, geese and ducks would venture out from the farmyard.

The rice fields continued towards the Ticino along straight roads, then, further ahead, after a few sharp bends, they gave way unexpectedly to fields of maize. After a few small, built-up areas, there was a section of dense poplar groves. There, you could already sense the presence of the Ticino river. But you had to enter the woods, taking paths known only to fishermen and farmers, to find the river bank where the croaking of the frogs stopped dead at the slightest noise.

The river looked different in every season. The winter floods altered the riverbed, creating new islets and fords. The river flowed along the deserted shore past sandy coves, where the water slowed down as if to rest.

Often the coves were hidden by tree trunks uprooted during the floods or boughs broken off by the currents. These were the white heron's fishing grounds. It would arrive swiftly, its quiet flight punctuated by the beating of large wings, its neck and beak outstretched, its long legs trailing behind to act as a counterweight. After landing, it would take three or four running steps along the shore, using its wings to slow it down, before folding them. It would wade warily into the shallow water on its long spindly legs, pecking unexpectedly at the many fish swimming among the submerged twigs. It would take fright and fly off at the slightest noise or movement.

The white heron also belonged to my childhood landscapes, like the dragonflies dancing along the river.

It was about this time that Italian prêt-à-porter appeared on the scene. Many Italian firms began to establish business relations with the foreign market. I went to see one of the leading prêt-à-porter companies on the basis of my previous experience and my knowledge of English and French, and was given the job of liaising with foreign customers and with the press.

My first business trip took me to Japan, which was very exciting for me, but I had to prepare myself psychologically. Although many years had passed since I was a child and a teenager in China, I still had bad memories of the Japanese.

All kinds of terrible stories were told about the Japanese soldiers and their cruelty. People talked as if the Japanese had always been at war with the Chinese. This gave rise to mass hysteria, which frightened me. I saw the soldiers everywhere. They always went around in small groups: you could hear them coming from a distance by the noise of their shiny hobnail boots as they marched. They raised their voices when they spoke. People ran away. They sat at junctions near the trestles of barbed wire blocking the streets, checking that everyone had been vaccinated.

There was always some epidemic doing the rounds and my arm was often swollen and painful because of all the vaccinations I had been given. I wore a sanitary gauze mask over my mouth. The city was pervaded by a strong medicinal smell. Even our bodies smelled of disinfectant.

The Japanese rationed food and inspected everything, checking people as if the enemy was hiding everywhere. Once they even came to the mission. They counted all the girls, but the nuns cleverly moved them from one part of the building to another, so that it seemed as though the mission had twice the number of residents to feed. This dangerous stratagem enabled them to obtain extra rations. To avoid any trouble, I, on the other hand, had wisely been hidden among the eiderdowns in a cupboard in the corridor. I heard the soldiers walking past: I was sweating the way I did when I was suffering from malaria, because I was afraid and the eiderdowns were so warm.

If I had to go through the barbed-wire roadblocks and the checkpoints, I had learned to take certain precautions. With my heart racing, I would lower my oiled paper parasol over my face and cover my "different" nose with a fan.

It was a frightening time for everyone. The sirens often wailed. At night, we had to run to the shelters. I would tie my shoelaces with a double knot so that they did not come undone as I ran.

I remember the nightmarish atmosphere rather than specific political and military events. I do remember one incident, though. Sometimes, in the darkest moments, someone offers a small ray of hope. All it takes is a smile or a gesture to make everything seem more bearable. The person who offered me this ray of hope was actually a Japanese officer. Many people spoke well of him, marvelling that a Japanese man could be so kind. He seemed to want to cancel out, by his own behaviour, the atrocities carried out by the soldiers against the Chinese population. He had almost become a legend. I heard some wonderful stories about him, some of which might have been exaggerated, others probably invented. I did meet him, although I do not remember the circumstances clearly. He smiled at me with a mouth full of gold teeth and looked me straight in the eye. He suddenly asked what my name was, as if he suspected something. I did not know whether to reply or not. I thought I would give myself away by telling him my name.

So I lowered my eyes and saw the shiny buffalo leather boots that all the Japanese soldiers wore. I was very frightened; I stood there, rooted to the spot, mesmerised by those boots, too afraid to raise my head. The officer came closer—and this was the real surprise—patted my head. This gesture gave me renewed strength and courage, and I ran away, embarrassed but no longer terrified.

The missionary nuns to whom I told the incident, reassured me: the officer was a good man and the exception that proved the rule. So I plucked up my courage and began going to the officers' mess to ask for extra rations of sugar, as the nuns had suggested, thinking I was the best person for the job. The officer wore a square signet ring on his finger. He pressed it onto the red ink pad and stamped the mission's ration card to show he had no objection. Then he smiled at me with his gold-filled mouth, as if to say: 'There, I hope you're happy now.'

One day he disappeared. People said he had been transferred because he was too lenient. A great many stories continued to circulate about him and his unexpected departure for quite some time.

Somewhat comforted by this memory, I prepared for my first trip to Japan. Shortly after we took off for Tokyo, the hostess reappeared in an elegant kimono and began handing out hot, moist towels to the passengers to freshen up. Then they served green tea and an array of chopped foods in lacquered boxes: it looked like a colourful graphic design.

I began to make peace with my memories. The Japanese passengers did not have the cruel look of the Japanese men I remembered. Many were with families and children. They all seemed happy, to judge from the smiles around me. I noticed that many of them had gold teeth, like the officer.

The children became restless and began running up and down the aisle of the aeroplane. A little girl in a kimono crawled towards me along the corridor on all fours. Seeing her gave me a start. I thought it was Momoko, the girl I had played with when I was six.

Momoko, Peach Blossom, was the daughter of a Japanese officer occupying Ningbo. I cannot remember how we met.

She did not speak Chinese and I did not speak her language. We would play among the bombed-out ruins. She wore a kimono, and I was dressed in a floral padded jacket.

From a distance, we looked very similar; we both had the square fringe that my Amah gave me to make me look more Chinese. We were the same height, and we may have been the same age. Although we did not share a language, we communicated partly with gestures, partly with the understanding that children always have.

One day, Momoko decided to show me her toys and beckoned me to follow her. Of the two of us, she was the "leader", a worthy daughter of a Japanese army officer.

Oblivious to any possible danger, I followed her. My features had not yet become too European in appearance, because the shape of my nose was not obvious.

We tiptoed across the courtyard of the barracks and, when we came to the open door, Momoko signalled that I should follow her on all fours past the furniture and high writing desk where her father was presiding over an officers' meeting. They were talking so loudly in that incomprehensible language that I thought they were arguing. Because of the noise, we managed to reach her bedroom unnoticed. Momoko had the confidence of someone who regularly slipped out to do what she wanted, despite being watched.

Her room was full of dolls, celluloid toys and other strange objects—all made in Japan. The dolls looked like her and wore exactly the same clothes. To my great surprise, she gave me one of them; I was very happy at this token of friendship, but perplexed because I did not know how I could take the doll back with me under her father's nose. Momoko, perhaps sensing my hesitation, immediately reclaimed the doll. I was disappointed. I thought that she might only have wanted to show it to me and had not had the slightest intention of giving it to me. Suddenly, still holding the doll, she motioned to me to follow her. I crawled after her silently, but she was moving so fast that the doll's head banged her father's desk. The officer jumped up, muttering something.

Terrified, I gazed at his buffalo leather boots with spurs. I stayed there, my head bowed, not daring to raise my eyes and crouching even lower, in an attempt to hide. Momoko jumped up and rattled off something to her father. The officer smiled and gestured to me to get up. From Momoko's gestures, it seemed she was trying to cajole her father into letting us play outside for a little while longer; and she succeeded.

When we were outside, where we usually played, she gave the doll back to me. I was very pleased with this gift, which I had begun to think had just been a figment of my imagination. Making signs and speaking her language, Momoko arranged to meet me the next day, in the same place, to play among the bombed ruins. But Momoko did not show up then or on any of the following days. All I had left was the doll that was so like her: I named it Momoko, after her.

After landing in Tokyo, we travelled to Osaka on the monorail. The president of the company with whom we were doing business, was polite but very formal. Sipping seaweed tea during a break in the meeting, he asked me if I was married. I replied that I was and that I had a little girl. He looked at me with a mixture of amazement and disapproval, then asked me why I had not remained with my family in Milan. I immediately replied: 'Because I wanted to visit Japan.' He did not say anything, but his silence exuded disapproval; the Japanese culture believes that a woman should be a wife and mother. At dinner in his house that evening, his wife and three daughters knelt in a corner on their own. They only came over to the table to serve us or to prepare some speciality, such as *shabu shabu* and *sukiyaki*. One of his daughters poured us tea or sake; but they never ate with us.

That trip to Japan was the first business trip of many. I particularly remember one evening when we were having dinner in New York a few tables from Pierre Cardin and some of his guests. At a certain point, I realised that Cardin was staring intently at me and sharing his curiosity with a petite Japanese woman at his table. After a few minutes, the woman stood up and walked over. 'Excuse me,' she said, 'Monsieur

Cardin is fascinated by your face. I have wagered with him that you have Asian blood. Am I right?' I told her I was half-Chinese. Satisfied, she returned to her table to report back: wide smiles and gestures were exchanged from a distance and the two tables toasted each other.

That incident gave me food for thought. In New York, I had been recognised as an Asian by a Japanese woman. I was still dogged by my "difference", my duality; but the wounds had healed. I no longer felt foreign: I felt instead that, wherever I was, I would always find something that would strike a chord in me.

I also met Irving Penn in New York. I went there with an Italian team for a photographic session. I was struck by the famous fashion photographer's contented air and his unhurried demeanour, which was very Asian. He seemed amused to find himself among rowdy, chattering Italians, who were never ready until the last minute.

He heard me casually say the word "*cucito*" (needlework) two or three times and he immediately adopted it for the rest of the day. "*Cucito*", "*cucito*", he kept repeating, enjoying the sound of the word that perhaps he thought comical or unusual. The next day at work, we walked into his huge study. As soon as he saw me, he smiled and greeted me with the words: 'Good morning, Bamboo. No *cucito* today?'

"Bamboo" is the name I decided to call myself in a fit of self-confidence. It came from an attempt to write down my thoughts in poetry. I compared my ability to react to hardship with the flexibility of the bamboo canes that can withstand strong gusts of wind. Since then, I have called myself Bamboo, in line with the Chinese tradition that allows someone to change their name if their circumstances change.

11

My daughter Nicole was born in Milan. I noticed she was smaller than the other babies in their chromium-plated cots, who reminded me of the baby girls I used to find by the front gate of the mission in Ningbo.

The cots in the mission's crèche were always full of screaming, newborn girls. They all looked the same, but they were always different. Almost as many died as were collected. The latest arrival wore the same clothes as the dead babies, and I had the impression that part of them lived on in this way.

Of course, I knew very well that they had died. I saw them carried away in rough little wooden boxes, as nameless as when they arrived. I was told they had died due to a shortage of sugar caused by the war.

They probably died because of the bitterly cold winter nights, because of the dysentery in summer or because of malnutrition during the hours they were left abandoned. In the morning, as soon as I found a baby, I put it in my apron, carried it to the crèche, then ran to the shop to buy some life-saving sugar with my *yuan*, coins from Mu-Mu or my "aunts and uncles" that I had saved up. I was always hoping to save the latest foundling. With my childish logic, I thought she was more likely to survive than the others because she was the most recent, so I raced to the shop near the Church of the Jesuit Fathers.

It was run by a woman, known as the "madwoman", who was in and out of the lunatic asylum. She sold sweets in all shapes and colours as well as the precious brown sugar. The merchandise was kept in front of the shop in glass jars lined up on a wooden counter, higher than me.

One morning, after racing enthusiastically to the shop, I put my hands on one end of the shelf and leaned there for a second to catch my breath. My weight caused it to tip over, sending the display jars flying. The world came crashing down around my ears along with the jars and sweets. Hearing the din, the woman poked her head out of the little window like an old turtle emerging from its shell. She cursed and screamed insults at me, contemptuously calling me a "foreigner". At the top of her voice, she demanded compensation for her spoiled goods and the smashed jars. At her shouts, all the other shopkeepers came out of their shops, looking at me in disapproval and adding other insults and tirades.

I was off like a shot, terrified by the incident, with the "turtle" in hot pursuit until she grew tired and stopped chasing me. On reaching the mission, still beside myself with fear, I took refuge in my bed, pulling the tulle mosquito nets around me to screen me from the menacing world outside. I stayed there so long that I fell asleep. Mu-Mu, Amah, and everyone were looking for me while news of what had happened quickly did the rounds.

I was found by Amah, who used to get my bed ready every evening, driving away the mosquitoes on the mosquito net with an enormous bamboo and dried lotus leaf fan. She knew what had happened that morning and, laughing affectionately, reassured me that the woman was completely mad.

The mission paid for the damage but, after that incident, I had to go to another sweet shop. It was further away and I had to run faster. I was always afraid that it would be my fault if the latest baby died because I had been too slow in getting the sugar that might save her. Unfortunately, to my great disappointment, almost all of them died. I held many of them in my arms while the missionary baptised them, but then they disappeared in little wooden boxes. The missionary nuns comforted me by saying that they had gone straight to heaven, where they were rocked to sleep by the angels and were no longer in pain.

There is an ancient Chinese legend that says when a little girl is born, a flower blooms akin to her in spirit.

And now another flower had bloomed on earth: my Nicole. I put the silver choker and two bracelets with little bells on her, as my Amah had done with me, so I could hear when she woke up.

I called her *Ling-Ling*, "little bell". When she grew plump, I called her *Yuang-Yuang*, "chubby little girl". Now she is a young woman, I use affectionate Piedmontese or Genoese nicknames, and I cook Chinese or Piedmontese dishes and make *pesto* like the Genoese, as if wanting to combine the three key places in my life for her: China, Acqui and Genoa.

My Chinese heritage has left its stamp on my relationship with her. I have never kissed her because, in China, people do not tend to kiss each other. And she, like me,stiffens, if someone hugs her: we both feel embarrassed and we both reply with a smile, like the Chinese.

I give her more subtle demonstrations of affection— brushing her hair, for example. Her neck and hair are very soft and strokeable. She no longer wants me to touch her hair, but I always find some excuse—it is tangled or has not been dried properly. For me, doing her hair is like caressing her, a way of taking care of her, a gesture of affection.

Her childhood passed by in a flash. If I had known, I would have paid closer attention to the smallest details, remembering all the colours of her birthday cakes, her games, her tantrums, or the sweet sound of the clarinet she was learning to play.

She is now a woman who borrows my dresses, my blouses and my earrings; a woman who still craves birthday cakes and Christmas trees.

I like her shyness and her gluttony. I do not like her anxiousness but, unfortunately, I know this is something she gets from me.

She likes knowing I am here. Even now, as soon as she comes home, before even looking around, she calls "Mummy": then, reassured, she goes about her business.

She has always had a mother in attendance; I soothed her small injuries, I gave her fish in ginger when she wanted it. Her father was the one who gave her permission to do things and set her an example. We had two completely different roles. From when she was a little girl, she always understood that my "be good" meant something completely different from her father's. When I said it, I was just being her mother.

12

It was a cold and rainy spring morning. I was in London again, as in the summer of 1962, but for a very different reason; I was in hospital suffering from a heart problem.

The doctors were preparing me for the operating theatre. They were bustling around, painting my chest with iodine, taking my blood pressure and listening to my irregular heartbeat with a stethoscope. The nurses were dressed in white from head to toe. Then I could not hear anything. I was weightless.

I woke up in the emergency ward, feeling as if I had been away from the world of the living for quite some time. I did not remember anything. I had lived part of my life without being aware of it.

I was in one of the many beds in intensive care, surrounded by people groaning and by nurses. One of these was the matron, whom I recognised from her status symbol, the little round fob watch hanging from her neck.

There were also volunteers on the ward. One of them wiped my face and forehead with a damp flannel, drying me carefully. Then she did my hands, wrists, and feet. She combed my hair as if she were stroking me. I did not have the strength to speak or thank her for these small caring acts that made me feel a little better. For twenty-four hours she lavished attention on me, twenty-four hours of comfort and tranquillity that I owe to a stranger. If I had to give her a name, I would call her Alice, because she reminded me of Miss Alice, at the hospital in Ningbo.

Miss Alice was a woman doctor from Philadelphia, who had

worked in China for over ten years.

She was like a character from a book by Pearl Buck: a Western woman whose generosity and missionary spirit had driven her to leave her country and devote herself to the life of others in China. She must have had to overcome many difficulties, being foreign and a woman. No one knew anything about her life in the United States, but everyone knew about her life in the hospital at Ningbo.

Initially people had accepted her through necessity. There were epidemics, the war, and the wounded. She battled against death as stubbornly as those who caused it. At times she won; at other times she was defeated, in accordance with the rules of war. Her devotion towards the wounded and sick eventually won over even the most suspicious of people. When there was a difficult case to treat, the Chinese came to her instead of to a doctor of their own race, as was their custom.

I was a difficult case, twice: the first time she cured an intestinal infection caused by my drinking polluted water; the second time she treated me was when I fell onto a large stone running to meet Amah. I still have the scar on my right temple.

Every summer, I went to thank her. We looked at each other more than we talked. She would ask me terse questions and seemed embarrassed. She knew I was there to thank her, not because I needed treatment. She was so tall that I could not see all of her. My eyes were level with her knees. If I wanted to look her in the face, I had to tilt my head back as if looking at the top of a tree. She would give me tea with English biscuits. I would sit on a chair that was too high for me and, feeling more embarrassed than she was, I would shyly hang my head and watch my dangling legs swinging back and forth. Her feet made me feel like laughing when I compared them to Amah's tiny feet.

Her rocking way of walking, like a camel, was also amusing and I would imitate her when I went back to the mission with Amah. But I often missed her. Her tender care, her coloured pills, and her raspberry-flavoured syrups seemed to recur later in the stories about Mary Poppins. And how different they were from Chinese methods, which were often primitive and empirical.

Certainly Miss Alice would not have cured my conjunctivitis by rubbing a special turquoise, almond-shaped "medicinal stone" over the edges of my lashes; she would have used those clear, painless drops that made my eyes shine without tears.

And she would never have used goats' bile. In China, the ritual for cleansing the blood in spring was to swallow little bags of goats' bile. You had to be very careful not to let it burst in your throat. If that happened, the blackish liquid left an extremely bitter aftertaste in your mouth.

Also, the time I had digestive problems after eating some sweet baked potatoes too quickly, Miss Alice sorted everything out with an effervescent pill. The Chinese doctor on the other hand had put me through real torture. After soaking two fingers in a bowl, he pinched my neck, back, and the bridge of my nose, leaving me covered in bruises for ages.

When I think about many of the methods used in Chinese medicine, I had more than one occasion to miss having Miss Alice around.

When I went back to my ward, there was no sign of the girl who had reminded me of Miss Alice. My head was buzzing continuously and I was in a great deal of pain. Half-asleep, I dreamed I had been launched like a satellite noisily turning on its own axis to escape the stones people were throwing at me. The world was rejecting me. The buzz only lasted for a few days before I discovered it was the buzz of the ward ventilator. The pain was just as bad; in fact, it seemed to be getting worse. They gave me some morphine to help me sleep for a few hours. When the effect wore off, the pain came back. I kept asking to sleep, but I was actually asking for morphine, because it was the only way my body and mind could rest. I had only experienced such severe pain once before, along with constant nightmares due to a high fever, when I had a bad reaction to a vaccination. That had been in China, just before I left for Italy.

I was 13, and I was about to set off for the unknown; I was as sad as a country bride being married off to a stranger.

I had pulled the curtains round the bed to cut myself off from the rest of the world which had suddenly turned hostile. I wanted to wrap myself up like a silkworm in its cocoon so that I could not see or hear anything, and so that I could warm myself up from the cold creeping into my bones. I wanted to be in my mother's womb so that I had never been born, or huddled in Mu-Mu's apron, held tight and rocked like a baby kangaroo safe in its mother's pouch.

My heart was pounding, I could hear my pulse beating at my temples. My ears were buzzing with frantic, dancing bees. I was confused by the fever brought on by the vaccinations I had been given that morning. I could not turn over in bed, my arm was swollen and painful. I could not sleep. I felt very heavy, like when I had eaten too much as a little girl and had suffered from nightmares.

I did not know where Amah was or where the red blanket was that she spread over me at night to chase away "the wild cat". Perhaps it was all a bad dream; for a second I felt calmer. But the wretched alarm clock on the bedside table was ticking the seconds so loudly that it brought me back to the harsh reality that I had escaped for a few seconds. It was already two in the morning and I still had not been able to fall asleep.

I reviewed my memories, beginning with the most recent. I had quarrelled with Jeanette, the friend I sat next to at the convent, and we had not had time to make up; I was upset about that. Mu-Mu and Amah were bound to be sad; I wondered who would comfort them. It was only then that I realised how happy I had been at the mission, how peaceful my summers in Kong-qiao had been.

It had only been a week since the preparations for my departure to Italy had begun. I had not even had time to get used to the idea of the journey. I wondered why everything happened in such a rush. I could not accept it. I kept thinking about it and wondering why my friends, who were more foreign than me, were allowed to stay, while I, Chinese by birth and by race, had to leave. Perhaps, I thought, it was because I was only half-Chinese, and that was regarded as a betrayal.

I was only 13, and there was too much I did not know. I kept returning to the conviction that I was "different", to the feeling of foreignness that would stay with me for many years and would influence my life.

I sensed that something inside was changing irreversibly, that I would never again be cheerful, light-hearted, even naughty. I wondered whether the round, white *tianjin* pear, with which I remembered treating Amah's conjunctivitis one day, would lose its magical, opaline transparency and its healing powers, when taken to Italy. Perhaps it would stop being smooth and round and become rough and square.

I continued wondering about these unanswerable questions thrown up by my flood of memories, until I finally fell asleep, still feverish.

The fourth day after the operation, they told me to get up. They had attached a piece of cord to the foot of the bed to help me. I was as weak as a kitten. I could not move unaided. A taut, painful swelling had formed under my left breast like a third breast.

I was very depressed. I thought I would never recover. Life seemed to be against me again. I thought about Nicole, who was five months old. I was afraid I might have passed on my bad luck to her, like a hereditary illness. I was even more afraid that she would lose her mother.

I thought about Elsie; our brief meeting, her words the evening before my operation. That day, they had made me sign a document waiving the doctors' responsibility in the event of my death. Elsie was recovering in my ward; she had sensed my state of mind and, coming over, had discreetly asked if I wanted to talk; she had seen me signing that document and had understood my anxiety.

She told me that this was the second time they had operated on her. After the first operation, she had been fine: she could finally go shopping and climb the stairs without difficulty. Now she was feeling breathless again, so she had to have another operation. She told me this casually, almost cheerfully. She finished by saying: 'I must go in before you so when you come out, I'll be able to talk to you.' These were the last words she said to me. I did not see her after the operation. She was taken behind a screen. I glimpsed her wired up to a machine at the foot of the bed.

She died that night. The morning after, I saw her husband from behind as he walked slowly down the corridor towards the exit with Elsie's bag hanging from his hand and his head bowed.

Elsie's death upset me deeply. I kept suffering from bouts of depression and thought I would never feel better.

I stayed in hospital for about two weeks. I was treated by an Indian doctor called Hari. His words and his Hindu philosophy helped me recover. He told me that everything passed and that we had to be patient, because illness, joy and suffering are cycles of life with which we need to make our peace. He told me that the mind is the seat of good and evil. It is not enough to heal the body—the mind has to be healed first. He spoke slowly, as if having a yoga conversation. He took my hand in his and sat by me. He asked me to help him and explained why. He took his time speaking; he was never in a hurry like the other doctors. He spent a lot of time with me. He told me that he was going back to India the following year—he had been in England for almost ten years. His presence gave me peace of mind and helped me to recover. As I recall, I gave him *Passage to India* by E. M. Forster.

Yvette, one of my French friends in Milan, was my contact with the outside world and she wrote to me about Nicole. She told me that her mother had come over from Paris, so there were two of them looking after my daughter. I was moved to think that Nicole had a grandmother figure close by. She told me that Nicole had cut five baby teeth, which she called *petites perles*.

13

When I came out of hospital, I went to a convalescent home in Midhurst, Sussex, where I met some fascinating people. I remember a Protestant theology student—once he had recovered, he was going to Cologne to finish his studies, then to take holy orders; a geologist, who had caught a renal infection in Mato Grosso; a Greek woman called Regina, who spoke very little English and made herself understood with gestures that were sometimes very comical.

Then there was Captain Morris of the R.A.F. He was a widower and he looked after me, accompanying me on walks, coaxing me out of my shell. His sense of humour helped me to laugh again. Once I laughed so much at one of his jokes that I burst some stitches; but laughing made me feel better. Those temporary companions helped me to recover my physical and mental health. We often met in the afternoons, and in the evening at dinner.

I was also visited by a squirrel that stood on the windowsill of my bedroom overlooking the vast grounds.

While I was there, the rest of the world seemed remote. This was finally a cage from which I did not want to escape. I was saddened by the thought that I would soon recover and have to resume the struggle. I wanted to remain a part of that little group, that family, forever. I felt we were connected by this shared desire to remain there indefinitely, so that we did not have to cope with the outside world and pick up where we had left off. I felt calm in that place; life was not a struggle. I was frightened by the thought of having to rebuild my former life. I was enchanted by the atmosphere of this "magic mountain" and I would have liked to stay with the others for longer, hearing their stories, even if they were invented.

I knew that Elsie had been buried in Alveston, a small village near Bristol, so I decided to go and find her as soon as my convalescence was over.

The bus dropped me near the church. I walked along the country lane to the church wall and opened the creaking iron gate, shattering the silence. There was no one around. I saw randomly scattered tombs overgrown with grass. Some were very old, others more recent.

The shade created by the trees, as well as their random planting, created a sense of tranquillity and intimacy; I felt as if walking on the grass among the tombs might disturb the peace of anyone lying there.

I looked for Elsie Hill's name for a long time, but to no avail. I went into the plain church, but there was no one to ask. Beyond the low wall, I saw a house surrounded by a garden full of flowers and trees similar to those growing in the cemetery. I thought that the vicar might live there and that he would be able to help me find Elsie's grave. When I came to the garden gate, I noticed a tricycle, a deflated ball, and other signs of children.

I rang the bell and the door was opened by three very blond boys with their mouths full, because they must have just jumped up from the table, and behind them came the vicar, a handsome young man. I explained the reason for my visit, and he immediately offered to accompany me to the church so that he could consult the register and the cemetery map in the sacristy.

We walked along the path to the church, the three boys running behind, until their father sent them home. He easily found what I wanted in the sacristy and showed me where Elsie's grave was. He then took his leave and left me alone.

This place awakened older memories of another visit to a cemetery, the Cemetery of the Ancestors in Ningbo, which I visited with Amah.

I must have been seven. It was a cold morning and Amah instructed me to follow her, because she had to sort out 'many important things.' There was something in the air, because people were talking loudly in the street, the shops were still closed, and the rows of rickshaws were stationary.

The outskirts of Ningbo had been bombed the night before. There had been a general walkout and people had rallied together as if they were attending a patriotic demonstration, or going to the temple to make offerings to the gods. Men, women, children and even the elderly were scurrying along. People were running and some were even weeping or walking around looking shocked.

From the different expressions on people's faces, and because Amah had not said anything as she was running along, I did not understand why people were gathered together like this. Unusually, Amah easily managed to keep up with me, despite her small bound feet.

I remember we walked for a long time until we reached the outskirts of the town, where the bleak countryside came into view. We headed for the cemetery, where we were greeted by an apocalyptic scene. The Cemetery of the Ancestors had been bombed.

The land was churned up and full of craters. The coffins were in pieces, white skulls and bones scattered everywhere. People were screaming, crying, and walking round the cemetery moaning like tormented souls in search of peace. Other people arrived; young and old, they walked to and fro between the tombs. The only thing missing was the angels with their trumpets, because it really seemed like the final judgement day that the missionaries had told me about. I even felt like a body that had just risen again, frightened by the thought of answering to God.

Amah began gesticulating wordlessly. She could not find the tomb of her ancestors, or her husband's. Until the bombing, they had been resting in peace in the cemetery. Now, the trees had been uprooted, the tombs were open to the sky, and a multitude of frightened people, like her, were looking for the mortal remains of their ancestors; but the skulls and bones all looked the same.

It was a tragedy for them not to be able to recognise the remains of their dead so that they could reassemble them. They were at a loss. No one wanted to believe that the Japanese had deliberately targeted the cemetery, because all Eastern peoples hold the cult of the dead sacred—more sacred than life itself.

After carefully inspecting the broken tombs and shattered gravestones, Amah looked around at the whole cemetery. She finally established that the tomb of her ancestors had been where there were some shrubs. Her husband's gravestone was also from that section, so she would be able to find "her bones" among the skulls and bones scattered around this area.

We then had to search for them. We had to rummage around in the nearby shrubs to reconstruct at least part of the skeletons. We only used the bones found near the skulls to reassemble these macabre puzzles, unaware that the bombs had scattered the skeletons from one end of the cemetery to the other.

I helped her to find them. I searched around and brought her the finest, longest bones, hoping that would make her happy. She then decided whether to keep or discard them, although I did not understand her criteria. Some were squabbling with their neighbours over a shard of bone, and their poor neighbours were devastated and weeping because they had not found sufficient remains, apart from the skull, to reconstruct their ancestor's skeleton.

Strangely enough, even when I think back to the incident, I do not remember feeling frightened or horrified. I even felt happy, because I was helping Amah to reconstruct the remains of her ancestors to some extent, and she looked calmer.

Once the skeletons were reassembled, she divided the bones into three piles and waited for the gravedigger to bring a coffin so that she could bury the remains and restore their disturbed peace.

We knelt down and prostrated ourselves in prayer, apologising to the ancestors for the disturbance and promising them that we would return for the Ching-Ming festival, the

"Festival of the Dead". On this occasion, the Chinese visit the tombs of their ancestors, bringing gifts of food and paper images of material goods (money, houses, clothes) which are then burned and reach the invisible world via the smoke rising into the sky.

Before leaving England, I stayed a few days with Agnes, the friend I had met in that Chinese restaurant in Mayfair some years before. She was now a widow with three children. She had undergone surgery on her breast. She told me about the other friends in the "group" and about their marriages, children, and divorces.

The only one of the group still in England was Mark, who had not been in touch with me for three years, that is, since I had told him about my impending marriage.

He had written me a letter telling me how happy the group was for me, but which also conveyed his obvious disappointment.

Agnes had told him I was in London, so he came to see me. He was married to an English woman and living in Chelsea. He had changed, perhaps because of the wrinkles around his eyes, and the fact that he was stouter; only his hands were the same.

He seemed embarrassed to see me. One evening, he invited me to have dinner with him alone. He took me to a restaurant in Soho. The waiters knew him. He spoke to them in Chinese. I thought that he was talking more than he used to. He asked me if I was happy. I smiled at him. He took my hand and squeezed it tightly, then dropped it suddenly, as if he had been given an order. I looked at him in surprise. He did not say anything. I thought back to his silences of old. Then he said the words that for a long time I thought he might say one day: 'Why didn't you marry me?'

PART THREE

1

Beijing greets me in the wide smile of Xiao Xu, the driver sent by my friend to fetch me from the airport. He bows deeply in welcome with a flash of white teeth that seems to symbolise the simple warmth of my native country.

I climb into the car, wasting no time in telling him that I was born in China and that my mother was Chinese. I do this because, deep down, I want to win his sympathy and affection, feelings that I fear no one here will have for me again. He asks if I am here to visit relatives. I reply they are all dead. It is simpler that way. His expression alters, as does his tone of voice.

I change the subject too, because conversation is becoming difficult. After many hours spent travelling, I have no desire to construct complicated Chinese sentences or try to fathom what might be meant by a simple change of tone.

I am completely dumbfounded to see a Chinese man behind the wheel. As long as I can remember, Chinese "drivers" pulled a rickshaw.

I left China with a suitcase and am returning with a bag; one thing I have learned in the intervening years is how to travel light.

At the hotel, I phone home to Milan to tell them I have arrived safely and reassure them about the outbreak of malaria reported in an Italian newspaper. I had the fever when I was a child, so I say I am more likely to freeze to death in the icy blast from the air-conditioning.

I had fantasised for months about sleeping in a bed

surrounded by a cloud of mosquito netting—instead, I sleep with a woollen blanket, beset by the irritating hum of the air-conditioning. I also tell my daughter that I am continuing to take the bee syrup prescribed by my Chinese doctor in Milan, and that my first purchase in China will be two boxes of acupuncture needles, since I have decided that, from now on, I will take care of my health in line with the ancient traditions of my ancestors.

It takes me a while to appreciate that I am in China because I am jet-lagged and because I immediately spend some time with my friend and her Western circle of contacts. Even on the way back from the airport in the car, I had been taken aback by the sight of Chinese men and women in Western dress—many of the women had short, curly hair. The modern, luxurious hotel with its lounges swarming with foreign tourists and businessmen—most of them Japanese startled me even more. I noticed that Chinese and Japanese physical traits were really quite similar: the same shiny, black hair, high, prominent cheekbones, flattened nose and almond-shaped eyes. I usually pick up on innate differences in cultural behaviour: gestures, bearing, facial expressions and smile. Lying there half-asleep, I thought about what I had seen in the past few hours and I felt as though I was in Tokyo not Beijing.

On my first evening in Beijing, I rediscovered my China in a bowl of vegetable soup! I had not eaten such a spicy, delicate green soup since I had left. This was my first real "taste" of China. I concentrated mainly on food in the first few days, because taste was the first of my senses to reawaken.

Escaping the comfort of the hotel frequented exclusively by foreign tourists, I decide to explore the city of Beijing. Early in the morning, I go looking for "my" China, following my nose, trying to pick up remembered scents, mingled with a thousand other smells. I walk over the bridge, cross the road and stop at small shacks where I eat fritters, water chestnuts, sesame cakes and a bowl of noodles. As I walk, my other senses are gradually brought into play. After taste and smell, hearing is the sense that largely rekindles my memories.

The clamour of the Chinese women in the markets stirs my emotions deeply. Each of these women cry their wares in the modulated singsong of the Mandarin language. Noises like the incessant ringing of bicycle bells are new to me, while others have disappeared. I follow another scent, the distinctive odour of spices, herbs, roots and healing plasters, and walk into a pharmacy.

Even my skin alerts me to the touch of a breeze saturated with moisture and heat that leaves it smelling of people, food and flowers. Of the five senses, sight is the one that has lost most of its memory.

Before I left Milan, I spent a long time examining the photographs of old Beijing in a book by the German photographer Hedda Morrison, who lived here between 1933 and 1946. During her long stay, she took hundreds of photos, which I studied to acquire some kind of historical background to a city I could not remember, having only lived here for a year as a child. Many of Morrison's photographs are snapshots of everyday life in Beijing in years gone by and I was eager to compare them with my own impressions.

There is a photo of Qianmen Train Station—the central gate to the south of the city: in it, rows of horse-drawn carriages and man-pulled vehicles for hire are lined along the walls.

Another photo depicts a street corner by the city walls with a train of camels laden with merchandise in the foreground.

The photo that made the greatest impression on me was the one taken on Coal Hill: its portico still stands, bearing ornamental motifs below, while in the background there are rows of dilapidated, ramshackle one-storey brick houses— one of the striking contrasts that are still to be seen in the city.

Another photograph shows a plum juice vendor with a bronze gong used to attract children's attention. At the foot of the Drum Tower, vendors are selling sugared hawthorn berries threaded onto wooden sticks. There is also an interesting photo of a bridal procession bearing an empty sedan chair to the house of the bride-to-be.

Morrison's book of photographs is like a bundle of letters from home. Now I live abroad, China is like a mother whom I generally think about fondly. I am proud of her.

I move from Morrison's black and white pictures to brightly-coloured images of the here and now. A stormy red sky hangs over Beijing and the weather is scorching. The long streets are lined by large mansions and modern complexes. People are walking in and out of these glass skyscrapers carrying bicycles on their backs. Many streets are now building sites, filled with the deafening din of scrapers, diggers and cranes. There is a heavy traffic of Japanese cars and motorbikes on the roads.

I set off to explore the city using a monument listed in my guidebook as a landmark. I enter the narrower streets of the Tartar City district, filled with tiny shops, houses and taverns. I go into one of the narrow alleys: the *hutongs*. These streets, lined with grey walls not yet defaced by modernisation, are the busiest part of the city, where even bicycles find it hard to get through. There are all kinds of discoveries to be made here: a deconsecrated temple used for a different purpose, an old pharmacy that still has its original sign, a shop selling masks and kites. In these lanes, home to almost ten million people, I feel as though I have my finger on the pulse of the real Beijing.

Prompted by uncharacteristic curiosity, I peer into courtyards—if the gate is open or ajar. In one, old men are playing chess, half-hidden by wicker baskets, birdcages, bicycles; barefooted children are chasing each other. I study the faces of the old men and wonder if any of them saw me when I was a child living in a *hutong* in this district.

Although unlikely, this could actually be the *hutong* where I spent the first months of my life and where the strong and lasting bond I had with Amah, my nurse, was first formed.

I walk through the city's alleyways between untidy groups of squat buildings, the smells of mould and dust alternating with the aroma of *youtiao*, strips of dough deep-fried in a large wok in the open air. I cannot resist the temptation, and return to the hotel clutching a packet of these delicious snacks.

I ask Xiao Xu to drive me to Tian'anmen Square, where all the narrow streets converge. I am immediately struck by the size and plainness of the square, which is so large that it makes you feel as if you are walking on the spot.

There is a tall column at the centre, dedicated to the men and women who fell in the struggle for independence. At its base sits an old man stroking his sparse white beard, seemingly oblivious to his surroundings— children laughing, a kite trying to lift into the air, a pushchair squeaking on the pavement. It is midday. The old man stands, leaning on his bamboo cane.

The square has always been a site for grand ceremonies and the point of departure for messengers bearing Imperial edicts to every part of China. It is now the people's square, where the anniversary of the People's Republic is celebrated. The mausoleum of Mao Zedong stands in the southern part and, seeing it, I realise the square is highly symbolic. Despite the fact that Mao's theories have fallen into disrepute, he does not appear to have gone down in the estimation of the people who stand in line every morning to visit the mausoleum erected in his honour.

While I am waiting in the queue for the mausoleum, I suddenly feel odd: I cannot catch my breath in the muggy atmosphere, my eyes blur and I grope around for something to hold onto. I slide weakly down the rough base of one of the columns supporting the mausoleum, while my driver, Xiao Xu, runs to retrieve my straw hat that is rolling down the steps. *'Bin le, bin le,'* ('I don't feel well') I call to him. Immediately a guard rushes over; ignoring me, he turns to the driver and says firmly: 'She can't stay there!'

'The lady doesn't feel well,' replies my driver, but the guard raises his voice and repeats: 'She can't stay there!' as if he has not heard.

I stagger to my feet and leaning on Xiao Xu's arm, I rejoin the queue and slowly and shakily make my way towards the room where the air is cooled by four large fans that immediately help me to feel better.

The spacious interior is dimly lit and the Great Helmsman lies in a crystal coffin wrapped in a red flag. Only his head is visible to the public. There is a rosy hue to his complexion and I remember his distinctive double chin. His black hair is combed back from his broad forehead, as in his photographs.

The crowd parts, walking either side of the coffin, and there is no chance to linger. We advance slowly and silently, dragging our feet like little lead soldiers.

Walking out of the room and into the heat, I begin feeling ill again. I lean against a column and again slide down to the ground. This time, no guard intervenes, probably because I am already through the exit.

I hear someone calling: 'Miss Bamboo, Miss Bamboo!' It is my driver offering to give me a piggyback to the car. I do not have the strength to get up and I feel faint. I think with irony: 'See Mao, then die'.

My driver starts carrying me on his back to the car. I remain in this position for a while, then ask him to put me down. As soon as he sets me on the ground, I collapse and hear Xiao Xu calling again: 'Miss Bamboo, Miss Bamboo.'

I lie on the ground thinking that perhaps it is my destiny to die in China, having been born here.

A petite woman with a child comes over to me. She sits down and shading me with her parasol, she instructs her little boy to fan me. The little boy quietly obeys. My driver goes off to fetch the car. The shade from the parasol and the breeze from the child's fanning immediately make me feel better. I want to thank this unassuming woman, the only person in the mass of people to stop and offer help, so I weakly stretch out my hand and, in reply to her question, tell her that I come from Italy. 'Ah, Italy,' she repeats, as if Italy had a particular meaning for her, and then, more loudly, orders the child to concentrate on fanning me. She is a peasant woman from Shanxi, in northern China, and the boy is her little brother. They have come to see Mao.

The driver returns and thanks the woman for taking care of me. I tell him to offer her some money, which she firmly refuses, despite my insistence.

I climb onto Xiao Xu's back for the second time, and he speedily makes his way across the square through the crowd and settles me in the car. The air-conditioning immediately revives me.

I have grown fond of my driver, who knows how to be quiet when necessary, but considerate and efficient, too. He is chatty when I speak to him and understands everything I say in Mandarin. He also corrects my accent and suggests the right words to use. Although he can also sing well, he does so in an irritating falsetto, like the singers who perform arias from Chinese operas.

He says that he likes Pavarotti, whom he calls "Pavalotti", and keeps repeating: '*pang le, pang le,*' calling him fat. I reply that he has lost weight; he does not believe me and releasing the steering wheel, continues to hold his arms out wide, repeating '*pang le,*' and laughing heartily. Perhaps he likes the fact that Pavarotti is fat.

Among other things, I have been curious to find out how much Chinese women might have changed and how popular the Western model is here—not only with young women, but also with their mothers. Until now, my concept of Chinese women has been influenced by the women of my youth: my nurse Amah, my mother, grandmother and great-grandmother, and my many aunts, my *ayis*. Back then, the ideal woman was a practical wife and a wise mother. A woman's most heartfelt desire was to be a mother. The ideal Confucian society was one in which there were no unmarried men or women. During my childhood, young girls had a much stricter upbringing: they had to grow up quickly and they began to learn feminine traditions well before their teens. They rose earlier than their brothers, they dressed with more care, they helped with the cooking and with feeding their younger brothers and sisters— they played less and worked more. They spoke in submissive tones and their movements were always graceful. Women were not allowed to laugh, only to smile. They did not allow strangers to see them. The more they kept themselves to themselves, the more they were worth.

They learned embroidery and, in cultured families, they also learned to read and write. In their first dalliances, they never took the initiative; at most, they made their feelings known by allowing a glimpse of the tip of their red shoes or by going to the Lantern Festivals. The importance placed on having sons had encouraged the practice of keeping concubines. If a wife had borne her husband numerous daughters and no son, she herself would urge her husband to take a concubine. Marriage was regarded as a family matter, not a personal affair. Anyway, Chinese wives always maintained their social status under these circumstances.

I discover, by watching women and particularly by talking to them, that there have been many changes.

One of the major innovations concerns the marriage laws; it is now decreed that the union must not only be agreed by the parents but also by the daughters, who finally have the right to choose their own husbands.

Almost all women marry: they do not stay single by choice. For the Chinese, the most reprehensible "sin" in the West is the large number of unmarried women. Other new measures include monogamy, divorce and, within the field of birth control, abortion, the use of the pill, the coil and sterilisation.

Many women now also work in typically masculine sectors like engineering, aeronautics and the merchant navy, as well as in public and governmental offices. The Minister for the Textile Industry, for example, is a woman, as is the President of the Bank of China.

Women are allowed to go to university and those who pass a special selection exam are sent overseas to take lengthy postgraduate courses. All women graduates are keen to move to the big cities. None of them want to go back to their native province or look for work in a small town. They are career women and as ambitious as their Western counterparts.

However, die-hard male-chauvinist attitudes continue to assert that woman are the weaker sex. Male candidates who may have graduated with lower grades end up being selected in preference to women graduates, for no good reason. As a result, some universities have even reduced their intake of women students. I found this out by talking to many young girls at the university of Beijing.

The craze for all things foreign has speeded up the modernisation of all kinds of traditions: from bound feet to bikinis. Thanks to the brazen transparency of nylon, I have noticed that women wear padded bras to increase their bust size to something approaching European measurements. They curl their hair and follow Western music trends. They stroll hand in hand with their "boyfriends" or with their arms around each other's waist. One way or another, it is always foreigners who show the Chinese how to modernise. Every house I visited had a refrigerator and a television. The Chinese frequently go to the cinema: it is not expensive and the films inject a little luxury and colour into a dull, monotonous world, which in turn gives family planning a boost. Women live in a highly controlled, almost Orwellian society. They still have a "big sister", called a *danwei*, which is the work or study unit to which they belong. It monitors the woman's behaviour at all times, particularly during the "five periods of frailty": menstruation, pregnancy, breast-feeding, weaning, and the menopause. There is no personal privacy. The Constitution states that a woman's duty is to work to build her country and raise a family. A new social consciousness has now superseded erstwhile family considerations. This social spirit is a new concept. For centuries, the family was paramount—it was the only system, the point of departure for every moral code of conduct enforced by Confucius.

In the late 1970s, the family structure changed. The traditional large Chinese family used to be composed of a family unit of three or four generations living under the same roof. Improvements in the standard of living and increased mobility has caused these large family units gradually to disintegrate and has led to an increase in the number of small family units. The government now encourages single-child families, although there are still not many of them. Family planning has given women greater freedom to devote themselves to productive paid work.

For a week, I leave the hotel regularly at eight-thirty in the morning as if going to work, even on Sunday. Looking at people's style of dress on the day of rest, I notice that Chinese men prefer almost see-through nylon socks with embroidery up the sides and shoes with built-up heels that make them look a couple of inches taller. I also notice that almost no one wears shoes with cloth soles any longer. They have been replaced with trainers and leather shoes. The rustle made by cloth soles—a slow, heavy noise, like footsteps shuffling over wet leaves—is a thing of the past.

Chinese men have abandoned the ancient ritual of bowing, and now shake your hand. They only smile and make a slight bow when apologising, and I cannot help regretting the disappearance of this ancient, respectful custom. Not only that, but young people from small towns that have stayed the same for thousands of years, now speak and act like youngsters who have grown up in the big cities. Young female tourists walk around with bare legs, although Chinese men do not look at them.

The female body, which in Western culture has always been a means of seduction, had no importance in China, except for the parts that can be seen: head, face, hands and feet. At one time, pale complexions, even if obtained with layers of face powder, and small feet—no longer than four inches— were greatly admired. In fact, in Chinese art, women's clothes are not depicted to accentuate their figure but to complement it.

The Chinese still appreciate delicate translucent skin and I noticed that the women in southern cities wear tubes of fabric on their arms and wide-brimmed hats to protect them from the sun. I asked a young man if he liked blonde girls. He said that he did: 'They should have large breasts and small feet.'

The three years I recently spent studying the Chinese language have made it easier for me to talk to the Chinese about simple subjects like family, marriage, and children. The women seem more open than the men. Here is a transcription of a snippet of conversation I had with a woman, waiting for a bus.

'My husband works in a governmental office in Nanking and we have not seen each other for four months.'

'Why don't you change your job to join your husband?'

'You cannot change jobs in China—you have to follow the path laid out for you. I'm lucky—one of my friends has not seen her husband for three years because he has been sent overseas to specialise in engineering.'

She smiles and continues: 'That's life— in China.'

'Is it easy to get a divorce?'

'Yes, very.'

'Are many people divorced?'

The terse reply comes from the only man I have managed to engage in conversation.

'A great many.'

He must be in his thirties, but he looks older. There is something childlike about his serious face that gives him the air of a cheerful dreamer. The Chinese always look young until they reach their thirties, then they begin to look ground down. Their serenity reappears when they are nearing sixty, when they appear more graceful and dignified, and it becomes impossible to tell their age.

'There are three reasons for divorce,' he explains. 'The first, these days, is the women's salary, which is often the same as the man's, so they are no longer dependent on us. We part because they become too domineering and want to give the orders. The second reason is having only one child—women pay more attention to their child than to their husband.'

He shakes his head in resigned disapproval.

'The third reason is that the daughter-in-law and mother-in-law often fight, and the husband is entitled to take his mother's side.'

In this respect, I share the opinion of the concubine Pan Chin Lien who, in the erotic novel *Chin P'ing Mei*, writes: 'Have you ever seen two spoons jostling in the same bowl without striking each other?'

273

The railway was introduced into the Chinese transport system very late, which is why I had never seen a train before I came to Italy. Before the railway, people used to travel inland on the river. Until a few years ago, the lack of a road network also made it difficult for lorries and other wheeled vehicles to get from one place to another. The Mandarins have always objected that the vibrations of the railway disturbed the spirits of the ancestors, while the foreign powers ignored them to satisfy their own commercial and political ambitions.

I have bought a railway ticket for Lugou Qiao in "soft class". In the "hard class" corridor, rowdy travellers are leaning against each other, smoking and spitting on the floor. Some labourers with thermos flasks of hot water are cooking noodles in an enamel container. Teenagers are playing portable radios at top volume. None of this surprises me. In China, the working classes have always been rowdy and chaotic. What does surprise me is to find myself for the first time on a train in China.

There are only Europeans and a few party members in "soft class". The latter can be recognised by their wristwatches and the fountain pens in their breast pockets, small status symbols that set them apart from the labourers packed into the adjoining carriages. The nine grades of the former Mandarinate are kept alive in the 24 ranks of the current civil service, whose members spend the summer in Beidaihe, together with foreigners, and are entitled to drive a car.

Travelling in "soft class" means that I could cross China from end to end and almost never find myself sitting next to a Chinese person. There are a few party leaders, but this class of people find it hard to strike up a conversation. An ancient sense of apartheid divides the foreigner from Chinese travellers. This dichotomy also exists in restaurants, and shops, as if the discrimination instituted by the colonialists has now come in useful for those who were once on the receiving end.

I climb down from the train and encounter a small silent crowd accompanying a funeral. When the funeral cortege begins to move, the professional paid mourners, dressed in white with white hats, begin to strike a gong. Two men carry on their shoulders a coffin tied with a thick rope. Despite the novelty of the train, this funerary scene takes me back to the past.

I have come to Lugou Qiao, a small town that seems fashioned out of mud and fossil coal, to see the bridge dedicated to Marco Polo, who is remembered throughout China. Every now and then, his name appears at a crossroads, or beneath the walls of a citadel. I find it moving to think that a young man who came of age in China so many centuries ago has left his mark on this bridge. The Marco Polo Bridge is elegant and arched like a musical instrument. The marble balustrades are the colour of antique ivory and its refinement and grace are only enhanced by the dreariness of the surrounding landscape. Every pillar is topped with a carved lion cub and there are larger lions at either end of the bridge, many of whose arches were wrecked and swept away by the tragic flood of 1890.

Lugou Qiao is a strategic site situated a couple of miles from Beijing and Fengtai. The latter is a busy railway hub with lines from Mongolia, Manchuria, Tianjin as well as the Nanking-Shanghai line. Seizing possession of Lugou Qiao and Fengtai is tantamount to isolating Beijing from central and southern China, which is what the Japanese did during the invasion. It was exactly this danger that accelerated my flight from Beijing to the south when I was a little girl.

When I visited temples as a child, people always made offerings of fresh food. Modernisation seems to have caused the gods to change their "diet". This is apparent in the Temple of the Lamas, the ancient residence of the prince who became Emperor Yong Zheng in 1722. Converted into a religious temple, it became a Lamaist monastery—the home of a living Buddha surrounded by three hundred orange lamas. It was closed during the Cultural Revolution and is now home to monks who recite long prayers in their cells, though some of these have been converted into tea rooms. In the rooms of the temple, Tibetan and Lamaist Buddhas are seated among plastic flowers with their Chinese counterparts.

In the side courtyards, there are friezes, wooden dragons, pedestals and statues of Buddha. Some pavilions have recently been rebuilt, their windows varnished and their roofs retiled. There are offerings on the central altar: bottles of orangeade, jars of fruit in syrup, branded wrapped sweets, fruit jellies also in wrappers, and sesame cakes.

Beside the altar stand statues of warriors and guards, some with blue faces and fierce expressions, others with red, angry faces, and one with a pink face, playing the flute. Behind the central altar looms a 54-feet-high Buddha which almost reaches the temple ceiling. Many tourists offer incense; I put a *yuan* in the alms box. The monk thanks me by handing me a brush dipped in ink and the visitors' book, in which I write "Bamboo, Italy".

Around the temple, tourists are assailed by all kinds of booths and shops selling drinks, clothes, fruit, fox furs, and sheepskin jackets.

Taoism, Confucianism, Buddhism, Marxism and Maoism: China seems to have lost these "religions", at least to some extent. What still lingers on is the time-honoured, unanimous belief in the afterlife. I have again seen burning braziers and parasols placed before the tombs. I will never forget the sight of the poetic ritual that took place on the Grand Canal that still links Beijing and Hangzhou—hundreds of small lit candles floating on the water to illuminate the Path of the Spirits.

2

I did not originally plan to visit the city of Xian, but a trip to China is not complete without a visit to the birthplace of Chinese civilisation, the city that contains the ancient Imperial past of eleven dynasties. It became world famous after the discovery of the terracotta army, created to guard the first emperor of China for all eternity.

With their capital in Xian, the Han and Tang dynasties held sway in the most glittering period of Chinese history. In the 20th century, the Chinese Communist Party established its base in this province, and led soldiers and civilians to great victory in the war against the Japanese.

The Chinese stretch of the Silk Route starts from Xian, in the province of Shanxi. I was not overly impressed by the rolling loess tableland around Yanan, but I was delighted by its relics and monuments. The Imperial tombs alone number 72. Only a quarter of the soldiers from the terracotta army in the tomb of the first emperor of the Qin dynasty have so far been unearthed. Looking at these martial figures, I feel a great sense of pride in my ancestors. The majestic city walls from the Ming dynasty, as well as the Big and Little Goose Pagodas, are steeped in history and stand as a monument to the ancient city's prosperity.

The bonze tells me why it is called the Big Goose Pagoda. 'Some pilgrim monks from India stopped here once, exhausted by their arduous journey and weak with hunger. A flock of wild geese flying above noticed the monks and their pitiful condition. The largest and fattest sacrificed itself by plummeting to earth just where the monks were standing, enabling them to satisfy their hunger. Fortified, the monks could continue their pilgrimage. That is the origin of the pagoda's name.'

After listening to his explanation, I make an offering and the monk immediately alerts everyone to my gesture by striking loudly on the gong. After that, the gong rings out repeatedly as other tourists follow my example. The monk, perhaps to show his gratitude to me for gaining him some unexpected offerings, allows himself to be photographed with me. This is highly unusual, because in the other temples you were not allowed to be photographed with the monks.

Before leaving, I ask him how one becomes a bonze. I was amazed to learn that you simply need to apply to the Association of Bonzes; if you are accepted, the initiation ceremony follows immediately—there is no need to have been a seminarian. Young men must have done a stint as seminarians in suitable temples, whereas adults can become bonzes straight away. They are free to have a job, but must spend several hours praying in the morning and evening. Funding for the temple and the monks comes from their work and the offerings made by the faithful.

On the central altar of the Seated Buddha are rows of bottles, all the same size, filled with fruit in syrup and drinks. The flowers are plastic.

Choosing to experience China at close quarters has meant that I have occasionally eaten food of dubious quality, and in my years of absence from China, I must have lost the "local bacteria" that used to protect my digestive system. As I cannot shake off this tiresome gastric complaint, I need to find a doctor. I also take this opportunity to seek treatment for a persistent cough, probably caused by the frequent sudden changes in temperature.

The doctor I have been recommended is in a pharmacy behind the bank. I immediately notice his pale face and thin hair as he mixes up some healing herbs. I look at the shelves: there are pieces of deer antler that look like potato crisps, and hundreds of lizard skins with dried heads. All the containers are placed in rows according to size and shape. To the right, on the walls, are dried root masses and bundles of twigs—all the same dusty colour; the only variation on the theme is something shaped like an octopus. To the left are macabre-looking fragments that appear to be little pieces of vertebrae-shaped bone threaded on a string that makes me think of a spine. There are lumps of moss to ease pain and place on wounds, as well as plant seeds, including the different parts of the lotus flower, which are used as a tonic and as an aphrodisiac. Assorted two-litre bottles hold a mixture of dried insects, like millipedes, large bluebottles, many varieties of beetles, and crumbling hornets. Others jars contain powdered pearl. There is also ginseng—known for its rarity, cost and much-vaunted properties—not to mention dried seaweeds, various types of lichen, mushrooms and cultivated mould.

There is never any lack of sticking plasters, which are very popular with the Chinese. As children, we used them for minor injuries, as well as rashes and insect bites. My nurse also used to put them on her temples and forehead when she had a headache or rheumatic pains. These sticking plasters, smelling of camphor and ginger, instantly take me back. It was in those years that medicated plasters with ingredients that are absorbed into the blood through the skin, came to the attention of the Western world, and began to be used by all the leading European hospitals. In China, this was already a time-honoured technique.

The names of doctors' pills in China reflect the Chinese knack of giving everything poetic, imaginative and whimsical names: "One Hundred Delights", "Forever Spring", "Banish Old Age", "Return to Youth", "A Myriad Harmonies", "Stimulate the Yin and Strengthen the Spirit". All these medicines sound far too tempting not to buy.

There are also pills aimed at men like "The Mongolian General Takes Command", and "The Five Tigers", which is made of juniper juice, dragon blood, sesame seeds, flowers of sulphur and other ingredients, the ideogram of which I do not understand.

While I am looking at "Pills for the Seven Great Values and Thick Whiskers", the doctor-pharmacist comes over and says: 'That isn't for you, it's for your husband!'

'I have a persistent cough when it is hot, and I sweat,' I tell him.

'Where do you live? Here in China?' he asks.

'No, I'm a tourist.' 'May I ask how old you are?'

'Of course.' I tell him.

'Oh, you look younger. Perhaps you take a lot of ginseng?'

'No. Perhaps it's because I am half-Chinese.'

He opens his eyes wide, Chinese-style, to show his surprise.

'How long have you had this cough in the summer?'

'For at least ten years,' I reply.

'I need to treat you at least four times, at weekly intervals.'

I reply that this is not possible because I am leaving. He then disappears into the back of the shop and returns holding a twist of paper, which he opens on the counter in front of me. It is the blown-up illustration of an ear, covered with ideograms. While I look at the illustration, he listens to my bronchi, making me breathe deeply.

'Can you read Chinese?'

'A little,' I reply, carefully looking at the paper.

'Do you see these letters?'

'Yes, this is *qi,* which means "air".'

'Good, and the other two here?'

'I don't understand those.'

All three ideograms are shown inside the ear.

'In line with these three ideograms, I shall implant three subcutaneous mineral beads in your ear. You will not feel any pain or nausea. When you cough at night, press the area with the beads between your thumb and forefinger and you will immediately find that you're able to breathe more easily and you will stop coughing. This is only a temporary cure though. When you go back to your country, go for some acupuncture: only then will it go away.'

He carries out the simple operation, covering each bead with a tiny almost invisible piece of sticking plaster. I notice that a long queue of patiently waiting people has formed behind me. The pharmacist obviously does not lack work. I thank him and pay ten *yuan* for the three beads, which are already making me feel better at the thought that the mere pressure of my fingers will stop me coughing.

The beads definitely helped. I took them out when I got back to Italy—they were easy to remove by pressing down on them with my nail. Now I am waiting for auricular therapy with needles, confident that the treatment will be a success. Having the point of a needle threaded through the earlobe is painless, inexpensive and effective—I have seen it done.

3

The third leg of my journey is to Chengdu, where, as a child, I had taken refuge with Amah and had hidden from the Japanese for a time. I had been longing to see this landscape of little bridges and waterways, huts built of leaves and bamboo canes, fertile fields and winding paths. We had a one-storey house, like most traditional Chinese houses. I was in my element there, sometimes just watching a mouse scurrying about on the floor. During the war, I had no toys, and everyone around me—adults, other children and domestic animals—were my playthings.

Chengdu is the regional capital of the province of Sichuan, a territory to the east of Tibet situated between two mountainous regions and surrounded by peaks and beautiful countryside. The Taoist monks were the first to come to these heights, seeking refuge and philosophical answers to the problems of existence. Sichuan is composed of the words "*ss*" meaning "four" and "*chuan*" meaning "stream". The province of the four streams is the richest in China. It is a world apart, continually fought over by north and south. It has been called the "Garden of China" for its well-ordered, varied and abundant crops; many of its hills are still dotted with sugar cane plantations.

Amah would give me a piece of sugar cane to chew and suck, and she would leave me sitting at the foot of the trees while she helped in the fields. Chengdu's natural isolation had protected the city from the Japanese invasion.

Comparing it with the scenery I remembered, the most

obvious change was the two-storey houses that have now replaced the squat huts in the built-up areas. I am not disappointed because these changes mean that the peasants and the poor have finally cast off the yoke of poverty. During my short stay, I did not see any barefooted children running in the fields as before. Their clothes were good, and clean, and the women's dress was similar to the clothes worn in the big cities.

I did not remember very much about the city. I had heard it called the "monkey city" because monkeys can still be seen on the paths leading to the famous Mount Emei. People here were so close to nature that they used to say they could hear the monkeys "weeping or laughing", depending on their mood. I always wanted to own a monkey, but no one seemed to know where they lived and where you could buy one.

Chengdu was an important centre around 400 B.C., and under the Han dynasty it became famous for its brocades, silk, filigree objects, umbrellas and paper lanterns. It has now become a picturesque tourist destination.

The province of Sichuan is renowned as the homeland of one of the four most famous types of Chinese cuisine. Chengdu is particularly known for its varied dishes, which are spicy, inexpensive and quick to make. In the past, there were only salted vegetables, and even the rich only ate pork twice a month. Now dishes made with chicken, duck, fish and rabbit are more common.

At Amah's house, I ate a great many cakes, and at nightfall she would dress me in red pyjamas to go to sleep. Red chased away demons.

In the morning, she would give me rice porridge with vegetables in brine that she had bottled herself. I would go out to play in the courtyard that was full of baskets and bottles. I was particularly fond of the old hen house, which always smelled of lime and things hanging up to dry.

Mount Emei with its greenish black peaks is one of the four sacred Buddhist mountains in China. The Yellow Emperor had his pills of immortality prepared here. The area is about sixty miles from Chengdu.

The clouds are very distinctive—dense, low and swollen with rain. On cloudy days, the peaks poking through look like volcanic islands in a flat, grey sea. The waterfalls and rivulets murmuring in the valleys create a sensation of coolness. The wonders of the landscape have always drawn men of letters and have served as a source of inspiration for the Chinese masters of painting.

Local buses provide transport to all the picturesque places and they are a good vantage point for watching the monkeys. Some pester the walkers visiting the 170 temples dotted about in this group of mountains. A monumental arch leads into the sacred places, the tranquil atmosphere of which prepares the pilgrim's soul for the mountain ascent. The arch provides a glimpse of a fourteen-storey pagoda with a copper roof, surrounded by thousands of carved images of Buddha. The pilgrims came back after the Cultural Revolution. They mingle with the tourists on their way up the seemingly endless stone steps that wind their way between pines dripping with clear, crystalline resin.

Near the Elephant Bath Temple live families of "civilised" monkeys that do not molest the visitors; they are actually called "gentleman monkeys". I have seen them sitting between the Buddhas watching the tourists, contenting themselves with imitating them, moving in groups and gazing around. Others calmly stroll around inside the temple, occasionally standing up to take a look around. About 12 of them crouch in a line under the porch, sheltering from the rain. They are not easy to photograph because they run away, or attack people if they try to get closer. The boldest or hungriest will deign to pose for the camera for food, but there is always the danger that they will suddenly snatch your camera out of your hands. The group of monkeys near the Cave of the Nine Old Men are usually badly behaved. They block the street like a picket of strikers and threateningly stretch out their arms under the pretext of asking for food. Some have also been known to rummage through pilgrims' pockets or try to snatch tourists' hats. The members of this particular group are nicknamed by locals "the bandits".

The Cricket Festival is being celebrated at the temple today. I walk over to a man sitting in a corner, surrounded by curious passers-by. This unusual artist is weaving blades of grass with deft movements of his fingers and wrists, making from memory perfect models of insects and small animals; there are some arranged in aggressive stances on a little table. He has a wide range of different grasses to unravel and explains that, before beginning his models, he cures the grass in boiling water, then lets it dry in the open air. When he gets a certain type of grass, he soaks the stalks in warm water to soften them and make them flexible. He cuts off the parts he needs with scissors and throws the rest away. He adds coloured seeds for eyes and it takes him less than fifteen minutes to construct an insect that is immediately claimed by a patiently waiting customer.

Someone shouts: 'Now do a locust for my daughter,' and someone else: 'A dragon for my son!' I bought nine, including a butterfly, a bee, a dragonfly, a cicada, a locust and, of course, some crickets.

The artist is weaving a lot of crickets because it is the Seventh Moon, the Cricket Festival, and, according to custom, people are walking around with crickets in small bamboo cages. Anyone who does not own a cage, keeps their cricket in a small empty pumpkin up their sleeve.

The cricket is regarded as an antidote to evil spirits, who apparently cannot bear its song. There has always been a flourishing trade in both chirping and fighting crickets. The cages with crickets are selling like hot cakes on the stalls, as they did in my time.

The tradition of keeping crickets was already thriving during the Song dynasty, when the Chinese kept caged crickets for their song. The custom became so popular that caged crickets were even found in the Imperial court. Certain people specialised in catching crickets, which they then gave to the emperor in exchange for lavish gifts.

As well as being taken on walks, crickets were carried on

river boats and trains. I have even met women in aeroplanes keeping tight hold of their cages, having entrusted their fate to these noisy good-luck charms.

During the Song dynasty, cricket-fighting became a national pastime. There were various opinions on what to feed fighting crickets and you can buy books which give detailed instructions. Some suggest a varied diet to ensure their strength and stamina while fighting. A rice-based diet, with lotus flowers and prawns is recommended. Others state that hard-boiled eggs are better and others again expound the macabre theory that crickets fight better if fed with the crushed legs of their last victim. If the cricket becomes ill, you should give it a consommé of butterfly wings. If they catch a chill (how do you know?) they should be given a mosquito infusion. If they have a fever, they must be given pea stems every two hours, while for other kinds of respiratory problems, they merely require a little powdered millipede.

Fighting crickets are classified into heavyweight, middleweight and lightweight; before the fight, they are weighed on a small pair of scales. The fighting arena is an unglazed earthenware bowl or one made of unsanded wood. The inside of the bowl has to be rough so that their legs can find a good hold. There is also a referee, the "fight director", who lists each of the two opponents' victories before the start of the fight. When the crickets meet, their natural instinct is to run in opposite directions, but they are manoeuvred and prodded by the referee with a mouse whisker inserted into the end of a bamboo shaft. The fight can last anything from three minutes to half an hour.

There is a large full moon, the August Moon. I am keen to do something out of the ordinary this evening, so I ask the hotel reception desk what they recommend. I head for the centre of town and the tea house at the foot of the Drum Tower. This is the first teahouse I have visited. Many have been demolished along with a large number of the old buildings in all of China's cities. It is an open-air venue and I sit down at the stone table on one of the wooden seats, shiny from years of use.

The audience, which includes a few foreigners, comes here to listen to the story told by a blind man with dark glasses, who sits on a stool on a wooden platform. Every evening he comes into the teahouse and tells an episode of a long story that traditionally accompanies the tea-drinking. The members of the audience sip their jasmine tea, which is continually being poured by a young waitress. Almost all the men are smoking long, thin reed pipes with metal bowls. No one seems to mind that the teahouse is very untidy, with empty boxes piled on top of each other and wicker baskets lying abandoned in a corner. People come here for the pleasure of listening to the storyteller's ballads. The blind man picks up a bamboo lute and bangs on the table with the end that is covered with a thin pig's bladder, then, in a monotonous voice, he begins to recite the story, singing parts of it at times. It is the story of an unfortunate mother who can no longer look after her baby son, so she abandons him in a basket near a bridge in the hope that some kind-hearted person will take care of him. An elderly couple find him and raise him as their son. The boy grows up and is told about his origins. He leaves home to find his real mother and succeeds. She warns him not to forget anyone who has loved him. However, when the young man becomes a Mandarin, he pretends not to recognise his adoptive parents and is struck dead by a bolt of lightening because of his ingratitude. This story was already doing the rounds in 12th-century Sichuan. Its plot forms part of the oral tradition and is similar to one we were told as children. It is a Confucian story about filial piety that often crops up in children's literature and I was amazed that, despite all the revolutions, this type of story still has such a large audience.

The blind man tells his story in ancient dialect, accompanied by the instrument. I am held spellbound by his beautiful voice. He has a young student with him, who is also blind. He sits at his master's side during the performance and listen attentively, as if memorising what he is hearing. I listens to only one episode—I was told that it would take seven evenings for him to tell the whole story.

Every cup of tea drunk earned the story teller a tenth of a *yuan*, and every evening, he managed to earn two *yuan*. On this evening of the full moon, I do not remember ever having drunk so many bowls of tea—it was enough to keep me awake all night!

4

I left Shanghai over thirty years ago. My last sight of the city was in January 1953 as my steamer pulled away from the banks of the Whangpoo. Shanghai forms part of China's more recent history. It owes its legendary reputation to the aura created by certain works of fiction and, later, by certain Hollywood films. Westerners who see Shanghai for the first time are expecting a city lifted straight from the *Arabian Nights*. The city grew out of Western greed—some streets were lined exclusively with banks, strongboxes built with valuable marble from Italy, unloaded by paupers with bare legs and feet. Shanghai was a Western capitalist myth that remained unchanged until the advent of Maoist Communism.

My memories of the past tremble like a mirage. What I see in Shanghai does not tally with my memories and this fills me with disappointment. The city before me is devoid of its past charm and glamour. That is the price of historical change: a type of colonialism has been replaced by social progress, but the city's appearance has suffered in the process.

This phenomenon arouses the sort of contradictory feelings that I have often felt during my trip. I am consumed by regret for my memories of the past, yet comforted by the knowledge that the country has cast off the yoke of poverty. I constantly waver between these two emotions.

People who have become corrupted by the West stand in front of shops selling radios, televisions, and domestic appliances; they flock to the cinema and almost come to blows on the buses, shoving and pushing to get on; they ride up and down the escalators of department stores for fun. Along these very streets, right in the city centre, I once saw lines of tanks flying the flag of the Rising Sun, make their way through a silent, frightened yet inquisitive crowd, preceded and followed by motorcycles with sidecars equipped with machine guns.

In the old city, in the tea house where I stopped for a break, some elderly men are sipping tea, oblivious to the milling tourists. The woman selling popcorn is explaining the mysteries of this unusual snack and the American machine that makes it, to a Chinese woman who is gripping a child's hand. The woman listens engrossed, while the popcorn seller works the machine and fills a paper bag. She hands it to the woman and her child, who wander off through the crowd eating this unexpectedly greasy, salty snack. Although there are many shops selling Western articles, they are still outnumbered by picturesque, traditional shops selling local goods. Modernisation has not yet managed to stamp out the evocative sights of a skylark in its cage, a beautiful fan held by a woman, or a crown of paper flowers hanging on a shop sign.

Near the port, the city has resumed its trading activities as if the past thirty years has never happened. Strolling along the Bund, I realise that everything has changed. A bank has been converted into a textile company and there is pop music coming from the Customs House. I also see, with great disappointment, that the two lions of the British Empire that used to flank the entrance to the Hong Kong and Shanghai Bank whose majestic paws I often stroked when I was a child, have now been replaced by two guards wearing trainers as green as their uniform.

The onetime prestigious Shanghai Club is now a smoky social club for labourers waiting for their shift to start in the nearby port warehouses. I paid a *yuan* to visit the gardens where there was once allegedly a sign stating: "No Chinese or dogs allowed". The Great World, where people played roulette in evening dresses and tuxedos, has now been abandoned: the caretaker informs me that they will soon be starting the construction of a hotel for Western tourists. The famous Racing Club, the most exclusive club for Europeans, has now been converted into a public library—a clear sign of the changing face of the city.

However, the luxurious Cathay Hotel, where the playwright Noel Coward wrote *Private Lives*, still has its stained-glass windows, while the Art Deco banisters and lamps can still be seen in the foyer.

There is a typhoon brewing. The wind has whipped up the waves, the clouds are racing along and the sky is dark. What does Zikawei say?

I wonder how many times I heard that question. In 1891, the Jesuits began to found and build meteorological stations around China to monitor typhoon activity and forecast their course. All year round, the Zikawei Observatory near Shanghai, published bulletins distributed in the city and nearby ports. The name—Zikawei—always fascinated me, perhaps because it could bring the city to a standstill with an announcement like: "Gale-force winds and imminent typhoons". At the convent in Shanghai, the nuns occasionally took us to visit Zikawei. There was complete silence in the observatory—the only noises were the ticking of an astronomic instrument and the rattling of a pane of glass shaken by the wind. Blue-clothed peasants worked in the vegetable gardens around Zikawei, the way they might on the threshold of a temple they did not dare to enter. The Jesuits showed us the course taken by the typhoons on geographical maps. On top of all the horrors of war, I thought the typhoons were monstrous creatures that spent the summer months hatching the havoc they would later wreak. Their nest lies deep in the Pacific near the Philippines; from there, they race across vast tracts of ocean, heading west, with a south to north drift. Shanghai was always hit full on, followed immediately by Qingtao. The typhoons would fling thousands of boats into the air. The junks would split open like shells between the flying shards of wood and shreds of sail. Doors and windows cracked, and roofs lifted off houses causing the same sort of damage to buildings as an air-raid.

What has become of Zikawei today? I think about the missionary priests, many of whom were Italian. As well as doing their job, they were the only ones not to lose face at a time when there were so many examples of colonial degeneracy. For many years, they worked in very dangerous, dramatic conditions. The Chinese politicians strove in vain to show that the missionaries were instruments of capitalism and Western Imperialism. Only the Chinese poor, abandoned by everyone, knew they experienced the same degree of hunger, poverty and humility as they did. The priests managed to ease the countless hardships of the poor and founded schools and orphanages for abandoned children. I clearly remember one hundred iron beds lined up in the vast bedroom of an orphanage. They were cots, but they looked big because of the tiny, abandoned, almost weightless, children that laid their heads on the thin pillows. It was as still and silent as a mortuary. All the blank, mute faces of these children bore the scars of poverty. Their sleep was troubled by the constant threat of hunger and illness and their waxen faces looked prematurely old. Few survived, but the missionaries said: 'Let us at least save their souls so they can ascend to heaven to pray for the many poor people of this nation', then they made the sign of the cross.

In the first days of my trip, I hung on every word said by my driver, Xiao Xu, who gave me Chinese lessons with the pronounced retroflex "r" sound characteristic of the Beijing accent. That, coupled with the four pitched tones of the Chinese language, made me gloomily aware that I would never speak the language fluently, despite my origins. I had been taught in my Chinese lessons in Milan that a Chinese man, woman, person of importance or child should be addressed as *tongshi* or "companion". In China, I used *tongshi* just as I had been taught, but received the impression that everyone I addressed in that way was looking at me rather condescendingly. So I cautiously began to abandon this form of address and reverted to my childhood habit of calling a man "eldest", a woman "aunt", a salesgirl "little sister", an office worker "little brother", and an elderly man "grandfather". People's expressions immediately softened and they were more courteous. It crossed my mind to wonder whether *tongshi* as a form of address had disappeared along with the Little Red Book. Meanwhile, I continued to use my "baby talk". Other words have acquired or lost meanings with the rapidly changing times. The words "my man" or "my woman", which many people use with unshakeable certainty, do not exist. In the same way, no one tends to say "my girlfriend" or "my boyfriend" in China. The most widespread word after *mu* and *fu* ("mother" and "father"), is *ai-ren* which refers to a loved one—either a husband or wife. The word "concubine" can no longer be used in the sense of "lover", as it is too closely linked to the ancient official connotation of adultery. Engagements are so short in China that marriage follows almost immediately, usually leading to the word *haizi* (child) nine months later.

I am on the train to Suzhou, once called "Soochow", the Chinese Venice, which is two hours from Shanghai. A girl who looks as if she is made of porcelain is sitting opposite me, smiling and playing "little rat" with her white handkerchief. We used to play this when we were children to keep us amused. Years later, I did it to entertain my daughter, Nicole. When I notice her, she is just finishing the mouse's ears. I begin to smile, knowing I can do better. She takes the initiative and asks me, in English: 'Are you English?'
  'No, I'm not,' I reply.
  'Are you French?' she continues, undaunted.
  'No, I'm Italian, but I speak English.'
  'Good! I can speak to you in English and get a little practice,' she says happily, and continues, 'The only chance I get to practise is at the English Speaking Corner, where they hold English conversations every weekend.'
  The English Speaking Corner in the People's Park in Shanghai had a strange genesis. A group of elderly people, who had learned English as children in the missionary schools before the Revolution, met every Sunday in the same corner of the park to practise the language. They attracted the attention of some students wanting to learn and practise

English and in 1979, what started as an informal meeting, became a weekly institution.

'I'm staying in Shanghai all this week,' I tell her.

'I live in Shanghai. If you like, I can show you around and you can help me practise my English. OK?'

Her name is Blue Sky and she has recently graduated in pharmacology. Her good marks have earned her a scholarship and she is soon to go to America to take a postgraduate course at the University of Michigan, at Ann Arbor.

From the train window I admire the beautiful lush countryside. Barges transport timber along the canals bordering the streets; the banks are lined with poplars and supple weeping willows that trail their branches in the water. Arched bridges and neatly cultivated fields like gardens stretch as far as the eye can see. Burial mounds are dotted about on the hills like swellings that are no longer painful.

'My grandfather is buried here,' says Blue Sky, interrupting my thoughts. 'We have bought a small plot of land and my father has had our tomb built. But now they want us all to be cremated, because they say there are too many of us, even when we're dead!'

'Has the life of the peasants improved in these areas?' I ask her.

'Definitely, they are one of the classes that are better off. They rent the land from the government and sell the products they harvest. The "courtyard economy" was established during the reforms. Now many peasants can rent other fields, as well as the land they have been allocated, and raise chickens, ducks and fish so they can improve their income. The peasants work very hard though and have a hard life. I know a little about it because I experienced it. During the Cultural Revolution, when I was a child, we were sent to learn how to do minor chores, like feeding the pigs, even sowing. They wanted us to realise how hard the peasants' life can be.' She continues, becoming more engrossed in a subject that still interests her deeply.

'I was only ten. The schoolchildren spent a great deal of

time in the countryside because the government wanted to teach them what physical labour was like and give them a practical illustration of the Chinese saying: "The intellectuals take precedence over the peasants, but when there is no rice the peasants take precedence over the intellectuals." Others were sentenced to live and work in the countryside as a punishment. It has all changed now and, as a result, many students have now forgotten what hard work is. Some peasants, though, manage to build themselves houses in their limited free time, doing masonry and carpentry when they should be resting. Rice, wheat and pigs are the government's three blessings.'

I note down what Blue Sky is saying.

'Note-taking is better than a good memory,' she says

I think how Chinese opinions always end up sounding like proverbs. I tell her this and we both laugh.

Back in Shanghai, Blue Sky and I take a stroll before saying goodbye. We decide to walk to the Bund, because I want to have tea at the Peace Hotel, which used to be the Cathay Hotel when I went there as a child with my mother. I take photos of the interior without explaining to Blue Sky why I am particularly interested in this hotel. I order some *paotze*— round dumplings with 15 folds, a Shanghai speciality—that I used to eat when I was a little girl. Blue Sky orders a fish dish with mushrooms and bamboo shoots.

I watch her eating and notice that she looks as if she is meditating every time she puts some food in her mouth. I ask her why and she explains that when she eats she always thinks about what she is tasting. I tell her that, in my view, this is a very healthy habit. I, on the other hand, eat so fast that I sometimes have no idea what I am swallowing. I have completely lost the Chinese pace of life.

We go back outside. It is very hot and the traffic is chaotic. There are bicycles everywhere, people are pushing and shoving, and some, realising that I am a foreigner, whisper furtively: 'Change money? Change money?' English is the language of the world of petty finance here.

Suddenly, the Big Ben of the Customs House rings three times—the only sound that is still familiar to me after all these years. The loud chimes project me into the past, sparking off a flurry of thoughts that are more like feelings than ideas.

Apart from that, I feel almost like a stranger in Shanghai; the city arouses very few emotions, and having been born here is simply a personal detail.

We cross the bridge guarded by two carved stone lions to get to the Longhua Temple. Almost all Buddhist temples are made up of a series of three or four pavilions. The dormitories, individual monks' cells and the common rooms where they eat and cook are located at the sides. The Longhua temple is a fascinating example of the architectural development of these buildings. Notable features include the deliberate sweep of the rafters, the single load-bearing column and the square plan of each of the five halls. These elements represent an ancient heritage, recalling the nomadic tents of the Mongolian conquerors of China. The first hall is that of the "Laughing Buddha". Gazing up at him, Blue Sky and I return the reassuring smile he bestows on everyone, good or evil. His huge bulk is placed above a large altar and in this temple he enjoys the privilege of being the only deity in the room. In other temples, the large "Laughing Buddha" usually shares the room with the "Four Gods". These large, grotesque figures are minor deities, one-time demons who subsequently converted to Buddhism. Blue Sky reassures me that their fierce expressions are not directed at the onlookers, but represent instead the savagery they still harbour as a result of all the fights they undertook on behalf of the faithful Buddhists.

I came to the Longhua Temple as a child with my Buddhist grandmother and, today, I rediscover the Black Face God. They used to threaten to give me to the Black Face God if I was naughty.

When I had to go to the temple for a festival, I always wanted to avoid walking past the right hand side of the altar in the hall of the "Four Gods", so that I did not have to see his statue. Inventing some excuse, I would pull my grandmother to the left of the central altar and keep my head bowed to avoid looking at him; even a glimpse of his black feet with his large toes emerging from his coloured sandals would start me thinking about the countless punishments that, they said, "Black Face" would mete out to naughty children.

Today the temple has a different atmosphere. I notice that the monks are wearing grey tunics; it is not easy to tell them apart from the nuns, because they all have completely shaved heads and are dressed the same. This is the first time I have seen the temple for 30 years, and I carefully examine the Black Face God from head to toe. He looks more like a large theatre mask of a fierce warrior, or the guard of a tomb, than a god. In any case, he is the only god that is black. Now that I am no longer frightened of him, I want to find out why he is that colour. A Zen monk explains that he is the God of the Wind.

'Why does he look so angry and evil?' I ask.

'To show the wind that he is stronger than it, to frighten it and keep it far from the coasts, where it can cause so much damage to people and property,' answers the monk.

The peasants hold this god in great honour, particularly during the monsoon period. If they neglect to offer him incense and other "delicacies", they run the risk of endangering the harvest or the fishing, and bringing other disasters down on their heads. I gave him two red candles with words of good luck written in gold. I take two others with me, to Milan!

Blue Sky and I head for another of my favourite places: the Yu Garden, which I used to call "my" garden, when I was a child. I would go there with the class on special occasions and when there was no danger of Japanese air-raids.

This garden, which is in the old city, is ancient. It was built during the Ming dynasty in honour of a Mandarin, who was the Minister of Justice. Like China itself, it has had a chequered history. It was destroyed about 1856 during the Taiping revolt, then damaged by fires and vandalism during the Opium War. It also experienced other trials and tribulations like the Japanese occupation, World War Two and the Cultural

Revolution. "My" garden is just how I remember it, which makes me very happy.

I decide that I am finally ready to look for the most important place of my childhood. So, a few days later, I take the first step and go to the French Consulate. A polite woman comes over to meet me, and says:

'Can I help you, Madame?'

'Yes, thank you. I was born here in Shanghai and I attended a French religious institution; all I remember is its name—the *Couvent de Saint Joseph*. I think it must be near the Bund, because we were often taken there for walks. I would like to find out its address and visit it after so many years. I have a hazy memory of a street name: Rue Montaubon. I don't remember any other details.'

'Wait here, Madame, I'll go and ask our *attaché culturel*. He is bound to be of more help,' replies the woman politely.

I see through the glass partition that she is talking to a young official. She beckons me over and says: 'I'll hand you over to this gentleman, Madame.' The cultural attaché is called Eric Herfort. He seems very obliging. He invites me to sit near him, while he begins to rifle through old maps of the streets of the French Concession during those years.

Looking for my school is certainly not easy because the streets have changed their names. Patiently, he looks through the maps: Rue Lafayette, Rue Bourgeat, Boulevard des Deux Républiques, Quai de France, Boulevard de Montigny and so on. There is no Rue Montaubon on any of them. Perhaps I was mistaken about the name of the street. The official continues to look through the maps, murmuring various names. Suddenly, he says the name "Zikawei". 'Ah,' I exclaim immediately, 'the Meteorological Observatory! I went there occasionally, with the nuns, to see the Jesuit priests, the ones who watched out for typhoons. But my college was a long way from there!'

'If you know Zikawei, I can arrange for you to speak to an elderly Chinese man who lived with the Jesuits in Zikawei. His name is Joseph Hsieh, he's about 80 and he knows everyone. Perhaps he was there at that time.' He consults a telephone directory on the desk and picks up the telephone. He explains my request to the man he is speaking to, then passes the receiver to me, saying: 'Madame, Monsieur Hsieh is on the phone. Why not talk to him yourself?'

'Good day, Madame. I'm eighty years old and I know your convent well—it was built in 1896 by the French, but I don't remember the name of the street either. You probably know, Madame, that all the city streets have been renamed. Don't worry, leave me your name and your hotel phone number. I will make some enquiries and phone you tomorrow. A man of my age knows a great many people.'

I immediately think: why wait till tomorrow? I ask the official for the exact address of Zikawei. Meanwhile, Monsieur Herfort tells me there is still a cathedral near the Bund that is called Saint Joseph's. Perhaps it is a clue. I suddenly remember something. Yes, that is my cathedral, so the convent must be nearby. Fire! Fire! I thought, speeding into action, as in the children's game.

I rush to Zikawei in a taxi. All around I see houses being demolished and streets in a shambles. Everything is in chaos. I try hard to remember something, but cannot piece together any memories. Everything looks smaller. Time shrinks everything, mixes up memories and fades them, just as your mind does.

The church at Zikawei, however, is well preserved behind a locked gate that protects it like the walls of the Forbidden City. A sign says that it is open on Thursdays and Sundays.

I call out loudly and refuse to admit defeat until, finally, a man arrives.

'I'm looking for *Père* Wong,' I say.

I follow him inside, leaving behind the blinding light, the muggy heat, the people and the traffic fumes. The cathedral is quiet and cool.

I look at the altar. I am drawn by the light filtering through the round stained-glass window depicting a large bleeding heart: a representation of the Sacred Heart. This is really the church of the Fathers of the Society of Jesus, the ones that used to watch out for the typhoons. I sit on a bench waiting anxiously and breathing in the smell of the statues. Suddenly, the invisible organ breaks the silence, producing dense, quavering tones—not music, just tuneless vibrations. The notes bounce off the high walls and vaults of the church in resonant echoes, then the sound stops as suddenly as it began.

The *curé* comes to meet me, surprisingly dressed in a white T-shirt and grey trousers. He apologises for his style of dress and explains that the government does not allow him to wear a cassock.

I briefly tell him why I am here and what I am looking for. He tells me that all the French Jesuits left in 1955 and that the church has been closed for many years. The Chinese Jesuits remained confined to the diocese for all that time, but now they are all dead—he is the only one left. I take some photos of the altar and the stained-glass windows, a souvenir of the time I spent here; I also take a photo of him, because he is part of a place that provides a direct link to my past. I ask about the old observatory.

'It's behind you, Madame,' he says, pointing.

The building is unrecognisable. All that can be seen is the dial of the clock that I actually do remember. The rest of the red-brick complex is completely surrounded by new buildings, as if someone wanted to wipe out the past and hide it from view. A triumphant new eighteen-storey skyscraper soars to the right of the observatory.

'Father, who can I ask for the address of Saint Joseph's Cathedral? I must find my convent,' I say urgently. Unhesitatingly, he writes a name and address on a slip of paper, which I immediately give to the taxi driver. We leave Zikawei.

Near Saint Joseph's Cathedral, at 36 Sichuan Lu, the streets are also in a shambles and houses are being knocked down; there is so much chaos and noise that it looks as if the area has been bombed.

The cathedral has two bell towers and is surrounded by a low wall. I enter the only open door and ask to speak with Father Laurent Jiang. The women sitting near the door go to fetch a young man, to whom I tell the reason for my visit.

This is the third time today that I have told my story. He tells me to come back tomorrow at seven in the morning, at the hour for mass. In the meantime, he invites me into the church, my church, which is silent and feels empty, as if no one has ever set foot inside. I recognise the Saint Joseph over the altar, but I do not remember him being so young. The vibrant reds and electric blues of the stained-glass windows here, also catch my eye. I immediately take some photos before these memories also fade from my mind. Outside the cathedral, the heaps of gravel, tools—and a few bricklayers, sweat running down their tanned backs and faces—inspire a feeling of desolation.

I turn to an old man sitting near the wall—perhaps he will know when I will be able to see Father Jiang. He has no idea, but wants to help, so he asks another old man. In a few minutes, I am surrounded by a crowd of people, because the story of my request has spread like wildfire.

Everyone here seems to want to help other people with their problems. It is an attractive characteristic that makes me feel less alone. Everyone agrees in the end that I should come back at seven tomorrow morning, when Father Jiang takes mass. I go back to the hotel, exhausted. It is almost evening, but I feel that I am on the right track. Fire! Fire! the voice inside my head repeats even louder.

The next morning, Father Jiang is waiting for me. He has been told about me by the whole community living within the cathedral's gloomy precincts. I follow him and he makes me comfortable in the sacristy, offering me tea and asking me to tell him my story. He does not appear to be in a hurry and listens carefully. We speak in French.

I notice that he is wearing a polo shirt and white trousers instead of a cassock. He is a thin, rather slight man, with spectacles that magnify his expressive eyes. He tells me that he was a seminarian near the Church, and has almost never left this area, not even during the Cultural Revolution. He says that the last French Jesuit left China in 1956, but there are still some Chinese priests here. During the Cultural

301

Revolution, he was also confined in a requisitioned institution.

'There are some old nuns in Zikawei, but there's no point speaking to them: they don't remember anything. Don't go back to Zikawei, Madame, you'll be even more disappointed,' he advises me, almost reading my thoughts.

'What with the war and one revolution after another, how are the poor people faring after all they have suffered, Father? Shanghai seems like a large village with countless people living and working on the streets. I don't recognise the city anymore,' I blurt out in disappointment.

Father Jiang replies that people are better off and that the reason why people spill out into the streets is that there is no room left in the houses. The most pressing problem these days is making sure that everyone has a roof over their head.

'But do they have enough to eat, at least?'

'Oh, yes, the problem of the single bowl of rice has been solved. Everyone has enough to eat now.'

'Father, I remember a street called Rue Montaubon. Does that mean anything to you?'

'Of course, it's the name of this street, only now it is called Sichuan Lu.'

'But that means my school must be nearby!' I exclaim.

'It's actually opposite. I will take you over, if you like, but I must ask permission; the government has not demolished the school, but the building has been divided into three separate institutions: a nursery school, a primary school and a workshop.'

I cross the street and Father Jiang points to the main entrance, which is at number 36. He asks a doorman sitting by the entrance if he can speak with the foreman, outlining my story.

A man with a kind smile arrives and shows us in. He is moved because I have travelled so far to see "my places": he offers to escort me himself around the building. I follow him, filled with the uncertain curiosity of someone who is retracing their footsteps.

'This was the parlour, Madame. Do you remember?'

'Vaguely. As I was coming in, I recalled that these rooms were used for visitors; but I remember the main entrance being larger!'

'This was your courtyard; in the middle there was the Madonna and Saint Bernadette,' says Father Jiang.

'Yes, we roller-skated here, and there, at the side, was a large hall, where we all used to assemble during the air-raids. We came down the stairs there, and walked down that corridor to end up down here. There were three dormitories, because we were divided according to age,' I add.

Despite these explanations, I cannot find my bearings: everything seems to have moved. I cannot pinpoint the rooms and the chapel. Meanwhile, the foreman politely invites us to continue on towards a corridor leading to another wing of the school. Father Jiang stops here and points to the former site of the chapel. Suddenly, in my mind's eye, I see instead, Father Thornton, the attractive Irish Jesuit who came to give the novena; I cannot remember his profile—just his distinctive tone of voice. Immediately his image disappears, like a cinematographic fade-out, and the cap vaults and capitals come back into focus, but not where I remember them. This place is no longer a chapel, but a workshop. I resign myself to taking photos in the hope that they will help me later to piece together the jigsaw of my memories.

We leave the building and head for the other door, hoping to recognise something on the way. There is a group of women sitting in front of the door. We visit the three floors that are now home to 300 children, including those from the nursery school and the primary classes. The headmistress, who is surprised and moved by the reason for my visit, offers to accompany us.

'These are the original stairs,' she says. I look at them and I do actually recognise the reddish colour of the wood, but they seem shorter than I remember when we used to slide down the banisters from the third floor when the nuns were not looking. I wonder how we could have had so much fun, if the flights of stairs were so short.

The headmistress points to another walled-up entrance to the chapel. The workshop was built on the other side. When we come to the first floor, I feel as if I am walking through a dream maze—the further we go, the hazier my memory becomes. On either side of a corridor, there are four rooms lodging the children from the nursery who, at a sign from their headmistress, clap to welcome me. This is the only pleasing note of my visit. I go upstairs to the second floor, then the third, where I meet some more children. From the window of one of the rooms, I manage to glimpse the two bell towers of the cathedral and take a photo. I am feeling increasingly disorientated. I cannot work out where my dormitory was, or the chapel and the rooms, while the few discoveries I make bear no relation to each other and only confuse me further. Father Jiang watches me as I wander among the rooms like a sparrow that does not know what season it is and is searching for summer food in the middle of winter.

'We change, Madame, and, although it's hard to accept, time will eventually wipe us out too,' he concludes, as we walk downstairs. I cannot believe I ever lived here. I feel like a failure. This place is pushing me out like a foreigner.

Despite my best attempts, I cannot banish the snatches of memory that fill my mind. I see the girl I used to be leaving the convent, a beret covering my thick black, wavy hair, a blue uniform swamping my slender frame. My pockets are full of the biscuit crumbs that I used to feed to the sparrows hopping around the courtyard. I always had something or other crumpled up in my fist, like a secret I had wrung from someone.

Thinking back to my past life in this convent, I realise I was leading a charmed existence—life was good to me and I was good to it. Then, I was a strange mixture of knowledge and ignorance, and the less I knew about life, the better I did at school.

We go back to the cathedral and I ask the taxi-driver to take a photo, a souvenir. Turning to the priest, I say: 'I don't think we can ever go back. My search for the past is a search for a utopia.'

'I understand, Madame,' is his only reply. The priest wants to take a photo of me by the altar of Saint Joseph.

'There were two large stoves here,' I say suddenly.

'Yes, that's right. We only put them there in winter,' he replies.

I am happy that at least this small memory has been borne out. Our conversation ends on this note. I give Father Jiang an offering for his church. With some emotion, he tells me that he is pleased that a former pupil has travelled so far to find her own church and the places that once meant so much to her. We look at each other in silence for a second and I hesitate to take my leave, embarrassed by what he has just said. To some extent, he is a link to what little I have managed to recapture. I make an effort, climb into the taxi and look back for the last time. I see the back of the priest who is walking slowly towards the church, and when we round the bend and the two spires also disappear, I heave a sigh of relief, as if a weight has been lifted from me.

Back at the hotel, I confess I spend almost an hour in tears. The *Couvent de Saint Joseph* is making a fool of me. I try to make my vague memories of the place tally with the one that was within my grasp a few hours ago but, as in a children's game, it dodges just as I am about to catch it, turning my memories to empty reminiscences that prove impossible to recapture.

Old Joseph Hsieh was true to his word. He gave me all the information I had asked for, and which I now knew, and left me a telephone number, saying: 'If you ever come back to Shanghai, call 377774.'

Watching the news on TV, I learn that the city of Ningbo, my next destination, has been devastated by a typhoon that has killed more than three hundred people. There is a shortage of water and an epidemic is feared. All lines of communication are blocked and I am forced to extend my stay in Shanghai until the situation improves.

I cannot sleep because of the heat, so I lie there thinking. Although I am not a fervent Catholic, the church was the landmark that enabled me to find my school again, fulfilling a thirty-year-old wish. The school was my family: it raised me

305

and I am upset that I could not recognise it—it is as if I have lost the ability to see. Places no longer look the same. My eyes and my mind cannot align the continually shifting memories that overlap and intermingle in confused patterns— it is like looking into a kaleidoscope. There is no landmark that will allow me to reconstruct my school-family the way I remember it and the way I was hoping to find it. I visited a different place, a place that no longer exists: a "non place", a utopia. I am upset by my disappointing failure.

Breakfast, reading the newspaper, everything I have planned for the day, help me block out the thoughts that come to mind every so often. I know I am leaving Shanghai forever.

From the top of my hotel, I can see the Bund, the skyscrapers, the old houses and gardens. I look at the panorama one last time. I can see the contours of the city, but I cannot look inside it. It is one-dimensional and flat— like looking at a postcard photographed against the light. I feel absolutely nothing. This circle of life has come to a close.

5

I arrive in Nanking, three hours late, but no one relies on the timetable in China, so there is no need to rush. As the ship draws nearer the river port, water birds take flight noisily. The closer we draw to the shore, the muddier the water becomes, giving off an unpleasant smell of rotting grass.

The Chinese passengers about to disembark gaze sleepily at the moon. They have not yet shrugged off their long journey, or the games of dice and cards played in smoky, secluded corners of the ship. The tourists stand at the railings to take in the panoramic view. The landscape is as flat as a calm sea. On the horizon, a few lights shine in Nanking.

From this vantage point, it is hard to think that the city was one of China's six capitals; nothing survives of ancient Nanking except the walls.

The Taiping Revolution and a hundred years of war have destroyed the architecture that Marco Polo described as magnificent, over a century ago. After the foundation of the New China, millions of dollars were sunk into the mass of modern buildings that can be seen today: houses, streets, bridges, public and commemorative buildings.

After 100 years of terror and destruction, the local authorities gave the green light to an extensive construction and reforestation programme and, after several decades of work, the city has more tree-covered land than the average city in China. Now Nanking looks as though it was built within an immense forest. There are numerous parks with countless lakes and islands sheltering in their shade. The city's gardens are a favourite haunt of tourists who like flowers and plants.

Brightly-coloured expanses of peonies, camellias, peach and plum blossom alternate in the city and surrounding countryside. The average summer temperature has fallen by three degrees owing to the tall plane trees, the cedars and the carpet of vegetation—which is quite a drop, if you consider that Nanking is known as one of China's "four ovens". It is now one of the most modern cities in the country, and also the shadiest.

I am strolling in a park, under the shade of the trees. I feel very sad, perhaps because of the heat or the weariness caused by my solitary pilgrimage in search of the places dear to me. Suddenly everything seems too difficult: walking, thinking, making enquiries to find out things. I try to relax like one of the old men sitting in this park, to take in my surroundings and absorb a little of their serenity and idleness.

I sit under a gigantic weeping willow trailing its branches in the water. It is an ancient tree of great importance, because it bears a plaque carved with a poet's name. A butterfly lands on my lap. It stays there motionless for a second, then flies off, carrying my childhood with it.

I sit there, watching. You never see the Chinese taking a dog for a walk on a leash, but you often see someone Chinese, usually an old man, carrying a round wicker cage covered with a cloth. After leaving the path and reaching the trees, he removes the cloth from the cage and shows these natural surroundings to the chaffinches and nightingales he is carrying. He and his friends then enjoy this woodland scene, while listening to the birds' cheerful song. It is an ancient pastime.

These bird lovers often meet in small copses where, hanging their round cages on the lower branches of the trees, they delight together in this melodious chorus, walking self-importantly among the cages. They hang cages with females in front of the males to make them sing at the tops of their voices, and laughter spreads like wildfire as the males immediately warble in frantic trebles as if competing in a singing contest. Everyone goes home holding their cages with large grins on their faces. The rumble of two aeroplanes landing at the nearby airport does not seem to disturb them: they are completely oblivious to the noise. Their world is the park, the small wood, and the round cage holding these tiny birds, whose song is a joy to hear.

I also see that the martial art of *taijiquan* is very popular in the parks—it seems like a real craze. Old and young men, women of all ages, even students and foreign tourists are intent on slowly raising their arms, then one leg, rotating it, as in a game of shadows. After slowly turning one leg and putting it down, they raise the other, in a sort of trance. These solitary dancers, with the inner strength of their slow, fluid moves, look as if they are pushing against a dense space with their hands and body. They gaze into the distance with impenetrable expressions and breathe slowly and deeply as they perform the moves. They repeat these exercises every morning, at the same time. *Taijiquan* is an ancient discipline that improves mental concentration and physical coordination.

The parks also have children's playgrounds, and teenagers come here to walk, in couples or in groups. The peaceful atmosphere of the park seems infectious and they are all calm and cheerful—it is rare to see groups of teenagers being rowdy or upsetting the children or the many elderly people. I have noticed that respect for the elderly has remained unchanged since my childhood in China. I think this is the only country where the old can still feel comfortable in modern society. This widespread respect for old age is worth far more than their meagre pensions or rest homes. Elderly people can be happy with very little if they have all the material essentials they need and if they are surrounded not only by their family's love, respect and understanding, but also those of society.

The teachings of Confucius still run in Chinese veins! The sage said of the elderly: 'Those who love their parents dare not show hatred towards others. Those who respect their own parents dare not appear coarse to others.'

If I had to come back to China, even for a single day, I would not revisit the past, guided only by my emotions; instead, I would allow myself to be swayed by spaces and colours; I would stand motionless in the side courtyard of an ancient palace and run my hand down the banister of a white marble staircase. I would not take a tour, I would just stroll. After every trip, there is always a reason for going back to a place to check your first impressions. Reactions are very personal. If I were to travel with one of you, we would not be making the same trip. We could never come away with the same impressions.

6

Many Oriental cities are shaped by their monuments or architectural styles; China's characteristic features have been fashioned by nature.

As well as taking in the newness of the landscape, I have to decipher the jumble of dialects that make it impossible for me to work out someone's place of origin. While Mandarin—the country's official language—dominates in the north, there is a real mix of dialects in the south and this, along with the use of my Anglo-Chinese slang, makes it difficult for me to communicate.

The only familiar vocal sound I have come across has been the Ningbo intonation, spoken by a woman who was upset, exclaiming *ah là, ah là,* followed by other words. Their modulated inflection I recognised, although not their meaning. I looked at her inquisitively and, when I heard her voice, I stared at her intently. That tone of voice, which I heard so often when I was a child, brought back other voices and with them a flood of personal memories that filled me with melancholy. Every memory, even if it is just a sound, is an emotional recollection—a living language of everyday things. I have forgotten the names of the cereals I ate and the names of the herbs with which they treated me. Languages maintain a strong link with reality; by mutilating them, I restrict my feelings and thoughts.

Ning-po is now called Ningbo. When I used to travel there as a child, the crossings were almost always accompanied by rough seas and strong winds. It was said that the waters of the gulf we had to cross were infested by pirates who were based on the islands of the Chusan Archipelago. It appears that they have now returned. I would like to forgo the experience of meeting them.

When I was a child, the journey from Shanghai to Ningbo was always without incident. I usually travelled with Amah, and sometimes with my grandmother, who were both Buddhist and very superstitious.

Buddhism owes much of its success in China to its ability to relieve uncertainty and fear. The fact that Chinese women had very little knowledge of the sea, coupled with a great fear of pirates, meant that all my journeys became a continual lament, as they prayed—on this occasion—to Gwan-Yin, the Goddess of Mercy.

Gwan-Yin was originally an Indo-Tibetan deity, who was brought to China by faithful Buddhists in the 5th century AD. The iconography of Gwan-Yin shows her as the captain of a ship transporting the faithful over the hostile sea of human suffering to reach eternal peace. Gwan-Yin is also the patron saint of sailors, but is highly revered by everyone, particularly women.

The way my grandmother and Amah acted on the way from Shanghai to Ningbo was ample proof of this veneration.

I spent my most enjoyable years at the Jesuit mission in Ningbo. But my memories are not in any precise chronological order. They are as muddled as a freshly shuffled pack of cards. I wander through the streets at random, trying to find the comfort that kept me going in my many years of daydreams. The sultry heat continues, but in the evening there is a slight breeze from the sea.

There are new generations of pedlars on the streets of the city. They seem to be smiling at me with familiarity, as if they recognise me, like the dignified elderly scribe sitting at his little desk spread with all the essentials for writing on behalf of the illiterate; or the man selling dusty books arranged in two rows on the table, with pocket editions hanging precariously from string on a bamboo pole. There is the herbalist with makeshift shelves crammed with bottles containing dried snakes and twisted roots: at the centre, flowers and leaves are spread out on a sheet of newspaper. The pedlar smiles at me and looks round to call me over, but then desists.

The barber sitting under a tree with his stool and his basin, is busy shaving a customer. Everyone seems to smile affectionately at me. There is no sign, however of the pedlar selling tablets against snakebites; perhaps he fell victim to the ineffectiveness of his antidote.

The shops also look as they did before: the ones selling paper umbrellas have them open and hanging upside down to keep their oiled, impermeable coating even. There is still the shop selling effigies and the paper funerary accessories that are burned at funerals—there are clothes, chairs, boats; everything that these "silent customers" might need in the afterlife. The Chinese have always believed that the soul of the deceased needs all the material comforts that he or she enjoyed in life. With modernisation, these models now include additional articles that did not exist in my time, such as aeroplanes, motorbikes, cars and even telephones.

There are only a few fan shops left, even though the fan is still regarded as one of the most important objects to provide relief from the heat in summer. Its origins date back to antiquity. They were actually used to clear the dust raised by the wheels of the carriages. During my visit to China, I fanned myself continually to cool myself down. Everyone uses them—even carters when they take a break, fishermen in their boats when they are becalmed, as well as beggars.

I notice there are still beggars, but not many compared to when I was here before. Beggars believed that begging was just one way to earn a living. There were usually many handicapped beggars who had been thrown out by their families because they were regarded as unproductive, and also women who had often fled brutal husbands or a forced marriage arranged by their parents. They usually came from country areas.

I peer into a half-closed shop that sells gigantic masks with scarlet mouths and grotesque heads worked by strings. It looks like a murderer's lair. The masks are made of papier mâché. There must be a festival in the offing—it is a pity I cannot stay to watch it. As in every other city, the rickshaw pullers have disappeared. The streets no longer echo with the noise of bare feet running, accompanied by the sound of a hacking cough, as they used to do when I was a child.

I cannot shake off the feeling that the old scribe recognised me. Perhaps he felt the same. His mind would now be clouded by age, although there was a knowing smile in his eyes when they met mine. Perhaps my mind is clouded by the vain hope of finding at least one "survivor" from my years in Ningbo.

The mission, I remember, was a complex commissioned and built by the French Jesuits around the mid-19th century to take in foundlings. Like ancient Chinese structures, it was built symmetrically to form a single group linked by a series of courtyards and arranged in three parallel lines.

In my mission, Monsieur Corcouf, the Jesuit father—a French resident—taught me to read and repeat in French: 'Lalie a six ans, sa maman la mène à l'école...'

In the afternoons, Mu Mu helped me do my homework and to hold my brush firmly between my fingers for calligraphy exercises, as well as teaching me to recite French poetry by heart for the festivals at the mission.

I am now walking along streets that I once travelled by rickshaw; cars and bicycles race past, keeping pace with my vanishing desires. My disappointment at my incomplete search kills all feelings of nostalgia, leaving me thinking sadly about the many ghosts that are now gone forever.

My desire to keep looking fades, flickers, then completely gutters out in Ningbo, leaving behind a vacuum. And yet I have worked so hard to get here, weighed down by a burden of memories. The disappointment I felt in Shanghai is redoubled here and I realise that the world I was looking for now exists only in my mind; desperately wanting to find it again is pure fantasy, I have come looking for a utopia—that is the only reason I came back to China. The utopia I was seeking is like the compass needle, without which you are lost.

This makes me think about the fable that the Chinese have summarised in a single phrase: "The world beyond the Peach Blossom River"—in other words, utopia or "nowhere".

We were told this fable when I was a girl with a head full of dreams that could never come true because they were not part of our world: they belonged to the world of a fisherman who goes astray in his boat along the Peach Blossom River, as told by T'ao Chien during the Qin dynasty. The fisherman allows himself to be carried by the current through a rolling landscape filled with peach blossom, until the boat comes to a stop at the mouth of a cave. He moors the boat and ventures inside the rock. When he emerges on the other side, he is amazed by what he sees: a vast plain, hundreds of beautiful houses surrounded by flowers, clumps of bamboo and thickets of mulberry trees. The fields are filled with vegetation. The murmuring of the brooks accompanies the cheerful singing of the birds. There is an atmosphere of happiness, harmony and safety. People run to welcome the fisherman and offer him food and drink. However, although the inhabitants try to convince the fisherman to stay, he decides to leave this "heaven on earth" and go back to see his family and friends, having already been gone a long time. On his way back, he makes a mental note of the exact location of the cave along the river, as well as every bend and stretch of landscape covered with peach blossom along the way, so that he can find the cave again. The officials of his village, after listening fascinated to his account, and impatient to reach this marvellous place, ask him to escort them to the cave on the Peach Blossom River. The fisherman goes with them but, as with the "places" on my trip across China, the spot was never found.

Just as utopia is a "non-place"—a place that no longer exists—so was the Ningbo of the Jesuit mission and the shady garden, and the Shanghai of the *Couvent de Saint Joseph*, as well as all the other places I visited on the trail of my memories. I have now stopped dwelling on the past and have started to experience China as it is today; but I wonder if the world I was so keen to revisit ever really existed. If I could collect all the images of every flowering peach tree that I have ever seen and add them to those depicted by the poets and painters, I still would not find a match for the flowering peach tree before me today. I do not think there is any flowering tree more beautiful, perhaps because they are so widespread in China. They are a more familiar sight than any other, because a large part of my fascination for them resides in the "forgotten memories" that have left me with an enduring legacy of sadness.

7

I travel by train to Hangzhou, capital of the province of Zhejiang, southwest of Shanghai. Many years ago, my grandmother had a silkworm farm here and, with some relatives, co-owned a silk mill near the lake, ringed with green hills dotted with pagodas and temples. The tiny caterpillars would hatch in the spring at the same time as the tender young leaves sprouted on the mulberry trees. The creatures and the leaves would grow rapidly and, after about a month, you could hear a continuous rustling as the silkworms stripped the leaves as far as the eye could see. When fully grown, their bodies were almost transparent; they stopped eating and began to spin a silk cocoon around themselves. The peasants called the silkworms "little treasures". No light was allowed to enter the buildings in which they were bred and the sound of footsteps and voices was also avoided—I never played near there. During the Spring Festival, the peasants would make a sacrifice to the Silkworm Goddess in the hope that she would protect them. To this day, Zhejiang is known as the silk region and supplies a third of the national demand for raw silk, brocades and satin.

Walking round the markets today, I found spices, toilet paper and mosquito repellents as well as soft silks and delicate brocaded textiles. The poor districts are creeping up the hills, while luxurious houses are being built around the lake where once nobles from the Imperial court merrily passed the time with their courtiers on luxurious boats, sheltered by elegant canopies.

Thinking about crowded, noisy Shanghai and Ningbo, I am

not surprised that Hangzhou is now a favourite holiday and honeymoon destination. It has also been a very peaceful leg of my journey, because I visited it on a weekday when there were no swarms of tourists.

Before leaving Hangzhou, I visited three temples, one of which had a gigantic seated Buddha with twinkling eyes. There are at least three hundred Buddhas in the hills, seated in shrines carved into the rock, that were placed here by the Mongols after the Song dynasty was driven out. There is a God of Letters and another called the God of Literature who helps those who have to sit civil service exams. He holds a writing brush and a roll of paper which bears the words: 'The heavens decide literary success.' I offered him a stick of incense to ward off bad luck.

I took a sedan chair carried by two men dressed in period costumes along the narrow streets leading to the temples. On the way, I came across some village women with typical cushion-shaped hairstyles, carrying straw baskets over their arms. Their ivory complexions were flushed by the mountain breezes and their eyes smiled when they met mine. They were on their way to the tea plantations, and were gaily chorusing a song dedicated to tea—singing about the magical elixir that transforms our bodies into a weightless substance, like jade, a resistant to fire and ice, so our bodies can take up residence in the palaces in the clouds. When picking the leaves the young women's nails are neither too short nor too long. They actually use their nails, not their fingers, to pick the leaves, in order to avoid contaminating them with their sweat.

I stop in Shaoxing, not only to sample the perch for which it is famous, but also to visit its mountain. I remember this small city fondly from childhood walks in the "Garden of One Hundred Herbs", but prefer its Shan mountain with the Shanxi river flowing at its base.

Some of the citadel's houses and buildings have been built on the steep mountain slopes. All the larger streets are paved to avoid mud, while the alleyways have worn steps, shiny with centuries of use. When I was a child, I used to go for long walks with my girl friends along these paths and play hide and seek in the bamboo forests, watched by the women who came here to weave bamboo baskets, escape the muggy air of the plain and, sometimes, the air raids.

The fascinating method of cormorant fishing is also very popular in Shaoxing. The cormorant is as important for the fisherman as the buffalo is for the farmer. This time, perhaps because of the heat, I noticed a small detail I had never seen before—when the cormorants land on the boat after diving for fish, they stand motionless with their outspread wings exposed to the sun like two black fans; they do this, I discovered, to dry them in the sun's warmth. Unlike most water birds, their wing feathers are not water repellent. The longer their wings stay dry, the easier their task of finding and catching the fish under the water. A fisherman who owns ten cormorants is regarded as well-off. The birds usually breed before the Spring Festival and nest in the boats—they pile together pieces of dried twigs, rotten fish traps, scraps of string and bunches of grass to build a sheltered nest. The cormorant lays about ten eggs per brood; it is during this period that the roles between owner and bird are reversed! When the cormorant chicks hatch, the fisherman decides how many he will keep for himself and how many he will sell at the market or give away, traditionally wrapped in red paper for good luck. The fishermen tend to give tonics to the males to keep them in good condition, and to the females to encourage them to lay large broods. They seem to lavish unlimited care and attention on their cormorants because they are their family's meal ticket: fishing is their livelihood.

When I leave the district and the car drives along the banks of the Shanxi river, I realise that the road, lined by the mountain on one side and by the river on the other, is familiar to me. The river appearing and disappearing along the road seems to be playing hide-and-seek. The pagodas rapidly fade into the distance as I watch from the car. I think about my childhood. I travelled this road on various occasions, crossing an unfamiliar world. Now the past is behind me again. This is the same landscape that I will want to remember forever.

8

I arrive in Guilin around eight in the evening, because of a delayed departure. I am taking a short break after my pilgrimage through China in the summer heat and am counting on having a rest here among the green mountains and clear waters. I have come to Guilin because many of the tourists I have met on my travels in China have sung its praises.

Even from the air, the city looks magical, nestling among long ranges of mountains that rise individually from the water and the plain like spikes. In the half light, they look like statues of warriors. The countryside is sodden with water from the canals, lakes and tarns. In the valleys, the irregularly shaped paddy fields alternate with the darker green of cultivated fields to form an enormous jigsaw puzzle, while myriad reflections make this already unreal scene even more elaborate. In the moonlight, the Lijiang river winds like a silver ribbon between the peaks. It is dotted with barge lanterns and reflections from village lights.

The market sells all types of wares: from used tyres to various animals, including dogs, cats, monkeys and snakes. These latter are killed for food or medicinal purposes. There are also various types of freshwater fish for sale, as well as animals and insects that I had never seen before, but are regarded as delicacies here, along with caterpillars.

One stall is selling water chestnuts threaded like caramels on a bamboo skewer and I buy them immediately to recapture the flavours of my childhood. Your love for your native country is largely bound up with your recollection of intense sensory pleasures from childhood.

The most beautiful scenery I saw on my whole trip was a stretch of landscape between Guilin and Yangshuo, a journey of about fifty miles along the Lijiang river. Strangely shaped mountains line the banks: cones, pillars, pagodas. Some look vaguely like elephants, camels and fish, while others are situated in rows like a forest of cultivated trees. Solitary mountains soar skywards and there are rugged scenes and landscapes, thickets of gigantic bamboo trees, sheer cliffs, and sandy coves fanning open as far as the eye can see. The landscapes have inspired poetic names such as: "Carp Wall", "Nine Horses Mountain", "Five Fingers Hill". Bamboo rafts drift along the green water, while large junks sail upstream. Buffalos splash about in the coves with children and farmers.

As soon as we land in Yangshuo, I notice a fisherman on the quay, two cormorants perched on either end of the pole over his shoulders; two young men resolutely come over and insist on a payment of a few *yuan* for taking a photograph of the fisherman.

Yangshuo is a village with a great many crowded markets. Whole streets are given over to the "free" market, which is only a recent development. A small section of the uncovered market sells articles from the trunks of old families, together with objects that have been in use in homes for many years: small boxes made of precious stone, used seals, liqueur glasses, filigree hair clasps, elegant porcelain teapots and ivory chopsticks.

It is fascinating to stroll through this market. Pedlars catch hold of my arm shouting in English: 'This is old—Qing dynasty, this is Ming—fifty *yuan*! How much will you pay? Make me an offer!' Their final bargaining tactic is to give me a small piece of paper and a pencil and tell me to write down what I am prepared to pay.

This has been great fun until I realise that in a ten-minute walk my wallet has been stolen from my shoulder bag with my credit cards, dollars and lire.

The guide who was on the boat comes to my aid, while someone immediately alerts the police who are in the vicinity. They ask me to make a statement at the police station.

Surrounded by four men who are officers, I mistake them at first for peasants because they are wearing straw hats. The guide tells me that they are plainclothes policemen and that they patrol these areas to prevent crime. The police station is a small room with a square desk and two benches. I notice the ceiling fan because it is not working; each is fanning the other with their straw hats. While I wait on a narrow, uncomfortable wooden bench, I see a sticky fly paper hanging from the ceiling fan. Some of the flies are trying to break free, others, exhausted, have given up. In the end, none of them escapes. I would like one of them to fly off through the only open window, just as I would like to escape from this situation and the stench of people packed tightly into such a small place. The thought crosses my mind that I have seen those horrible fly papers before—in Grandfather Kon-Kon's country house in Kong-qiao during the hot summers.

I am dripping with sweat as I list the contents of my wallet. I have to complete a form with wide red lines. There are ten ideograms at the top. They make me press my right thumb on a red ink pad and put my fingerprint on the sheet where I have to sign, as if I was the thief.

They apologise for not catching the purse-snatcher. The guide informs me that it is against the law to charge anyone unless they are caught red-handed. The police inspector gives free rein to his irritation at this, uttering an untranslatable curse, whose meaning I know only too well. It was used widely by men from southern China.

I ask the guide to tell them that a thief cannot be arrested in Europe either if he is not caught stealing or if he does not admit his guilt, so apologies are unnecessary. Everyone there seems to look less embarrassed as a result of my words, because the Chinese are always afraid of losing face in front of foreigners. I leave the police station and retrace my route with the policemen along the street where I had been walking when the theft occurred.

I tell them that I stopped first in the shop where I bought a bracelet with a little bell, similar to those I was made to wear when I was a baby to attract my nurse's attention when I woke up. The policemen disperse the inquisitive crowd and question the shopkeeper and the other shop-owners along that stretch of street. But no one has seen anything; it was too crowded.

My anger at the theft of my wallet is appeased by distant memories of hearing about the cruel punishments meted out to thieves caught red-handed. Recent criminal and legal reforms have now led to substantial changes to the laws. Chinese society used to have no constitutional protection and the first criminal codes were only introduced in 1980.

In the past, the severity of a crime was judged according to the effect it might have on moral and social order. The citizens themselves assessed the importance or severity of an offence and the harm it might do to public order. The sentencing in the most serious cases was done by the emperors themselves or the local Mandarins, who avoided enforcing the laws as much as possible, for fear of inciting the people to rebellion. Several centuries ago, one emperor declared that anyone appealing to the courts would be dealt with in such a way that they would be disgusted by the laws and 'tremble at the mere thought of reappearing before a judge again.' In ancient China, judges were known as the "Kings of Hell"!

This discouraging attitude can be borne out in the county government office at Neixiang, in Henan Province, which has been preserved as a museum. The court where the judge passed his sentences can be visited; above the doors, there are two stone arches carved with ironic notices: 'The Governor is a public servant' and 'The People are in charge.' On the floor before the judge's desk, there are two stone slabs with four hollows called: "The stones of those who kneel", because both the accused and the accuser kneeled there, irrespective of who was right or wrong!

I might have had more chance of getting my "lost" wallet back ten years ago, when people would have chased the thief without wasting a precious second. Now all the "red tape" has excluded the people. I am well aware how patient you have to be in China when dealing with bureaucracy—and police stations.

I feel depressed. Being on my own all the time makes me wistful. I am tired of this trip and I think more and more frequently about going home. In my mind's eye, I keep seeing my daughter: her eyes flash, a shadow passes over her face, she smiles, then she says: 'Why are you there, all on your own?' As if looking in a mirror, I see my own face.

9

During my childhood years in China, I never ate snake meat, nor did I ever see anyone else eating it; but now I am intrigued by the idea of eating snake and would like to try it. In China, nothing is regarded as inedible, although the Chinese prefer eating prawns to locusts.

Having naturally good teeth, the Chinese never turn up their noses at locusts or snakes when there are no alternatives in times of famine. Snake meat is in any case regarded by many as a delicacy. Prejudices are innovation's worst enemy when it comes to food. Creativity widens the range of food placed by nature at our disposal.

In Guangdong Province, the capital of which is Canton, there are many gastronomic specialities that do not exist in other parts of China, so I make the most of my visit. The most sought-after specialities come under the heading of "game", which includes wild cats, tortoises, and civets, as well as various types of snake like cobra and rattlesnake. The Snake Restaurant, with several floors, offers all these specialities. One dish called "The Dragon and the Tiger" offers snake and cat meat. Popular choices include braised civet with herbs, and a starter of fried snails.

At night, this street becomes a busy market selling every imaginable speciality to seduce the palate. There is a kiosk selling different stews, while others sell jellies and various cuts of tortoise, considered extremely tasty by the working classes and an excellent antidote to impurities in the blood. It is very popular.

The woman selling the speciality stews greets customers with a broad smile, although she can barely be seen behind the clouds of steam that rise every time she lifts the lid of the pan.

I walk down a wide street named after the Taiping revolutionaries who fought against the European powers. This is the revolutionary city par excellence. Canton is a breeding ground for everything, even revolutions.

There are still ivory craftsmen in the old city's narrow streets. I enter this maze of alleyways and walk into a workshop. I am struck by the sight of girls and boys as young as ten who are already starting an artistic job that requires great dexterity and patience.

I am even more amazed by the adults' devotion. They seem to be aged around 50 and are sitting there, teaching the youngsters with words and the movements of their delicate hands, but they cannot see—their staring eyes are clouded by twenty or thirty years of eye strain.

My pity turns to indignation when I notice a sweaty, wealthy-looking man dressed from head to foot in white, sitting in an armchair in the cool breeze of a fan. Without rising, he asks if I am a tourist. When I say I am, he invites me to accompany him to his shop in the elegant neighbourhood of the city where, he says, I can see many beautiful works of art made by his artists, who are the best in Canton—blind and poor at 50 while he is rich, dressed in white linen and has a Malacca cane with a carved ivory pommel.

Most of Canton lies along the Pearl River. The large houses look as though they are copies of those on the Bund in Shanghai. The river feeds millions of Chinese, providing fish of every kind, which are sold dried or fresh. Canton is a floating city: its inhabitants are dependent on the low and high tides, besieged by mosquitoes and at risk from typhoons. The river is covered with countless boats that rarely move.

Finally the rain stops, the sun breaks through the scattered clouds, and the humid, suffocating heat returns. The fishermen begin fishing, many of them with cormorants. This river has not changed. The expanse of yellow water is like a moving lake; tree stumps carried from distant banks float on the water, representing a constant danger to the motor boats that make their way upstream with groups of passengers clustered together on heaps of cages and suitcases. While walking along the quay, I peer inside a boat through the curved opening of the deckhouse. Someone is asleep: these are people who can sleep in any position, despite the noise.

Inside, the family on board feels safe and cut off from the world. Near the old woman washing clothes in a bucket, a young woman is rinsing vegetables, and another is breast-feeding a newborn baby. Chinese children are well-behaved and do what they are told. When they are very small, they are tied to their mother's back with strips of cloth and then, when they grow bigger, they are put in a barrel like young Diogenes, with their arms and heads poking out, until they develop their "sea legs". You can hear the splash as nets, rubbish and buckets hit the same stretch of water. This image of China has not changed.

I have seen more beggars in Canton than anywhere else in China, despite the fact that the city is becoming increasingly like Hong Kong, with the construction of so many hotels and factories manufacturing electrical household appliances, stereos and other consumer products. In my time, beggars were a common sight and even had their own god and their own trade union. The god, who is called Chu Yuan Chang, was of very humble origins. He grew rich asking for alms, then became a merchant, and then an army general. As the story goes, when he was young, he entered an abandoned garden and satisfied his hunger by eating the fruit on the trees. Many years later, Chu Yuan Chang passed the same garden, this time at the head of his troops. He stopped, climbed down from his horse and, turning to his soldiers, said: 'Look at this tree: when I was hot it gave me shade and when I was hungry it gave me food. Gratitude is a great thing.' With these words, he took off his cloak and cast it over the tree, entreating it to accept the title of Marquis of the Ice and White Dew. Apart from these myths, the beggars' union was very powerful. They had offices in every city, where they discussed shop openings,

327

marriages and funerals, and there were people responsible for recruiting ulcerous men and crippled women. After a period of apprenticeship, they were given posts suited to their physical disabilities. Shops would pay a bribe to the local union to keep these unsavoury people away from their premises. The shops that refused to pay were persecuted by a specially handpicked group of the most hideous and grotesque beggars, accompanied by others who made annoying noises on a gong to prevent customers from speaking. During funerals and marriages, it was advisable to submit to this blackmail to ensure that the ceremony was not disrupted.

My "First Uncle", who did business with them to avoid being pestered during a funeral cortege, and his own wedding procession, said: 'I am very prejudiced against anyone who is blind, deaf, dumb, lacking a limb, or humpbacked. There is a strange relationship between a person's appearance and their soul, as if losing a limb can cause someone to lose a piece of their soul.' I do not share his opinion: if anything, I disagree with it. In my view, the soul becomes purer after losing a limb or a physical function.

Many of the beggars performed acrobatic contortions in the busiest city areas to earn enough to buy a bowl of rice. I saw them in front of the mission's church, walking on their hands, with their legs contorted so that their feet appeared behind their neck. They had a vast repertory of exercises and I enjoyed watching their performances. They were very skilled and at the end of every act the money collected ensured that everyone had a meal and a bed for the night. Scraping a living is also an art. As one Chinese proverb says: 'When has pride ever filled a bowl of rice?'

Spending a few days in Hong Kong convinces me more than ever that people want supernatural assistance to overcome the difficulties and psychological pressure of daily life in this busy city. Capitalist life seems to be extremely stressful; people are more in need of spiritual guidance than ever before. Western logic and psychology seem unable to provide the answers to the problems of Chinese society.

People are increasingly inclined to return to their own deep-rooted philosophy for comfort and reassurance. Many frequent the temples and consult the soothsayers who wait nearby, in their stalls. They include face readers, geomancers and chiromancers.

Soothsayers fall into two categories: those who are born with the power they say they developed in their past lives, and those who devote their time to practising the power learned from the arts of the masters and the *Book of Changes*, also known as the I Ching. These sciences have their roots in the I Ching, which is regarded as the source of all learning. The principle of the I Ching is based on the concept that the world is driven by two opposing but mutually dependent energies: yin and yang, which appear in the natural world as female and male, darkness and light, water and fire. The interplay of these two forces exists within countless natural phenomena and has an impact on all changes.

Heaven, earth and man form the trinity of the Taoist philosophy and the role of soothsayers, geomancers and chiromancers is to bring "human affairs" into harmony with heavenly and earthly influences in order to avoid conflict and achieve positive results.

One of these sciences is face-reading, because it is regarded as the most accurate way to determine an individual's character and personality. Face-reading is believable because it is based on diagnostic principles practised in traditional Chinese medicine. For face-readers, the face is an open book. Moods, memories, the subconscious and inclinations are reflected in the complexion, eyes, tongue, ears, lips, wrinkles, the shape of the skull and its contours—all of these factors are taken singly, then analysed one after the other in groups. Other factors can influence someone's destiny and good fortune: free will, spiritual forces, past lives and religious beliefs.

According to the *Book of Changes*, the face mirrors the spirit as well as the condition of the internal organs. Believing this, I go to the White Horse Temple to burn incense and have someone read my *qi*, the life force that should appear in my facial features.

After this face reading, I learn that my element is wood—I appear hard, but am very sensitive and altruistic because, like wood, I burn for others.

The two lumps on my forehead denote a sickly childhood, but are also signs of mental clarity.

The colour of my eyes—the contrast between white and black—shows that my health improved as I grew up.

My small ears show that I have not had much luck in terms of familial love. The two bulges behind my ears mean that I shall live about 66 years.

'Is that all?' I ask with some concern.

'I'll take another look—76!' he says, correcting himself.

My nose is my best facial feature because it is straight and regular: it governs the influences linked to the other traits.

The groove beneath my nose confirms the length of my life, but I need to monitor my arterial pressure during old age.

My mouth and chin indicate that I am moving towards a certain degree of serenity. I am advised to continue and not pull back from the initiatives I have undertaken.

My right hand—the swellings under my little finger, ring finger and middle finger reveal strong emotions and passions, which are kept under control by the central line on my palm that denotes thinking and planning.

The line leading from my ring finger to the first crease shows I have chosen a frivolous husband.

The line travelling from the main crease and heading towards my wrist indicates fragile health around twenty. The little fingers of both hands are shorter than my ring fingers, so I must perform a "cosmetic" intervention by growing my nails to lengthen my fingers. This change may influence my daughter who is, at present, surrounded by black clouds, but must continue down the path she has chosen.

Every day my travel bag grows heavier with another packet, box, garment, or gift for one friend or another. When I left Italy, it was almost empty—I just packed the essentials. I am only taking back things from China that provide some kind of link to my Chinese childhood. Objects that remind me of particularly happy times—things of no great value that I have collected on my journey. I am taking back little pieces of my China.

I have bought:
1 small cricket cage with a cricket, which I set free in a garden.
1 pair of embroidered shoes for bound feet.
2 red candles bought at the Big Goose Pagoda.
9 insects made of pieces of grass by a specialist craftsman.
9 Mao Zedong badges and a copy of the Little Red Book.
2 metal spheres for rolling around in the palm.
1 silver bracelet with a little bell for a newborn baby.
1 china doll, dressed in costume.
2 *qipao*—traditional Chinese dresses.
1 packet of moon cakes.
Needles for acupuncture and auricular therapy.

In addition, I bring back impressions of certain people, including:
The falsetto singing of my driver, Xiao Xu, in Beijing.
The anonymous face of the peasant woman who came to my help in Tian'anmen Square.
Father Jiang's words of comfort in front of the cathedral.
Blue Sky's laughter in Shanghai.
The old scribe's smile in Ningbo.

At the end of this long, tiring journey, I have the impression that part of me will always feel isolated and estranged. This is, to some extent, what I wanted: to exorcise a past that weighed heavily on me and that I could not always understand. However, the love that binds me to China is the one true thing that will never change: it is an enduring symbol of belonging.

OTHER TITLES BY LOKI BOOKS

LOKI INTERNATIONAL FICTION SERIES

DOLLY CITY
Orly Castel-Bloom

Paperback   ISBN - 10 -   0 9529426 0 7
                   ISBN - 13 - 978095294603
£7.99

An irreverent and witty satire, an original and timely tour de force about the Yiddish-mamma complex, and Israel today, by a triple prize-winning new young voice.

'A novel of Joycean insolence… A beautiful book whose non-conformism is a delight.' (*La Marsellaise*)

'Castel-Bloom writes with such freshness, such dash and panache that I was willing to follow her anywhere.' (Eva Figes)

APPLES FROM THE DESERT: SELECTED STORIES
Savyon Liebrecht

Paperback   ISBN - 10 - 0952942615
                   ISBN - 13 - 9780952942610
£9.99

Foreword by *Grace Paley*
Introduction by **Lilly Ratok, Tel Aviv University.**

Savyon Liebrecht's short stories are **classics in new Hebrew** literature. A broad panorama of contemporary Israeli society in **'bitter-sweet tales of fury, passion and disenchantment.'** *(Ha'aretz)*.

'...beautifully, affectingly plumbs profound and painful themes...Be sure to read them.' *(Washington Post, 1998)*

CHERRIES IN THE ICEBOX: CONTEMPORARY HEBREW SHORT STORIES

ed *Marion Baraitser* and *Haya Hoffman*
Introduction by Haya Hoffman
Supported by The European Jewish Publication Society

Papaerback ISBN - 10 -   0 952942658
            ISBN - 13 -   9780952942658
£11.50

A unique collection of twelve of the best, daring, young multicultural voices, writing in Hebrew today, these stories encapsulate the diverse mosaic of a society that is uncomfortable with itself, as it comes to terms with violence and dislocation, with wry wit and hope that counters despair.

'Excellent and stimulating anthology' *(**Jewish Chronicle**)*
'The easiest way to find out who will be the next Amos Oz' *(**Jewish Renaissance**)*

LOKI INTERNATIONAL PLAY SERIES

ECHOES OF ISRAEL: CONTEMPORARY

DRAMA
ed *Marion Baraitser*

Paperback   ISBN – 10-   0 952942631
**   ISBN – 13 - 978095294627**
£9.99

From the Royal National Theatre.

'Bold dramas...revealing the rifts and taboos in Israeli society at this crucial time in the nation's history.' *New Statesman*

A FAMILY STORY by **Edna Mazya**
Winner of the Israeli Theatre Award 1997/8
MURDER by **Hanoch Levin**
Play of the year and Playwright of the Year, 1997
SHEINDALE by **Rami Danon** and **Amnon Levy**
'*A vital subject .. an intriguing merciless play*' *Al Ha'Mish Mar*
MR MANI, a monodrama by **A.B. Yehoshua** . '*A fascinating insight into the British presence in Palestine by the Israel Prize winner.*' *Ha'aretz*

BOTTLED NOTES FROM UNDERGROUND: CONTEMPORARY PLAYS BY JEWISH WRITERS
ed *Linden S, Baraitser M.*

Paperback   ISBN – 10 -   0 952942623
**   ISBN – 13 -   9780952942627**
£9.99

From Sobol to Schneider—a barn-breaking collection of five popular award-winning new plays of excellence from London, New York and Israel. Features Israel's greatest living playwright **JOSHUA SOBOL's** *The Palestinian Girl* with **Carole Braverman, Sonja Linden, and David Schneider.**

THE DEFIANT MUSE: HEBREW WOMEN'S POEMS FROM ANTIQUITY TO THE PRESENT: A BILINGUAL ANTHOLOGY

ed *Shirley Kaufman, Galit Hasan-Rokem,* and *Tamar Hess*

Paperback ISBN –10 -   095294264X
**   ISBN –13 -   978095294261**
£12.99

Poetry Book Society Recommended Translation, 2000

Unprecedented in its scope, many of these poems are unknown to an English speaking audience. A unique volume of 100 poems by 50 writers from antiquity to the present, which transforms the perception of Jewish women's poetry in Hebrew.

- Unique bilingual anthology transforming the conception of Jewish women's poetry.
- New material, new translations.
- Introduction placing the poems in historical, cultural, and literary perspectives, and full bibliographic and biographical notes.
- Arts Council of England and European Jewish Publication Society support. Published in association with The Feminist Press at CUNY

Shirley Kaufman: prize-winning American Israeli poet and translator who has   published seven volumes of poems, as well as translations from Hebrew and Dutch.

Galit Hasan-Rokem: professor of folklore at the Hebrew University of Jerusalem, translator, scholar, and poet: **Tamar Hess**: teacher at the Hebrew University.

HOME NUMBER ONE: teen graphic novel
Marion Baraitser and Anna Evans

Paperback **ISBN – 10 -   0952942674**
          ISBN – 13 -   9780952942672
£8.50

A modern teenagers' life-changing journey through a war camp

Written by the award winning playwright **Marion Baraitser** with illustrations by Penguin Illustrator **Anna Evans**, *Home Number One* depicts the courage and survival of four teenagers in the Jewish ghetto of Theresienstadt.

'**This is a brilliant book, informative, funny in places and interesting**… I found the book was so brilliant I could not put it down.. I could relate to it as the characters are more or less the same age as me.'
Nicole Birley, 14, JFS (*Jewish Renaissance, 2006*)

All books available from good book shops or from amazon.co.uk, or LokiBooks, 38 Chalcot Crescent, London NW1 8YD:all@lokibooks.vianw.co.uk http://www.lokibooks.com. Trade: Central Books.99 Wallis Rd, London E9 5LN: tel: +44 (0)845 4589911 : fax:+44 (0)845 4589912: orders@centralbooks.com